BRITAIN IN OLD [

WEMBLEY & KINGSBURY

ADAM SPENCER

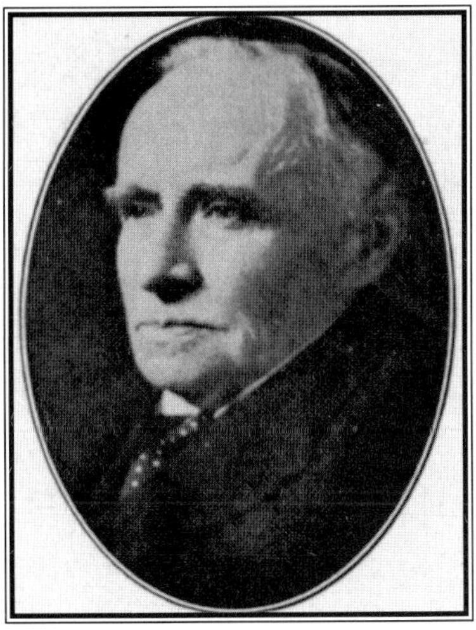

ALAN SUTTON PUBLISHING LIMITED

Alan Sutton Publishing Limited
Phoenix Mill · Far Thrupp · Stroud
Gloucestershire · GL5 2BU

First published 1995

Cover photographs: front: The Red Lion pub, The Hyde, Kingsbury, c. 1880; back: Wembley postmen standing outside the post office, c. 1905. Title page: George Titus Barham, 1860–1937

British Library Cataloguing in Publication Data
A catalogue record for this book is available from the British Library.

ISBN 0-7509-1014-3

Typeset in 9/10 Sabon.
Typesetting and origination by
Alan Sutton Publishing Limited.
Printed in Great Britain by
Hartnolls, Bodmin, Cornwall.

Dedicated to all victims of war 1945–1995
Adam Spencer, May 1995

Contents

	Introduction	5
1.	Wembley	7
2.	Kingsbury	85
	Acknowledgements	126
	Bibliography	126

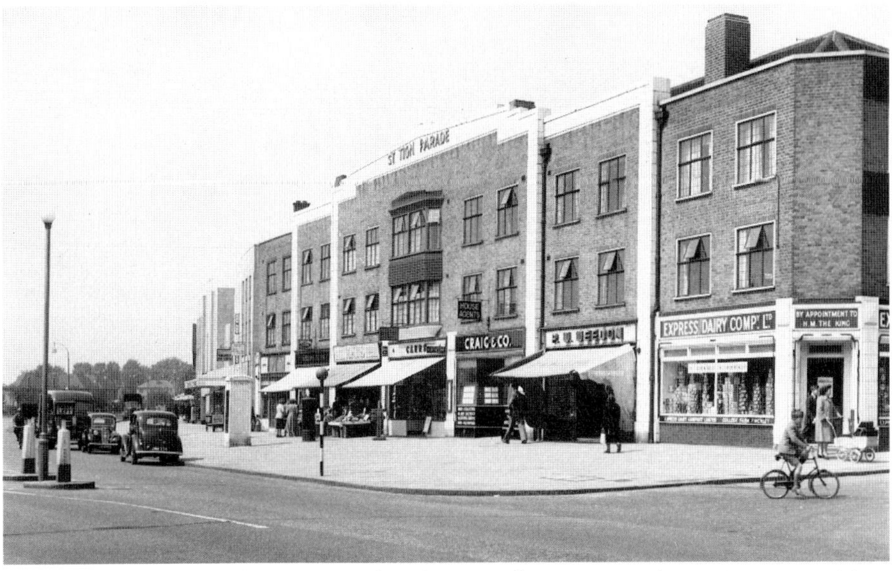

Kingsbury Station Parade, *c.* 1950. This photograph is opposite the station on p. 104.

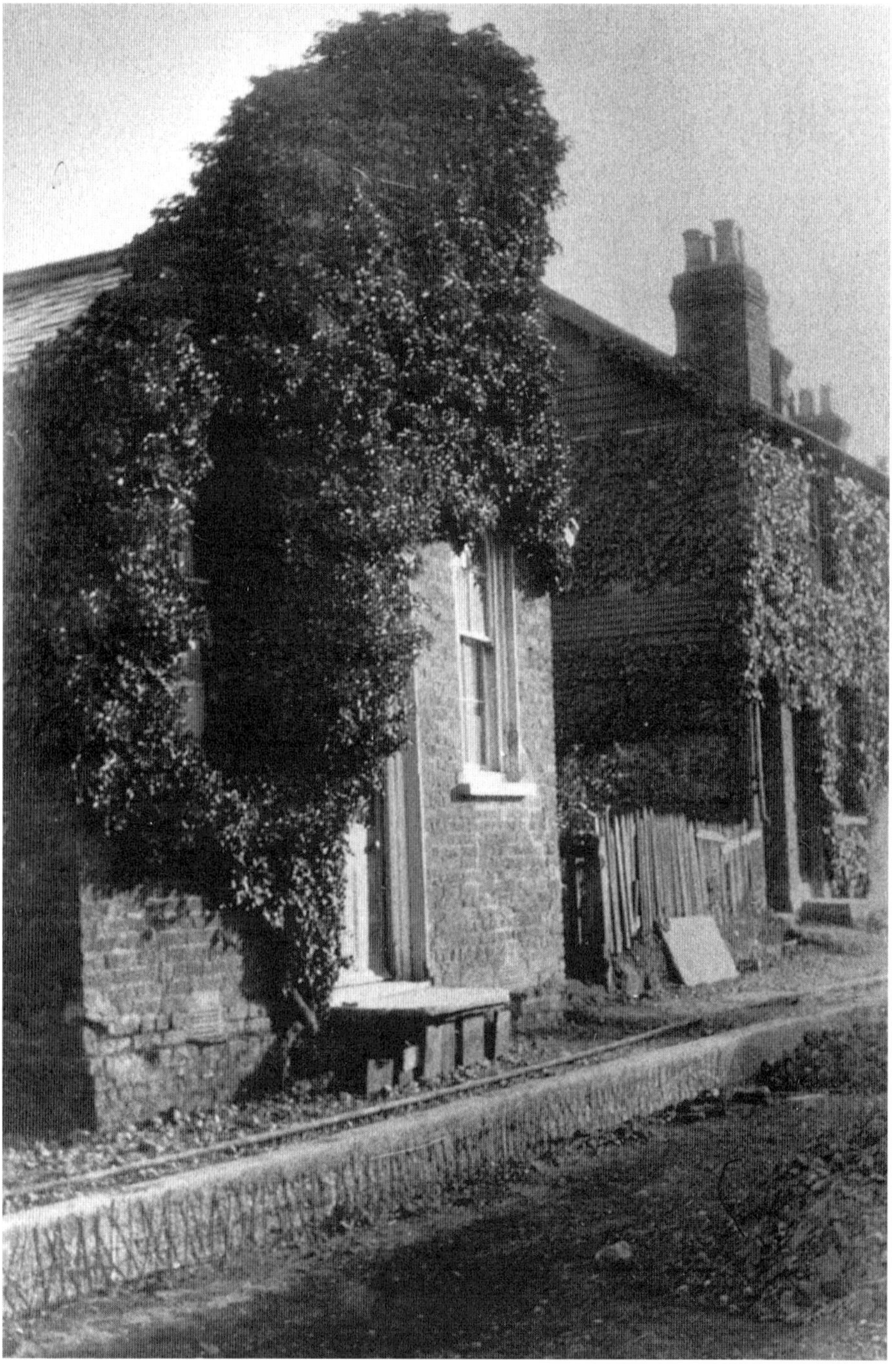

Ivy Cottages, Ealing Road, Wembley, *c.* 1930.

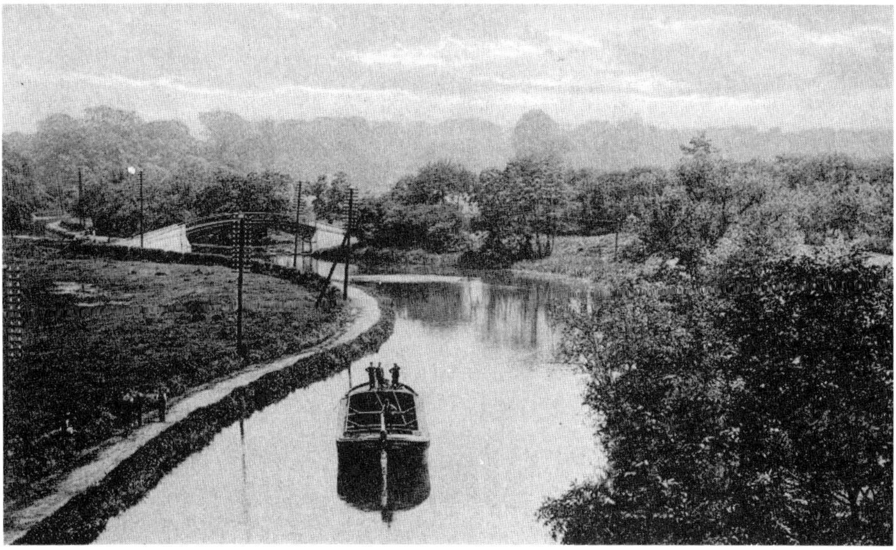

Valley of the Brent, Alperton, *c.* 1910.

Introduction

Wembley was first documented in 825 as 'Wemba lea'. The name means 'Wemba's clearing' and, although the personal name is not recorded, it is thought that it is a nickname derived from the Old English 'wamb' ('belly'). It gave its name to a thirteenth-century family and by 1212 was a township. Development and population growth were exceedingly slow: from the two tithings of 1316, almost certainly including Tokyngton, there were only six houses listed in 1547. By 1805 there were at least twenty-two houses and in 1831 the population was 208. But even the coming of the railway in 1845 made little difference: the population of Wembley and Tokyngton in 1851 amounted to just 203. A little development occurred at the end of the nineteenth century, when some large houses were built, but it was not until the first decade of the twentieth century that its development as a suburban centre began. Within three decades all that remained of old Wembley was the original street pattern, a skeleton beneath the maze of new streets covering the whole region.

Kingsbury, meaning 'the king's manor or stronghold', lay between two ancient north–south routes, Watling Street (Edgware Road) and Honeypot Lane (earlier Old Street or Hell Lane), and there seems to be evidence that Kingsbury pre-dates the Anglo-Saxon period, as Bronze Age cinerary vessels have been found in the Brent Reservoir. The boundaries of the parish were uncertain, the northern one with Little Stanmore not being fixed until after 1276–7. Even in 1536 the villagers were presented at the manor court for not marking their boundaries.

Kingsbury was never an area of nucleated villages: the settlement pattern was scattered and the Black Death decimated the parish. In 1350 there were at least thirteen deaths 'at the time of the pestilence' presented to the manor court. Consequently, property holdings became concentrated and many houses were abandoned; the settlement pattern changed, the most populous area now became Kingsbury Green while the southern part of the parish shrank to the church and one or two farms.

Population growth was erratic, trebling between 1801 and 1851, the number of houses increasing from 45 to 102. In 1901 there were 140 houses and the population stood at 757. The First World War and the British Empire Exhibition led to wholesale development. The number of houses grew from 140 in 1901 to 440 in 1921, 3,937 in 1931 and 11,776 in 1951. The view of one historian is perhaps a little bleak but none the less accurate: 'continuous suburban housing obliterates all distinction between Kingsbury, Harrow, and Stanmore'.

Wembley and Kingsbury developed in a similar fashion in that they changed from virtually rural communities to outposts of suburbia in the space of just a few decades, and in some areas within living memory. What this book seeks to do is to give a glimpse of the Wembley and Kingsbury that used to exist, and an idea of the individuals, communities and buildings that created the environment around us today.

A particular aim of this book is to introduce readers to the resources of Cricklewood Library and Archive, the provenance of the majority of the photos in this book. I have attempted to illustrate the history of Wembley and Kingsbury with as diverse and visually appealing a collection of photographs as is available. Perhaps their publication in this book will encourage people to visit the archives themselves. For every photo included there have been three or four discarded, which gives an indication of the breadth and depth of the collection. I will gladly receive further information about any photograph reproduced here.

I feel sure that I am not alone in lamenting the loss of some of the buildings and landscapes shown herein. However, progress is dynamic and it is important to recognize that where destruction is unavoidable then full and accurate recording must take place. It is increasingly incumbent on all of us to take part in the protection of our heritage: history is not only about yesterday but also about tomorrow.

Section One

WEMBLEY

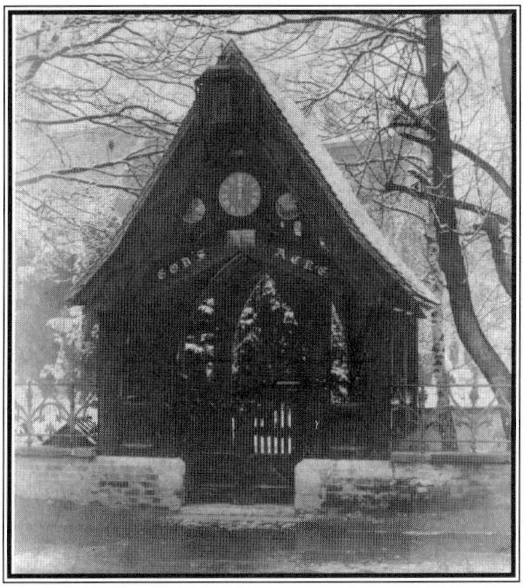

The lychgate of St John's Church. Wembley only became a separate parish in 1846, when the Church of St John the Evangelist, designed by George Gilbert Scott and W.B. Moffat, was consecrated. Built in the Gothic style, of flint with stone dressings, it originally comprised a chancel, nave, north-east chapel and wooden bell turret. Further additions consisted of a north aisle (1859), a south aisle (1900) and extensions to the west in 1935.

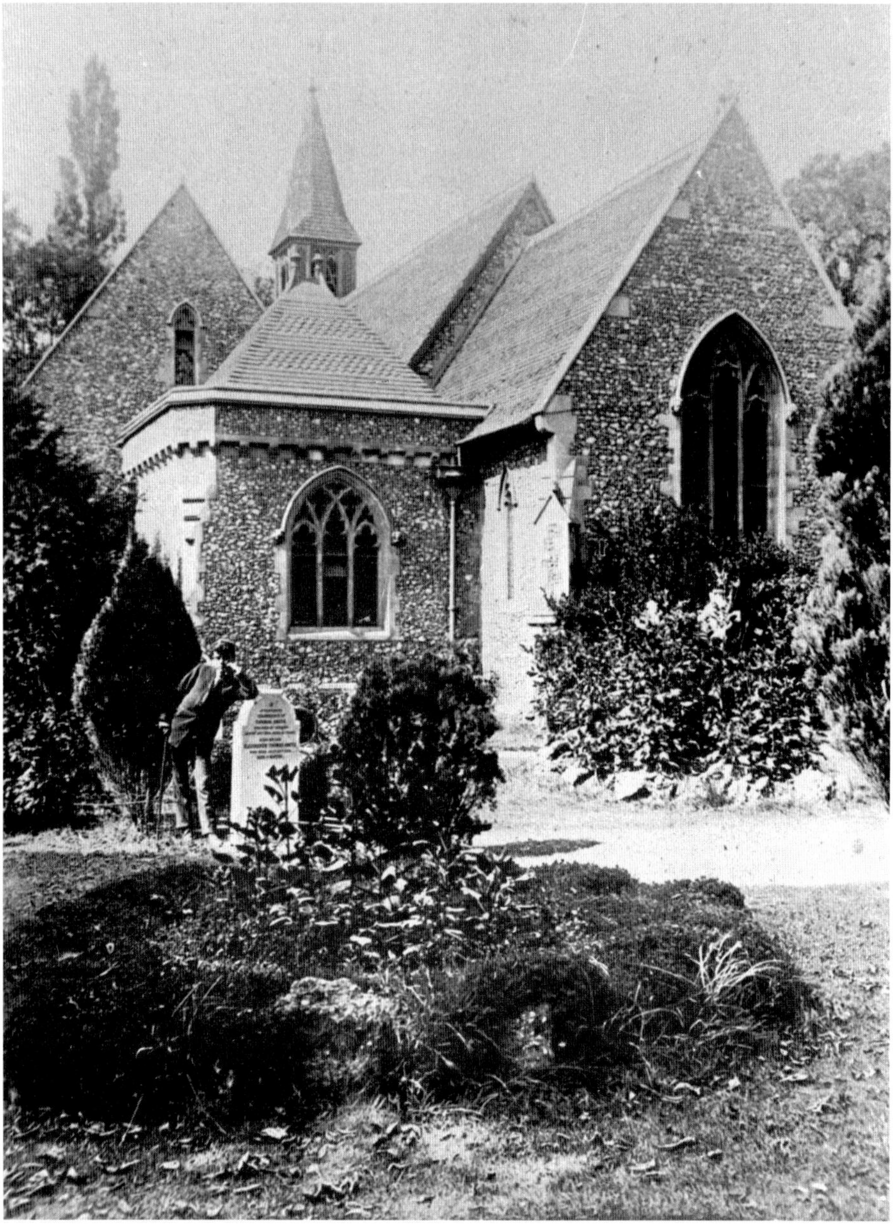

An informal portrait in the churchyard of St John's. This image comes from the photo album of Harold Groom, one time Harlesden librarian. He later moved on to Isleworth, becoming borough librarian for Heston and Isleworth until his retirement in 1954. The album contains some twenty images of Willesden, Wembley and Kingsbury (others can be seen on pp. 101 and 108). All were taken between 1903 and 1910.

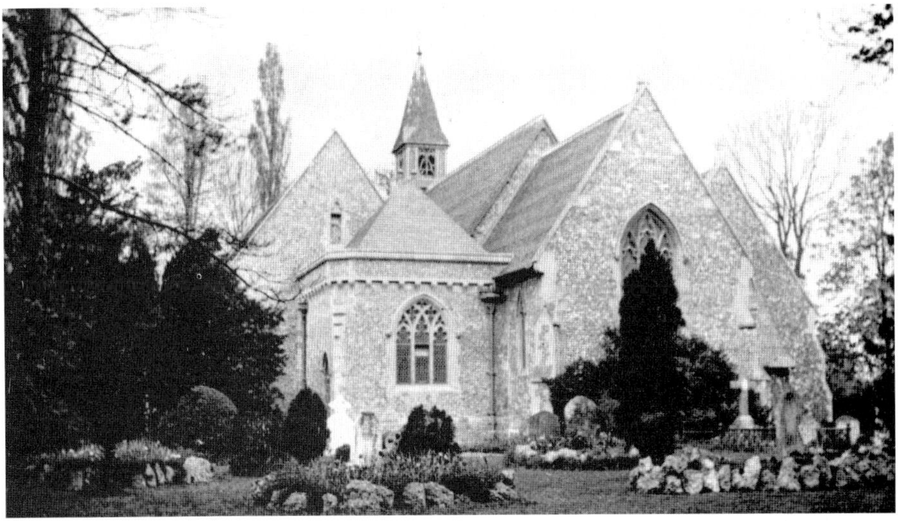

'Wembley Church Middlesex' in a more formal picture of around 1902. By this time the vicar was J.W.P. Silvester (father of band leader Victor Silvester) who came some time after C. Layard, the latter being renowned for his evangelical views. He had, for instance, instituted weekly meetings at Wembley Hill and Honeypot Lane and held services for men at the workmen's hall and for women at a house in Alperton. Consequently the High Church views of Silvester, who was vicar from 1896 to 1944, aroused some controversy.

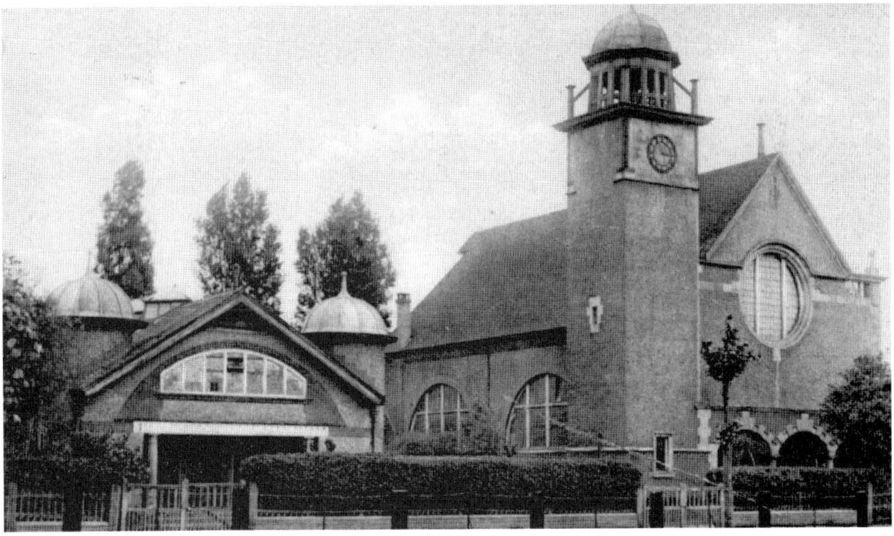

St Andrew's Presbyterian Church, Ealing Road, *c.* 1910. The foundation stone was laid in July 1898 and the church was officially opened in October 1899. Mr Hamp of Park House, Alperton was the main benefactor for 'not only did he buy the site and build the church, but he also gave the beautiful organ, the communion service, furniture and hymn books'. St Andrew's closed in December 1982.

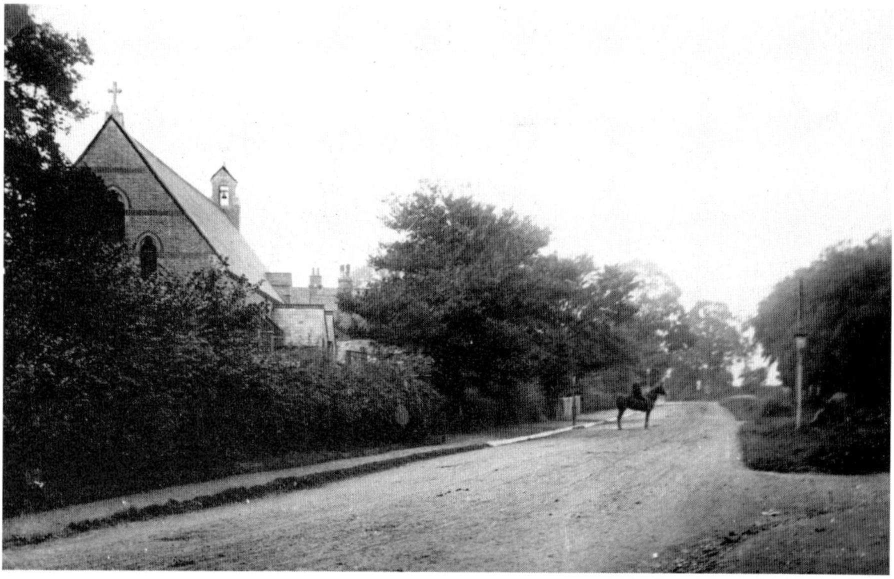

St Joseph's Church, *c.* 1910. Roman Catholics in Wembley had to worship in Harlesden until the erection of St Joseph's in 1901. The small brick chapel was moved from Harley Place (near Baker Street) and resited to Wembley Green where it remained until its demolition and replacement with a larger building in 1956–7.

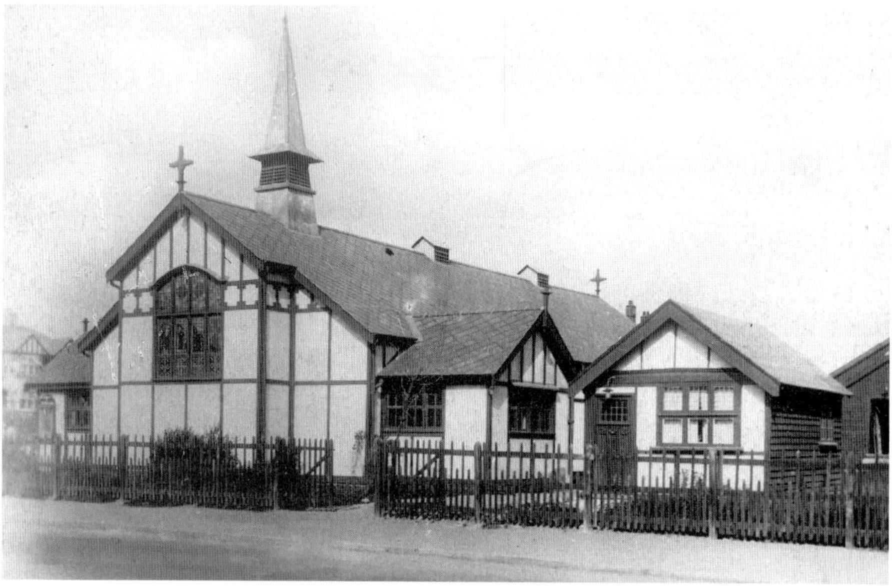

St Leonard, Kenton, *c.* 1930. This wooden building was built *c.* 1927 when a new parish in Kenton was formed from St Mary, Harrow; All Saints, Harrow Hill; St John the Baptist, Greenhill; and St Augustine, Wembley Park. This structure was replaced by a permanent church in 1936 dedicated to St Mary the Virgin.

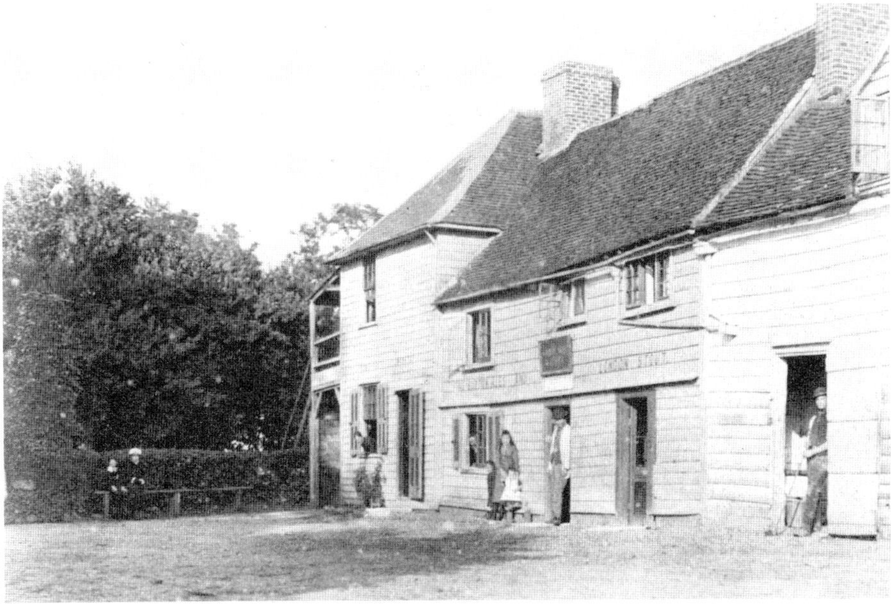

The Green Man, Wembley Hill. The earliest extant photograph of Wembley is thought to be one of this pub in June 1862. The picture above is later and, coming as it does from Frederick Augustus Wood's collection, is probably from between 1870 and 1880 (for more on F.A. Wood see p. 97). Sitting at the summit of Wembley Hill, the Green Man had been a pub since at least 1722. Over the years the name changed – from the 'Barley Mow' (1751) to the 'Red Lyon' (1774) until in 1785 Henry Goodes (who remained the licensee until 1828) renamed the pub the 'Green Man'. A late medieval house, with eighteenth-century weather boarding, the original building was destroyed by fire in 1906. The new Green Man (below) is an Edwardian building. Here a group of customers stand outside, including a dog and at least one chicken.

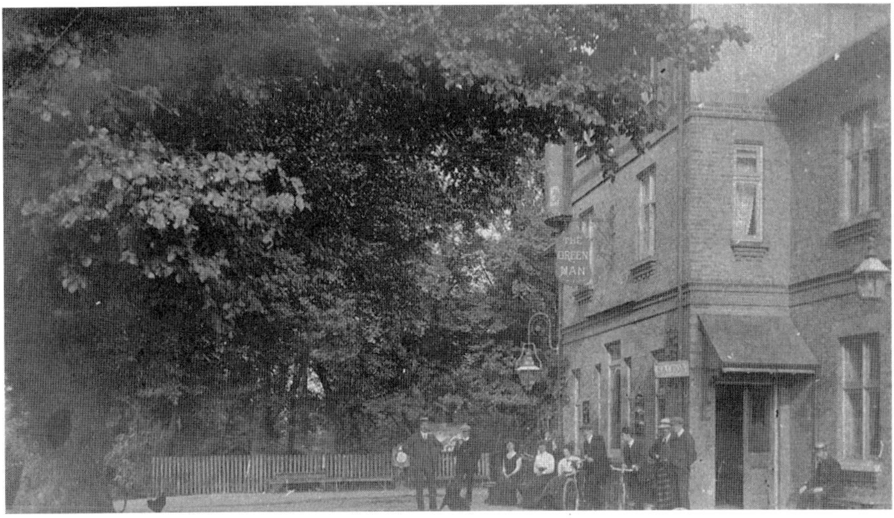

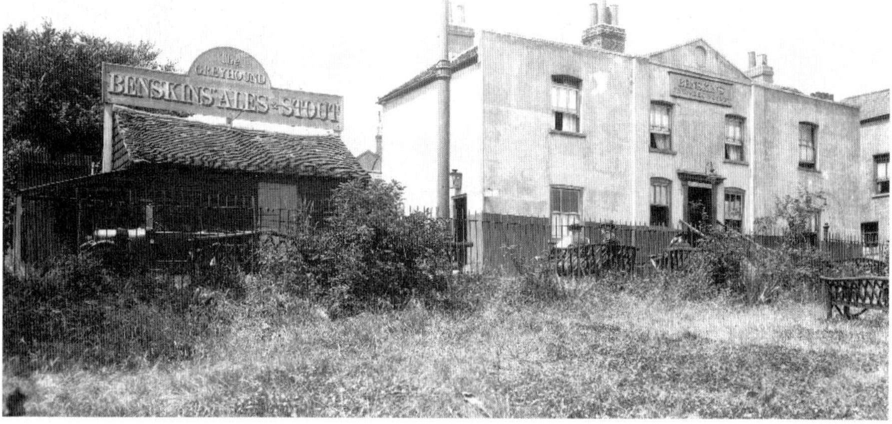

The Greyhound, Wembley Hill, *c.* 1920. Like other public houses in the area (see p. 91) this was originally a beerhouse. In 1841 it was run by a Joseph Goodes; his widow was listed in 1871 as a recipient of parish relief. The physical structure dated back some hundreds of years, but it was demolished in 1929, another casualty of the 1920s–'30s building boom. From 1923 onwards it was a popular meeting place for Cup Final crowds.

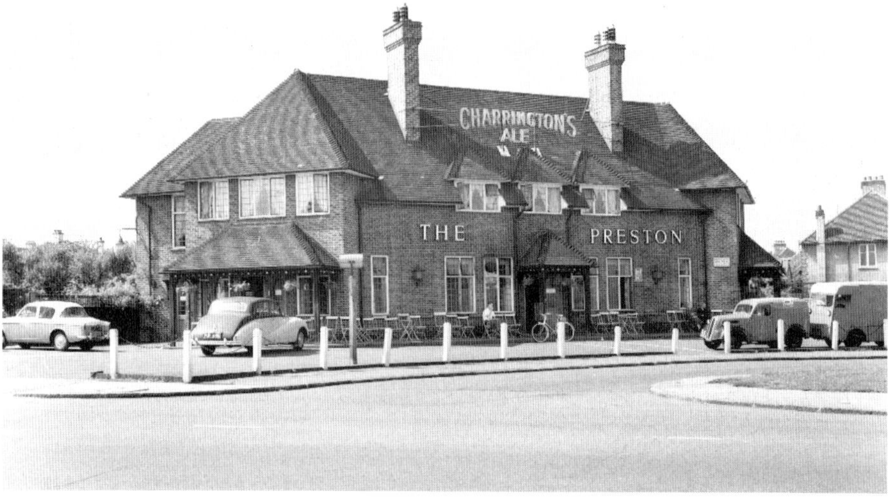

The Preston, *c.* 1950. Built in the late 1920s by Clifford Sabey, The Preston serves the public in the area around Preston Road and Carlton Avenue East and is virtually opposite Preston public library.

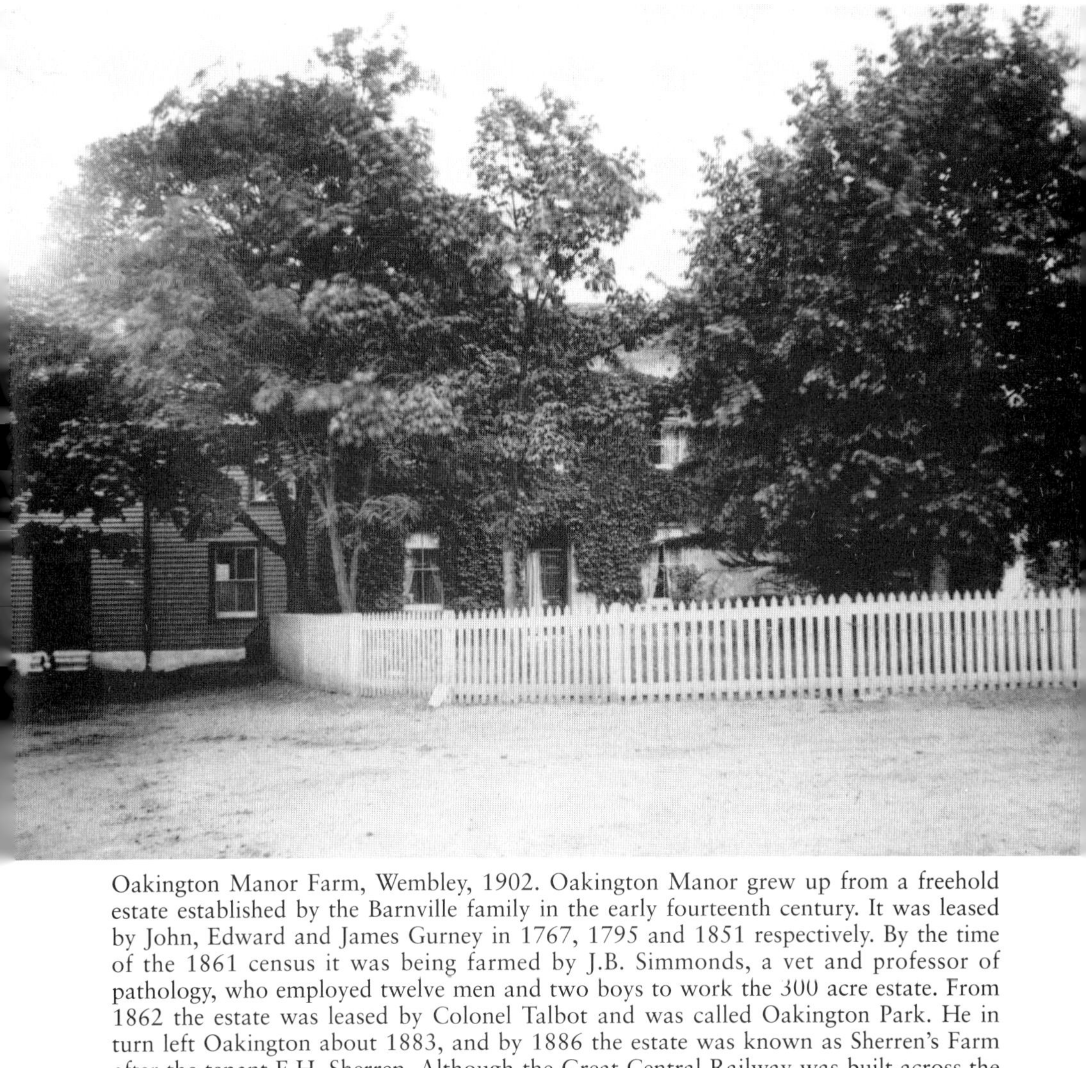

Oakington Manor Farm, Wembley, 1902. Oakington Manor grew up from a freehold estate established by the Barnville family in the early fourteenth century. It was leased by John, Edward and James Gurney in 1767, 1795 and 1851 respectively. By the time of the 1861 census it was being farmed by J.B. Simmonds, a vet and professor of pathology, who employed twelve men and two boys to work the 300 acre estate. From 1862 the estate was leased by Colonel Talbot and was called Oakington Park. He in turn left Oakington about 1883, and by 1886 the estate was known as Sherren's Farm after the tenant E.H. Sherren. Although the Great Central Railway was built across the north of the estate in 1906 the farmhouse survived. The subsequent construction of residential estates led to the end of arable farming by 1934 but Sherren remained until 1938 as a pig breeder. Sir Audley Neeld, the freeholder, had conveyed forty acres alongside the River Brent to Wembley Council for open space sometime after gaining agreement to develop his land along garden city lines in 1913. He followed this in 1938 with a further twenty-one acres, including the manor house, for additional open space. A proposal to use the manor house as a public library was unsuccessful and it was demolished in an Air Raid Protection (ARP) exercise in 1939.

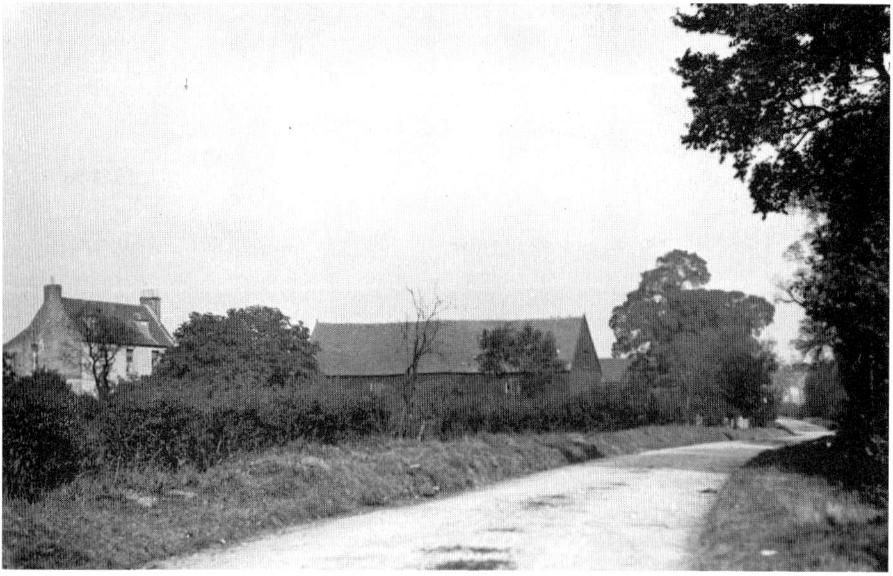

Manor Farm, Alperton, *c.* 1920. With its 175 acres Manor Farm was the largest farm in Alperton on the eve of enclosure in the early 1800s. It was then leased to Thomas Bowler, who also held cottages in Watery Lane and Honeypot Lane. He was convicted of shooting a farmer with intent to kill and although the victim survived Bowler was hanged in 1812.

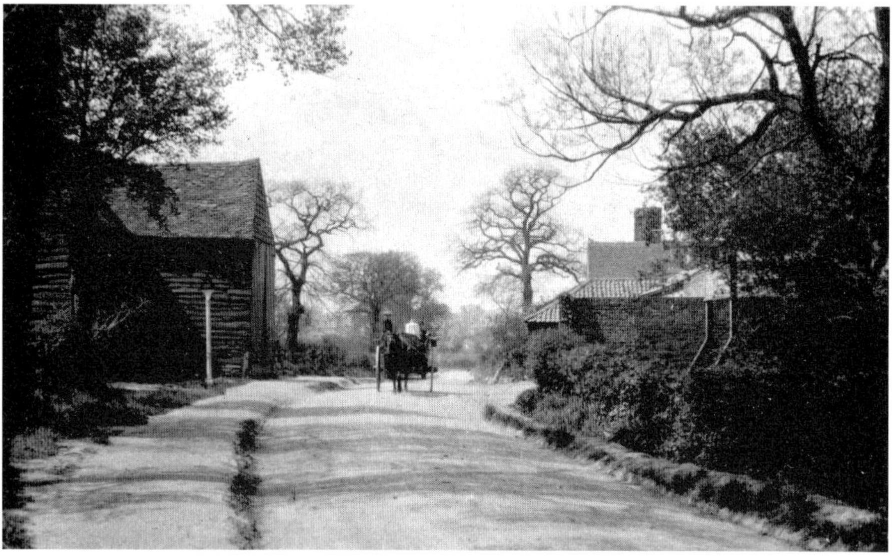

Wembley Farm or Padfield's Farm, *c.* 1920. It was built soon after the Enclosure Act of 1803. By 1811 John Read was in residence and the family remained there until 1874. They were succeeded as tenants by George and Frank Padfield, dairy farmers. As was often the case, the farm came to be known after the tenants and thus as Padfield's Farm.

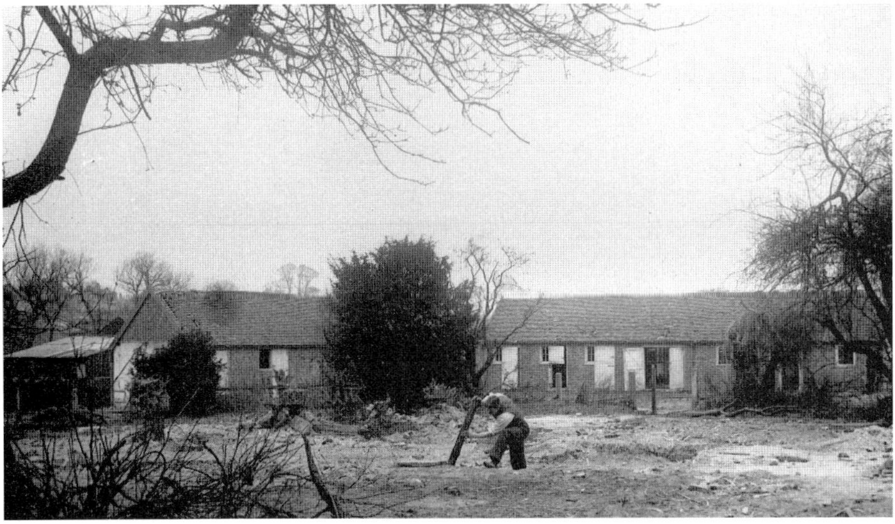

'The last of a Harrow beauty spot. Uxendon Farmhouse has been completely demolished, only the outhouses now remain standing', *Harrow News*, April 1929. Historically, Uxendon is largely known for its Catholic connection. After the Reformation the Bellamy family provided refuge for a number of priests, not least Anthony Babington who was arrested at Uxendon in 1586, for which the family paid a great cost. The estate was finally sold to John Lyon (a neighbour and perhaps a sympathizer) in 1600.

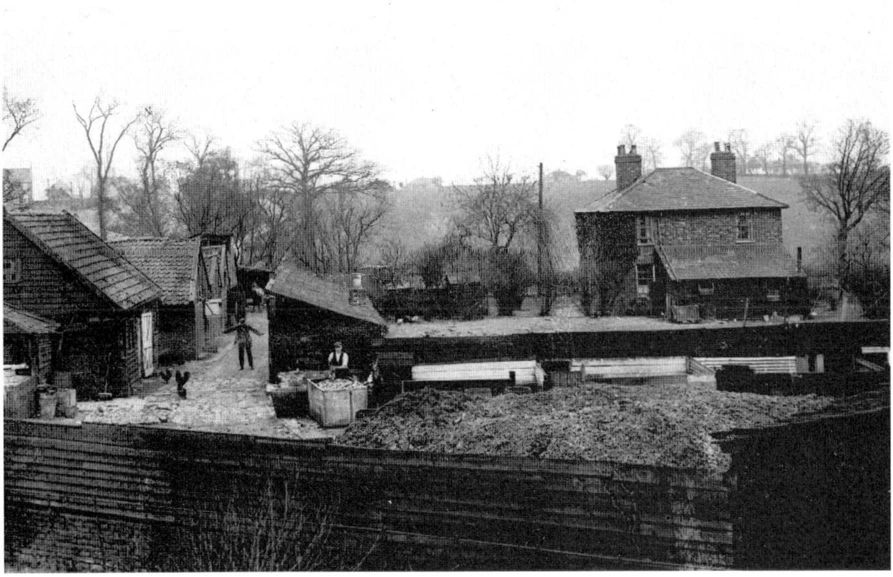

'Woodcock Dell Farm, which is now being demolished to make way for building.' The original caption for this record of the final destruction of the rurality of northern Wembley, as it appeared in the *Harrow Observer*, 10 April 1931.

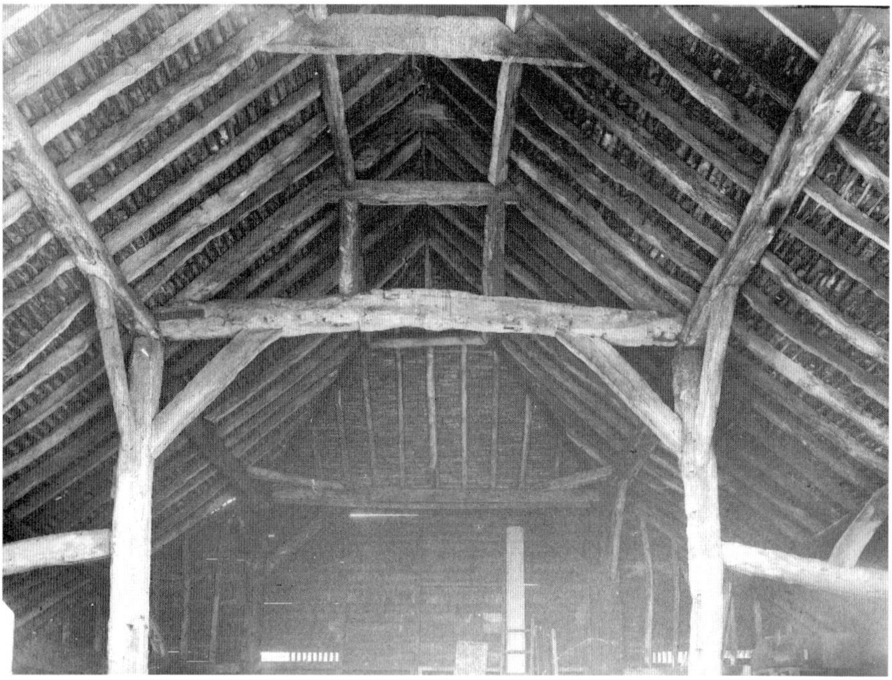

The seventeenth-century barn at Hundred Elms Farm, *c.* 1950 (above), and Elms Lane (below), a postcard view perhaps as late as the 1920s. Unfortunately the barn was partially burnt down in October 1951 and the elms that gave both the farm and the lane their names were lost in the late 1970s as victims of Dutch elm disease. The oldest brick building existing in Wembley is a surviving part of Hundred Elms Farm, the original usage of which is still uncertain. It may even have been a chapel for the archbishops of Canterbury visiting Harrow, although another possibility is that it was built by the owner of Sudbury Place.

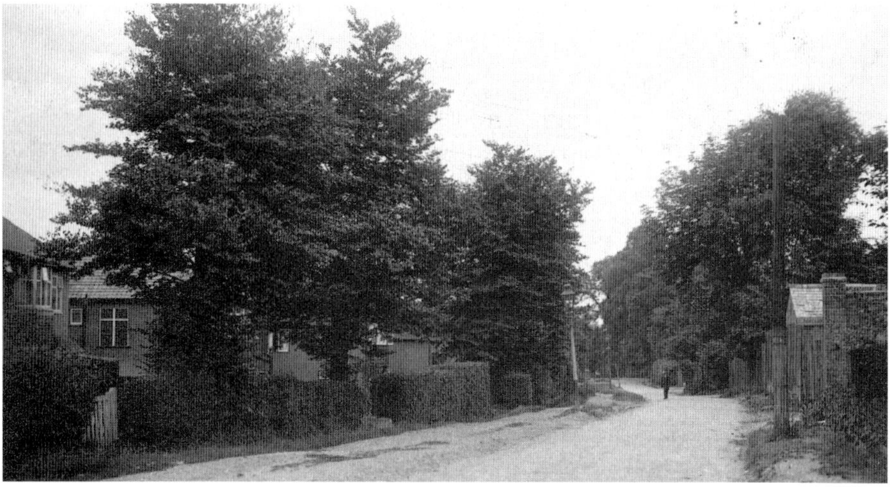

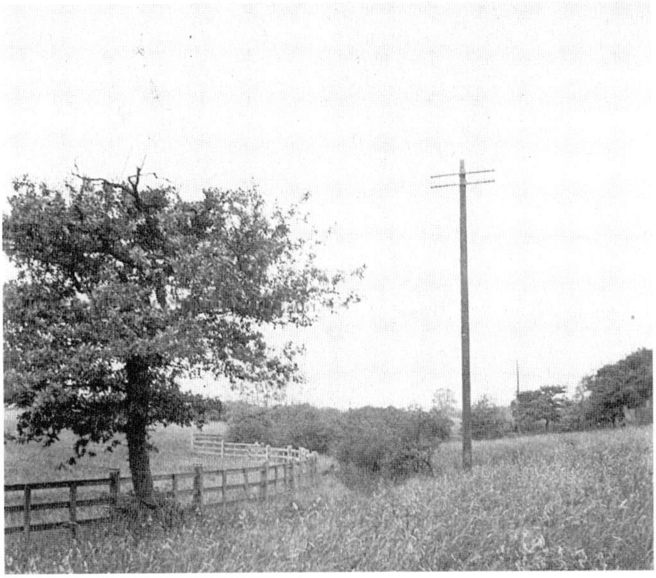

The Curtis Estate Dairy Farm, June 1904. These two views come from a collection of six taken by Charles Lancaster, gun and rifle manufacturer, 151 New Bond Street. He was opening a shooting ground on the farm. The views are included in a large legal archive relating to the estate which is currently being listed and will need some extensive conservation work. A note in the archive describes how the photographs came to be taken: 'Dear Sir, Since I had the pleasure of seeing you and during the time the grass was being cut at the Shooting Grounds, I thought it as well to take a few "snap-shots" so that you might see how imperfect, or I might say, a total absence there is of anything like a hedge around the field.'

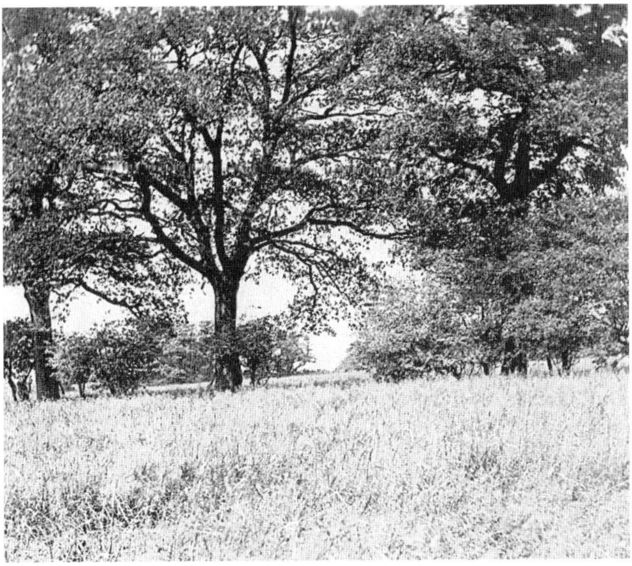

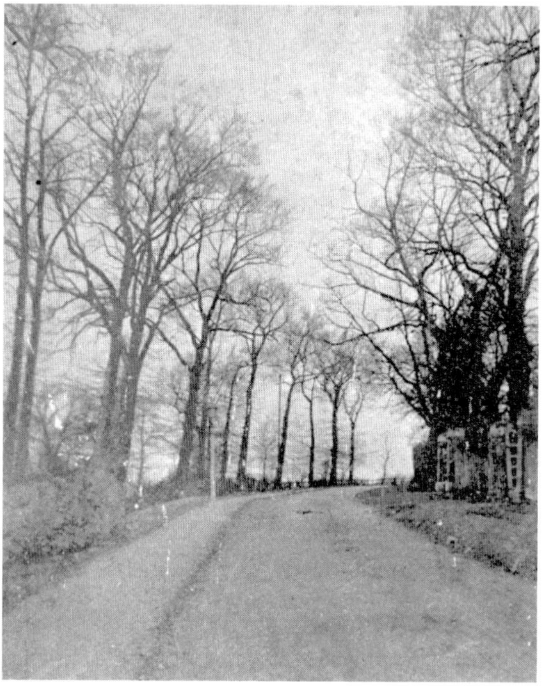

Blind Lane, Wembley. From a postcard postmarked 2 March 1907 which was sent to Mrs Hudson, 22 Cromwell Road, Alperton. The message, from Eliza, mentions the recent birth of a baby and concludes 'I shall come down as soon as you get well enough to see me but won't come until because of the childrens noise, for you no what kids are for making a row, so hoping you both well. Good luck this time, Eliza.' Blind Lane became Park Lane *c.* 1912 to indicate that it was a main route to Wembley Park (see pp. 68–71).

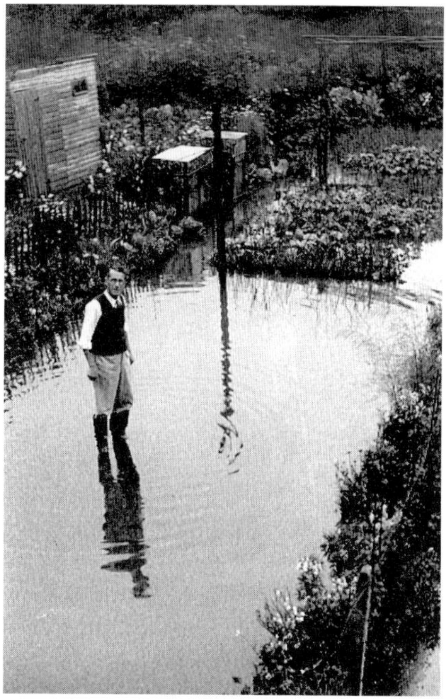

Flooding at 50 Charterhouse Avenue. A real rarity, this photo was posted to the Wembley borough engineer and surveyor with a letter dated 2 September 1941. The property was one of a number of homes that were affected by the flooding of the Wembley Brook, as the waterlogged condition of the garden clearly shows. From the available information it appears that the man is probably the owner of the property, Mr Joseph Coquard.

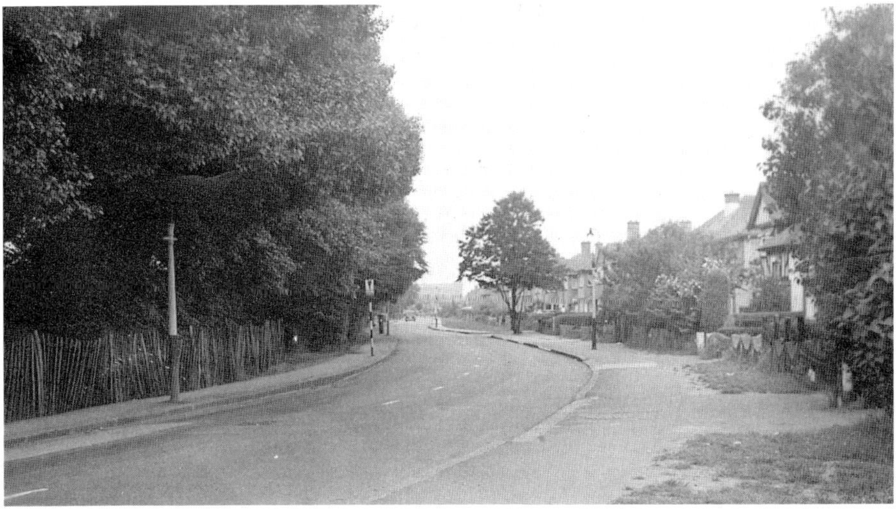

Woodcock Hill, Kenton, near the junction with Draycott Avenue, on 1 October 1959. The farmhouse on Woodcock Hill was demolished for building development, after being acquired by C.E. Costin in 1958. At one stage the farm occupied 179 acres, the land hosting no fewer than four railway stations (South Kenton, Preston Road, Northwick Park and Kenton).

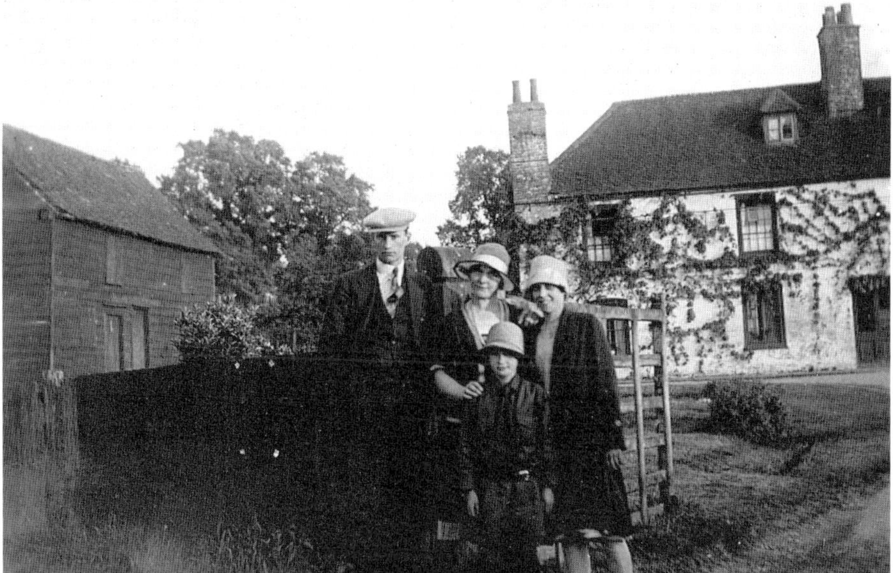

'At Kenton'. A picture from a family album, *c.* 1920 (see also pp. 23 and 25). Kenton, which means 'farm of the sons of Coena', was first mentioned as 'Kenington' in 1231. As no major road passed through Kenton village the road layout survived until after the First World War; the eastern boundary of the hamlet, Honeypot Lane, is a prehistoric track.

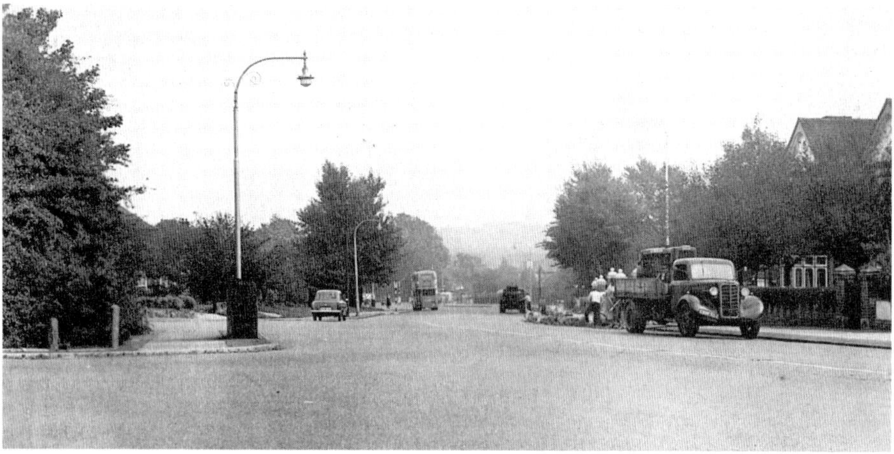

Forty Lane reconstruction in 1957–8. These photos take us on a short journey along Forty Lane, beginning at the top of Blackbird Hill looking back towards Neasden from near the junction with Salmon Street (above). Next we look up Forty Lane from just in front of the town hall (below), while the third photo, taken from the junction of Forty Lane, Forty Avenue, Barnhill and Bridge Road looks back up towards the site of where the previous photo would have been taken (opposite above). None of the images shows the town hall (see pp. 59–60) which would be on the left in the middle distance in the third photograph, though, of course, the building is set well back from the road. The photos were taken well before the redevelopment of the area to build the Chalkhill Estate. At the time of writing the Chalkhill Estate is itself to undergo redevelopment, including demolition of all the concrete tower blocks. Looking at the photo of the town hall on p. 59 will put these photographs in perspective as well as give a much clearer idea of the 'town houses' that existed before the Chalkhill Estate.

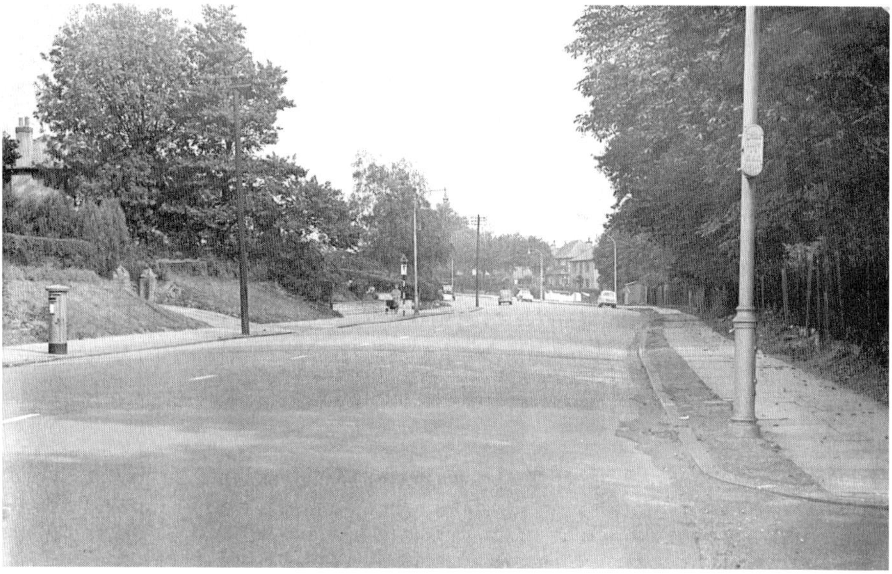

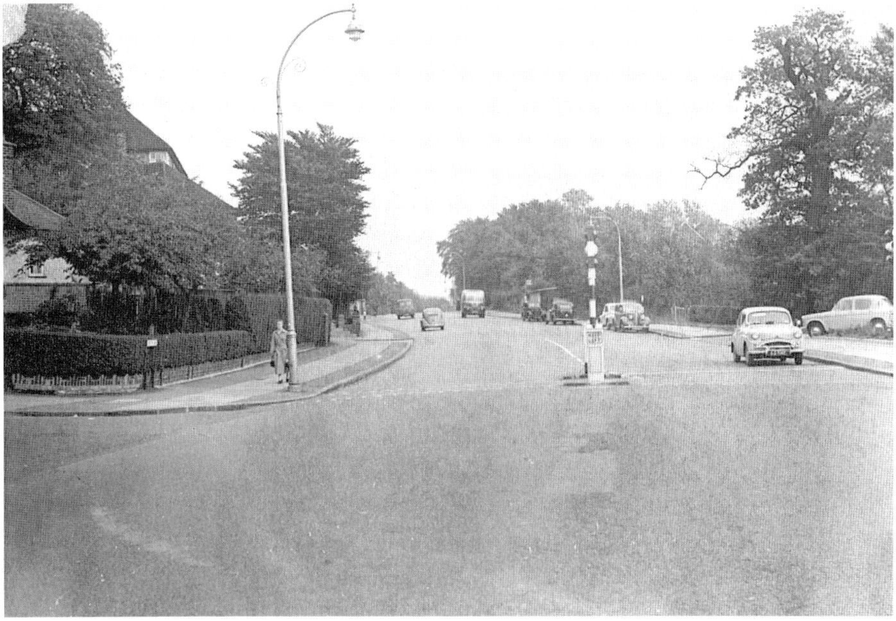

Forty Lane, 1957–8 (see opposite page).

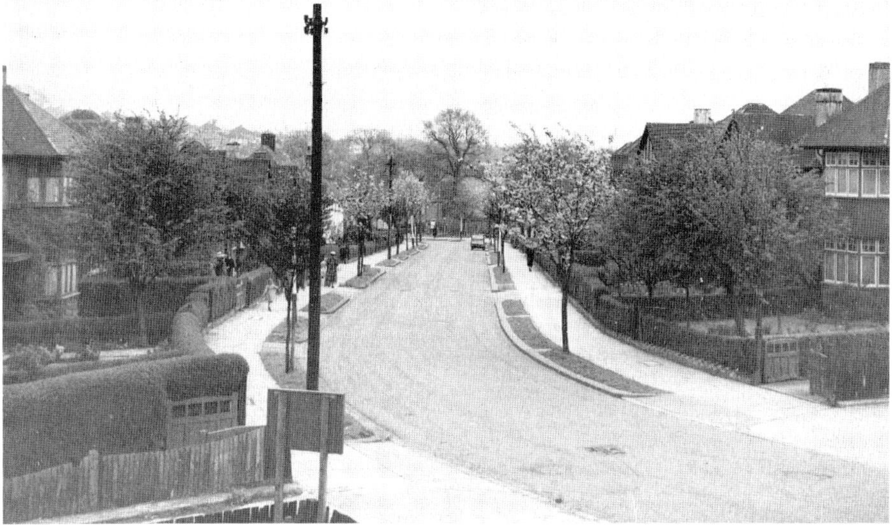

Uxendon Crescent, in Wembley Park. Named after Uxendon Farm (see p. 15) which was first documented in 1257 as Woxindon. The second element of the name is the Old English 'dun' (hill), and the name may refer to Barn Hill. But the first element may, as in Uxbridge, refer to the Anglo-Saxon tribe the Wixan or alternatively be Celtic for water. The Lidding Brook and numerous springs are near by. The presence of a Celtic earthwork and an ancient trackway supports this theory.

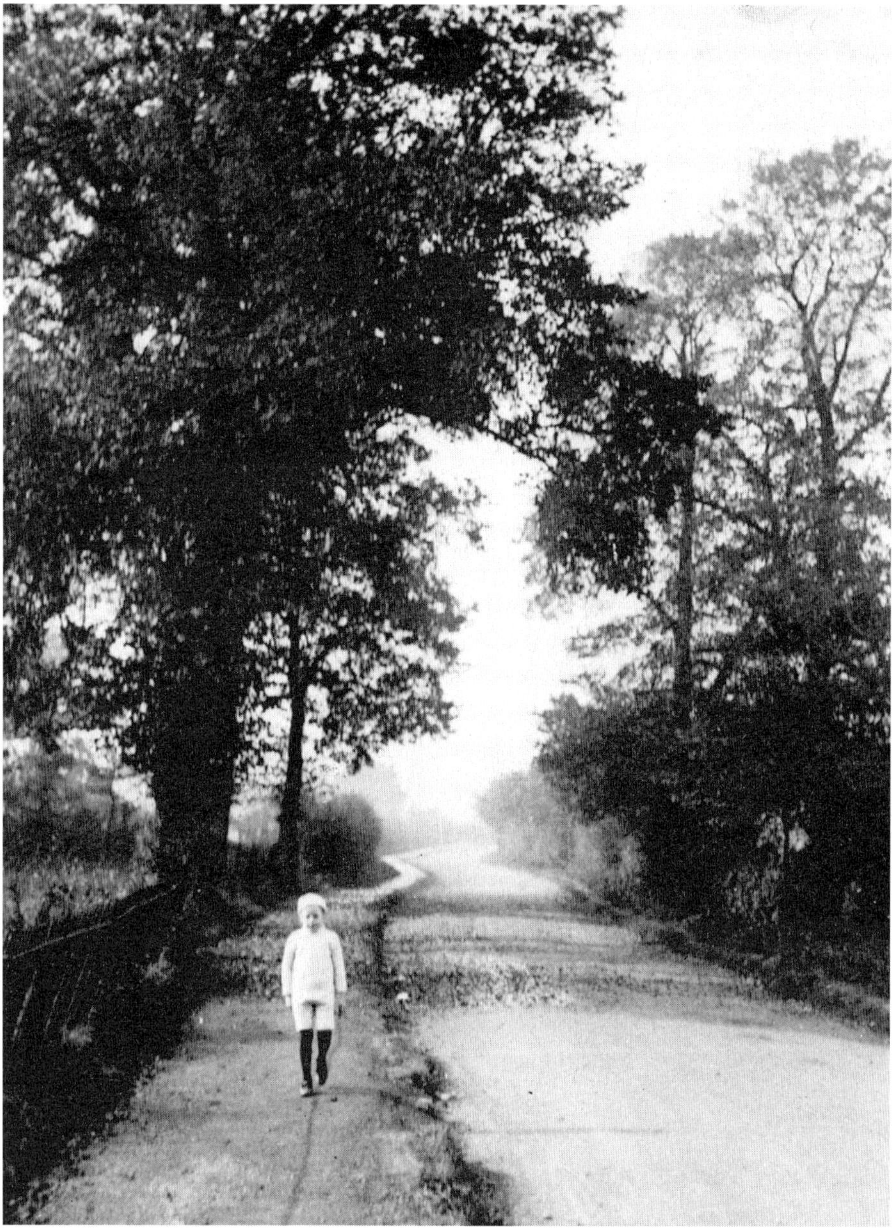

East Lane, 1912. Although East Lane appears in Tudor archives (listed as Est Lane in 1548) there were no houses recorded there until the nineteenth century. The first settlement was Wembley Farm and soon after this Robert Tubbs, of Harlesden, built cottages opposite what is now the GEC estate (see p. 80). The occupiers of the cottages were invariably agricultural labourers, although the advent of the railway did result in a number of railworkers living there.

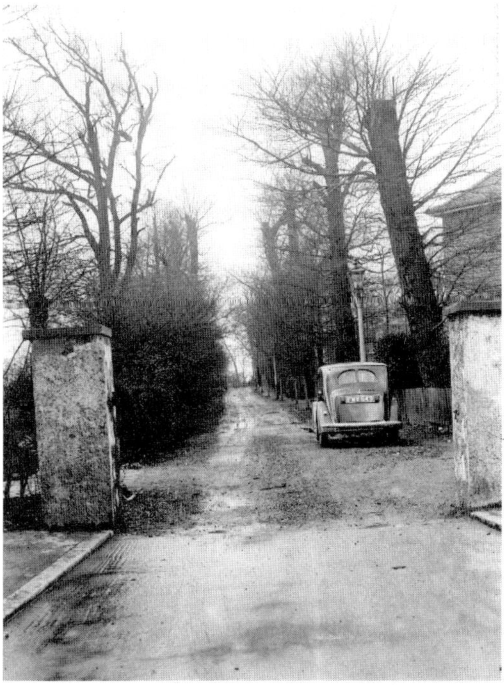

The Drive at the top of Blackbird Hill and running behind Forty Lane down to Chalkhill House (see p. 47), as it was on 6 March 1939. The Drive is the subject of one of the strangest and sadly unreferenced index cards in the London Borough of Brent's archive. A house in The Drive called 'Green Shades' designed by a Mr Candy was apparently the first 'all electric' house.

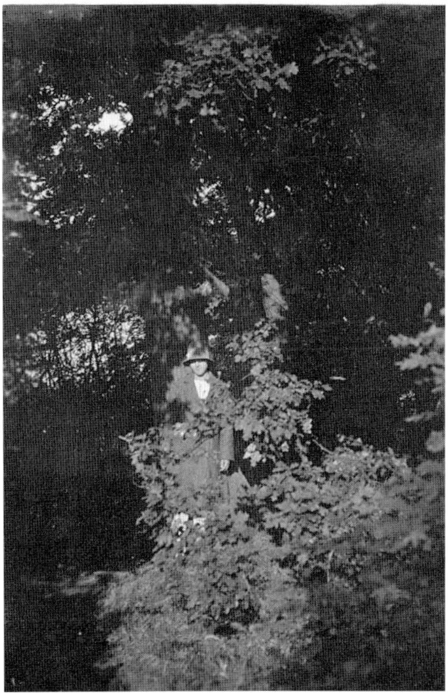

In the woods at Preston Road, *c.* 1925. A delightful image from a family album, alas without any provenance. Other views can be seen on pp. 19 and 25. Preston was a rural hamlet well into this century, and although the Metropolitan Railway passed through the area as early as 1880 there was no real station until 1931–2, although a halt was established in 1908.

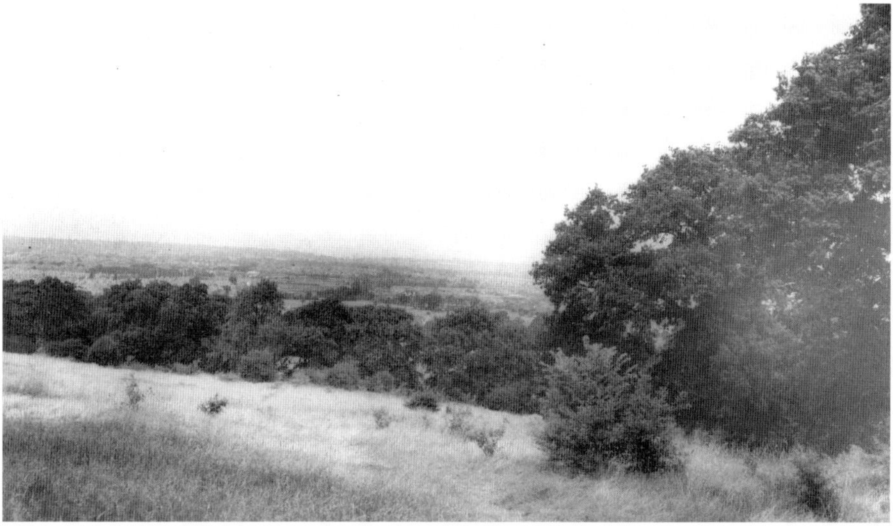

Barn Hill Open Space, *c.* 1950. The importance of parks and open spaces led to the retention of Barn Hill and Fryent Way, particularly as development was fast eroding what unspoilt areas were left. In 1927 Frank Bastable of Haymills conveyed fifty acres to Wembley Urban District Council for the establishment of Barn Hill Open Space. After the opening of Fryent Way in 1935 Wimpey's began redevelopment, proceeding apace with access and sewerage works. Middlesex County Council acted promptly and made a compulsory purchase of the area, with Wembley Council contributing 25 per cent of the cost.

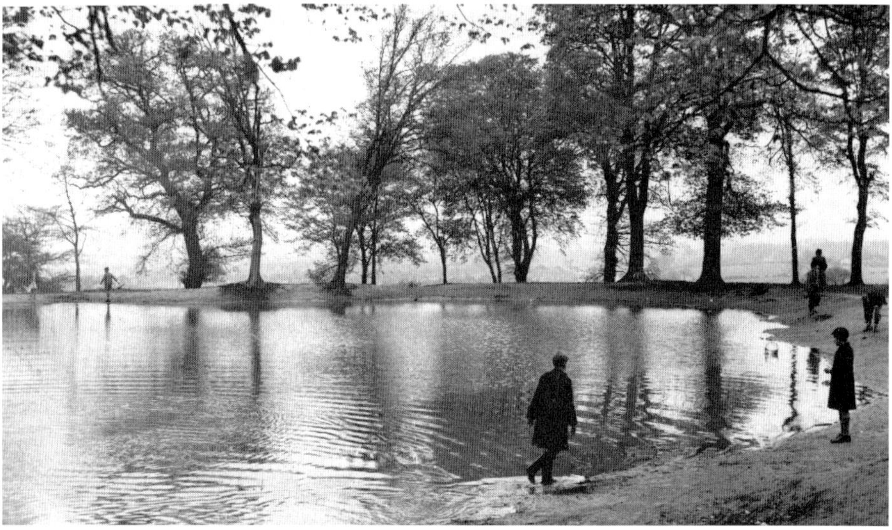

Barn Hill pond, *c.* 1950. The pond on the summit of Barn Hill is of doubtful origin; there was certainly another, smaller, pond which is shown on maps in the mid-nineteenth century. It does not share the characteristics of other common cattle ponds of the period.

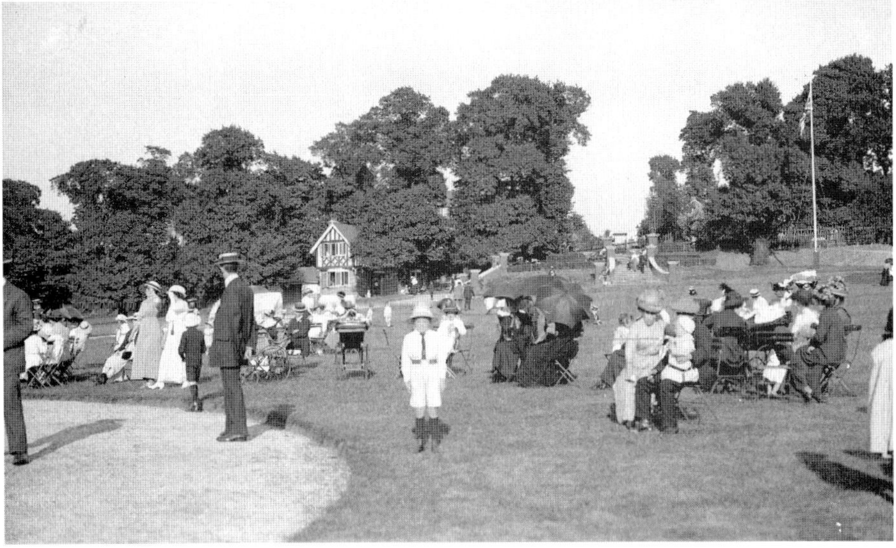

Listening to the band at the opening of King Edward VII Park, 4 July 1914. A photo by Kuno Reitz (see p. 35). The creation of King Edward VII Park was partly to recompense the public for the loss of the facilities offered by Wembley Park. The bandstand (not actually visible in this photo) was burnt down in October 1963.

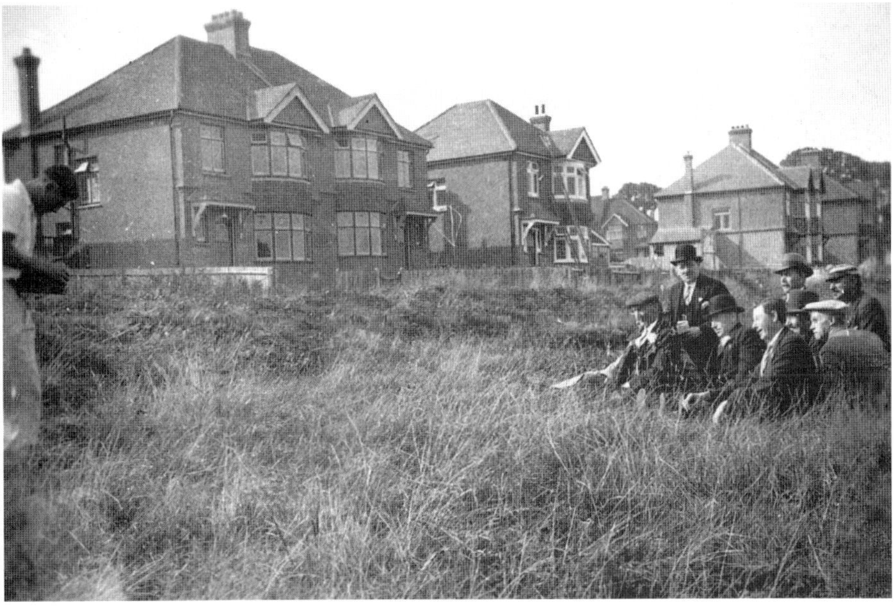

On the cricket ground, Preston Road, *c.* 1920. Another appealing image from a very impressive but undocumented family photo album (see pp. 19 and 23). Note that on the left of the image another photographer is patiently at work, and most of the people in this photograph are looking at him.

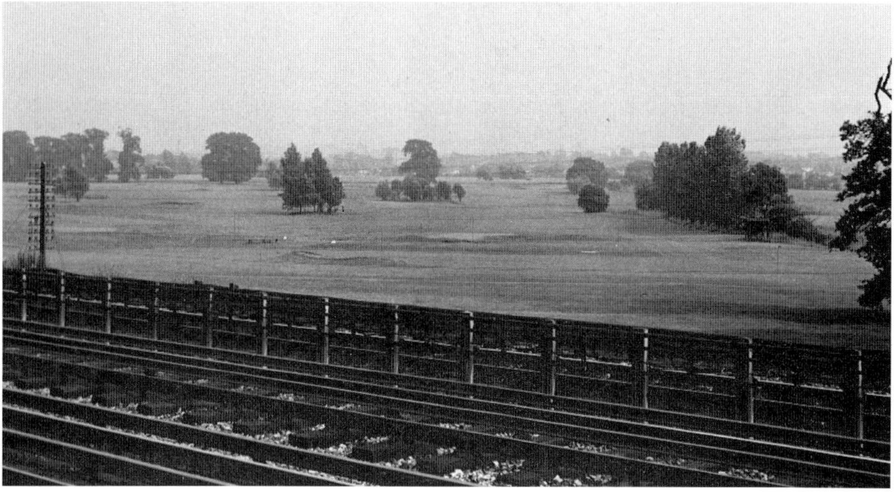

Northwick Park from the Metropolitan Railway, in the summer of 1953. The widow of the third (and last) Lord Northwick left Northwick Park to her grandson, Captain E. Spencer-Churchill, in 1912. By 1927 he was naming streets Pebworth Road and Paxford Road, after villages around his Gloucestershire seat. In 1936 Middlesex County Council and Wembley Borough Council agreed to the acquisition of the Northwick Park Estate (192 acres) as an addition to the regional open space.

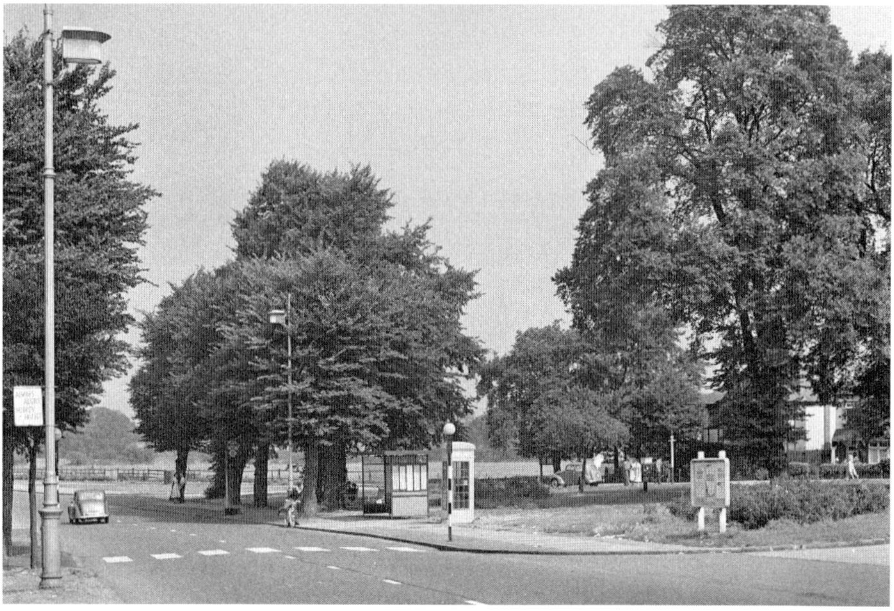

Watford Road and Carlton Avenue West, *c.* 1950. Watford Road was Pinner Road until the early twentieth century. This image shows the junction with Carlton Avenue West on the left and the corner of Northwick Park, which curves away to the right middle distance. The building to be seen through the trees is St Cuthbert's Church.

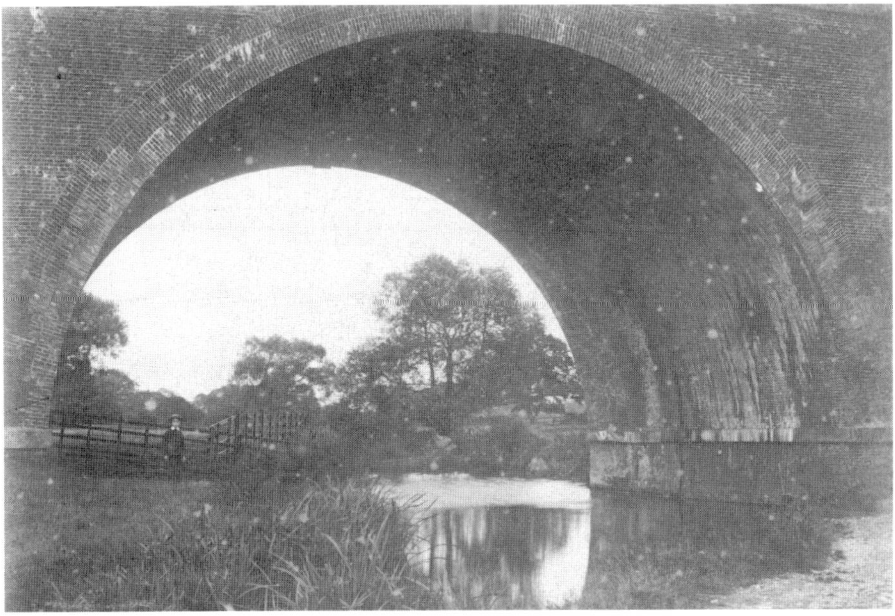

Bridge over the River Brent, *c.* 1880. The London and North Western Railway bridge over the River Brent from Frederick Wood's photograph collection (see pp. 11, 88 and 97). The London and Birmingham Railway built this bridge during construction of the line in 1835–7. Later the London and Birmingham became the London and North Western by acquisition and merger.

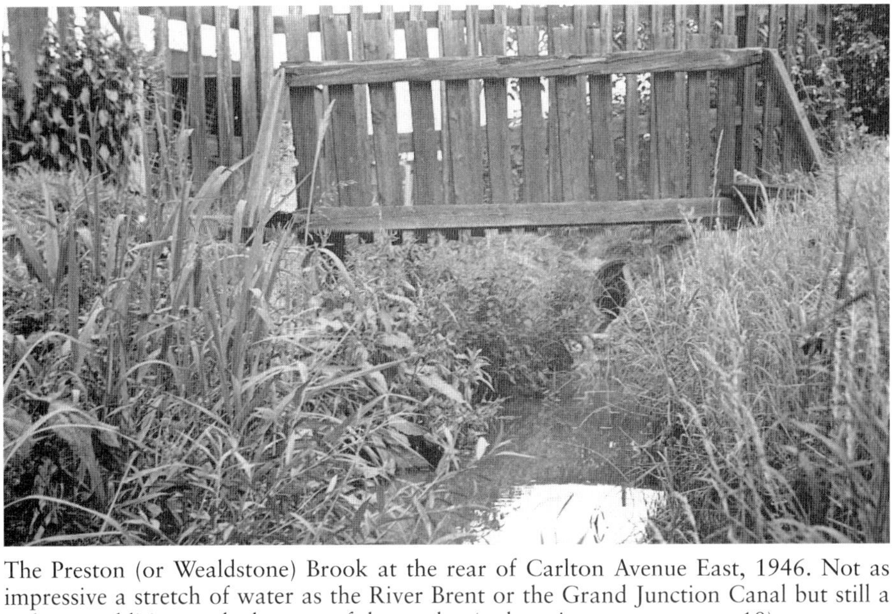

The Preston (or Wealdstone) Brook at the rear of Carlton Avenue East, 1946. Not as impressive a stretch of water as the River Brent or the Grand Junction Canal but still a welcome addition to the bottom of the garden (at least in summer; see p. 18).

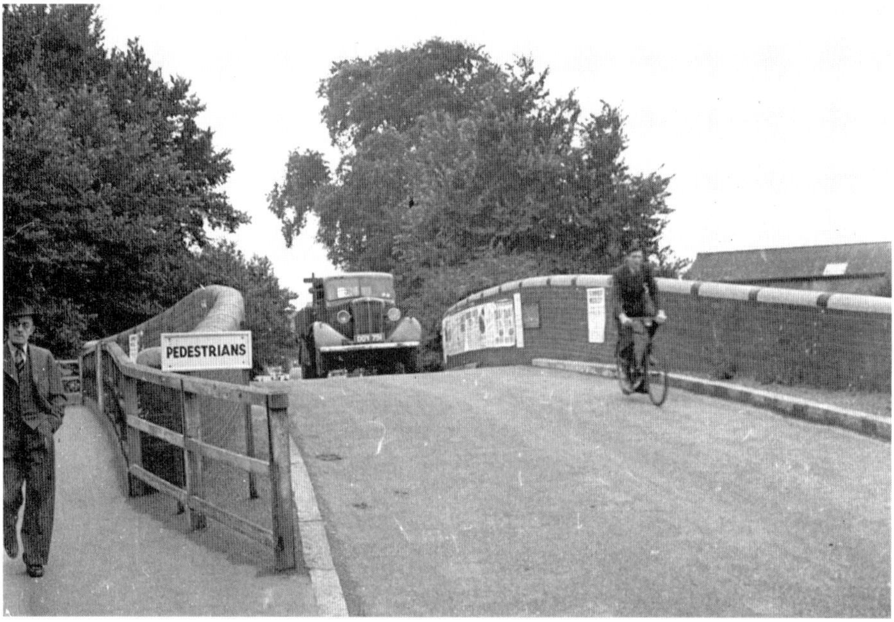

Manor Farm Road Canal Bridge, 4 July 1950 (above) and Canal Bridge, Alperton, *c.* 1910 (below). This is the bridge also to be seen in the background on p. 5, as viewed from the canal. It is clear that the Grand Union Canal, of which the part that flows through Wembley is known as the Paddington Canal, has always had a recreational usage as well as providing a commercial transportation infrastructure. The Paddington Canal was surveyed in 1794 and work commenced in 1797. The canal was added to in 1816 when the branch to Camden Town was opened and again in 1820 when the link to the Thames at Limehouse Basin was inaugurated.

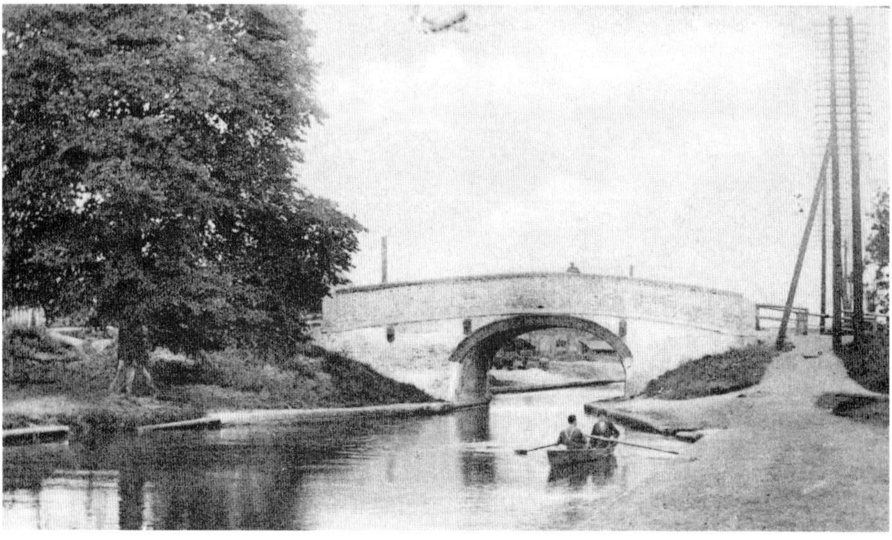

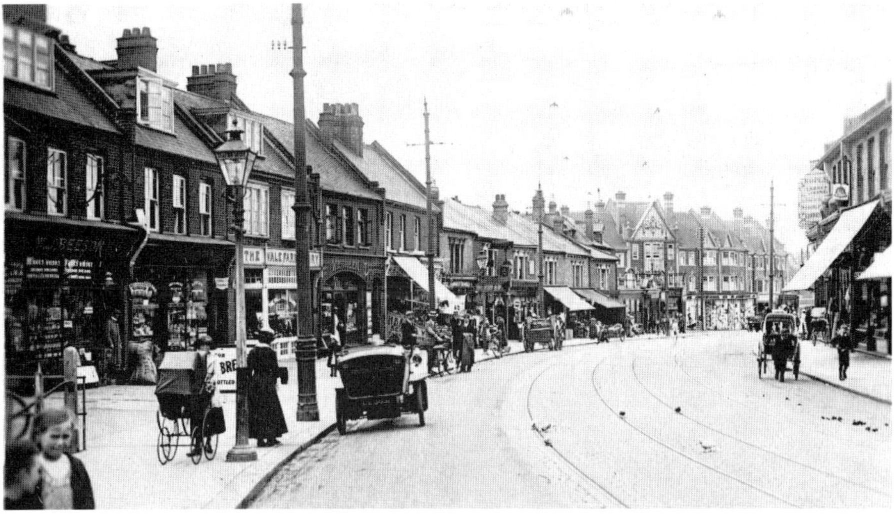

High Road and Quadrant, Wembley, *c.* 1910. Note the shops on the left: W.J. Beeson wine merchants, R.L. Whigham chemist, Vale Farm Dairy shop, W.T. Green bootmaker and, at the junction with Ealing Road, the single-storey Railway Tavern, the proprietor in 1906 being H. Harding.

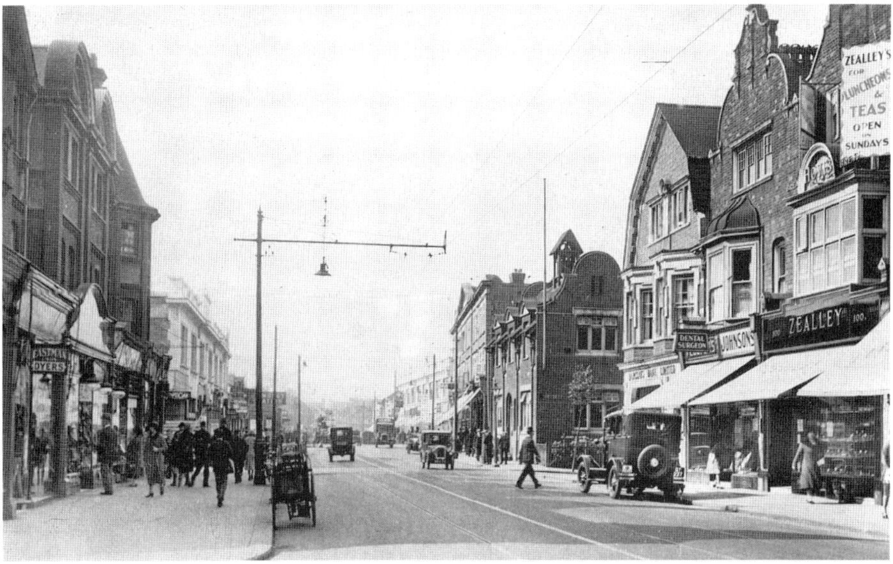

High Road looking west towards Wembley Central station, *c.* 1930. Taken from the junction with London Road, St John's Road is on the right hand side, and the building on the corner is the Wembley Borough Council offices (the site was sold to British Home Stores in 1962). Zealley's, at 100 High Road, is advertising luncheons and teas, and Barclays Bank is on the opposite corner to the council offices.

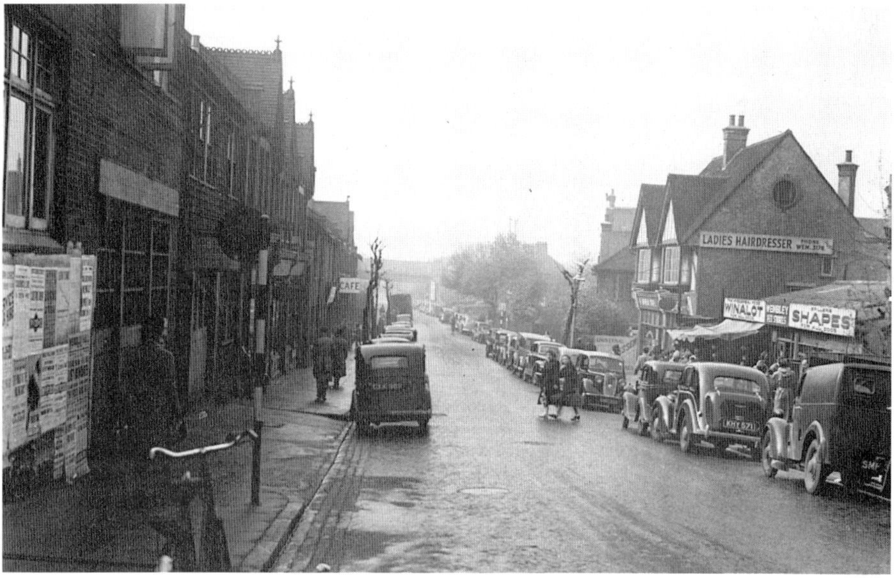

St John's Road at 5 p.m. on 6 May 1950. Notice the ladies' hairdresser's and the Wembley Pet Stores on the right, advertising Winalot Shapes. On the left is a café, which by 1956 was the Ritz Snack Bar (proprietor R.H. Dutton). The photographs were taken to highlight the problem of parking in the vicinity of the High Road.

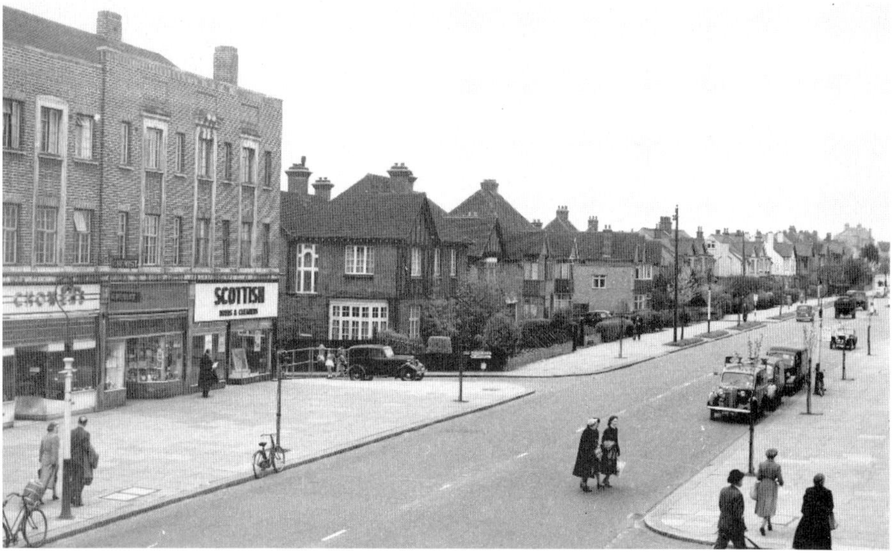

Preston Road looking north along the parade of shops up towards Preston Hill, with Preston Waye on the left. A typical scene of a quiet suburb going about its weekday shopping, *c.* 1950. The premises seen here are (from left to right): Chowens Bakeries Ltd, H. Haydon dispensing chemist, and Scottish Dyers and Cleaners (receiving office). For the shops further north, at the junction with The Avenue, see p. 33.

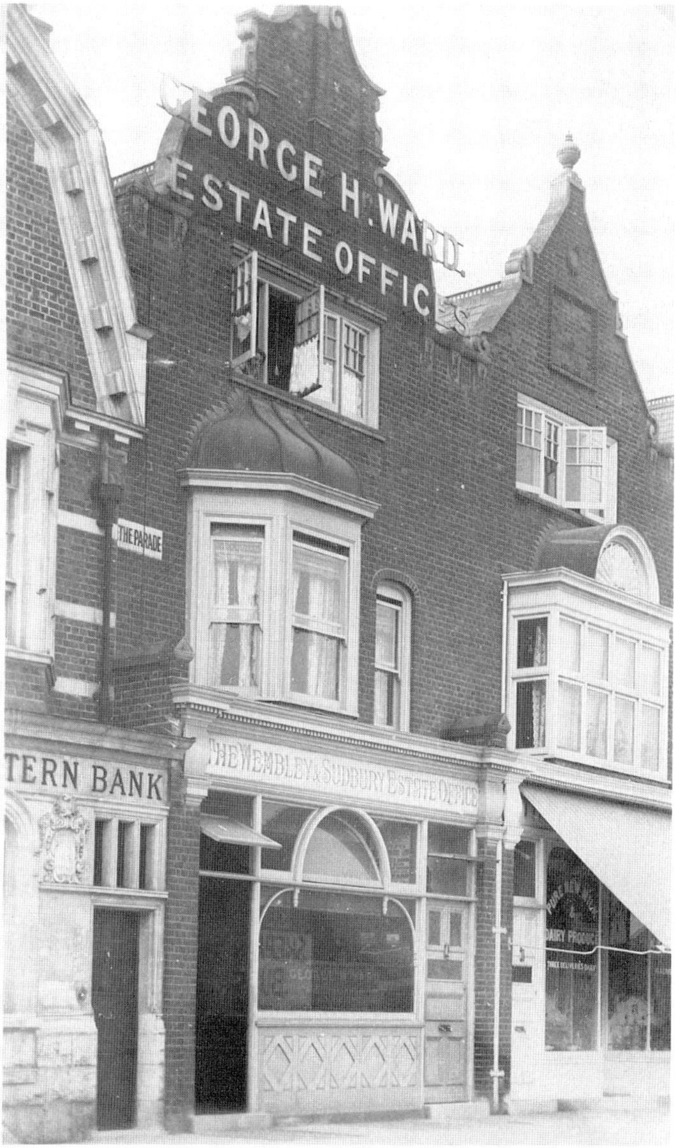

No. 1 The Parade, Wembley, *c.* 1900. Here it houses George Ward's estate office. This gentleman had sufficient influence to change the name of the now Wembley Central station from 'Sudbury and Wembley' to 'Wembley for Sudbury' in 1910. Originally the name of the station was 'Sudbury (for Wembley)'. As an estate agent and surveyor Ward was instrumental in the development of Wembley, suggesting the layout of Elm Road, designing working-class accommodation for Mrs Anne Ecclestone (hence Ecclestone Place) at Wembley Green, and eighteen houses for a new street, Park Place. As a prominent local businessman he had a leading role in the establishment of Wembley Rotary Club in 1930.

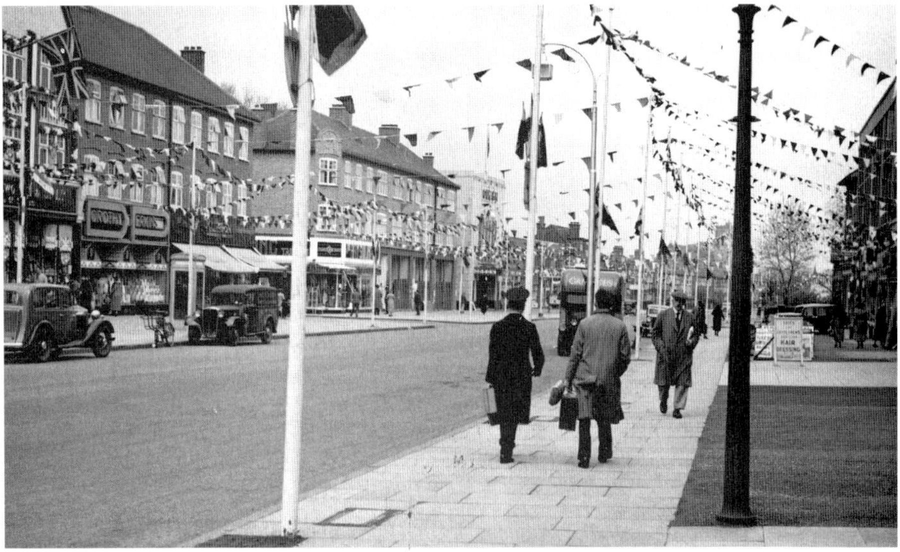

Kenton Road decorated for the Coronation, 1952. Kenton mushroomed in the 1920s and particularly the 1930s, its population increasing from 268 in 1921, when it was just a rural hamlet, to 6,171 in 1931, when all trace of the previous settlement had disappeared. After 1934 Kenton became two wards, the northern part in Harrow, the southern in Wembley. By 1951 the combined population was 27,680.

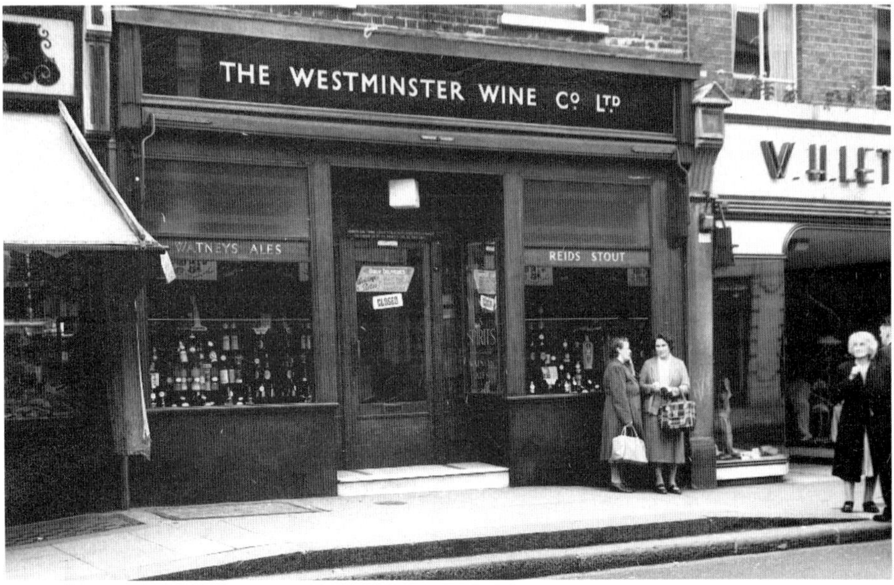

The High Road in the late 1940s. The Westminster Wine Co. Ltd and W.H. Letty milliner at Nos 118 and 120 respectively are shown (before the road was re-numbered). This photo was donated by the *Wembley News*.

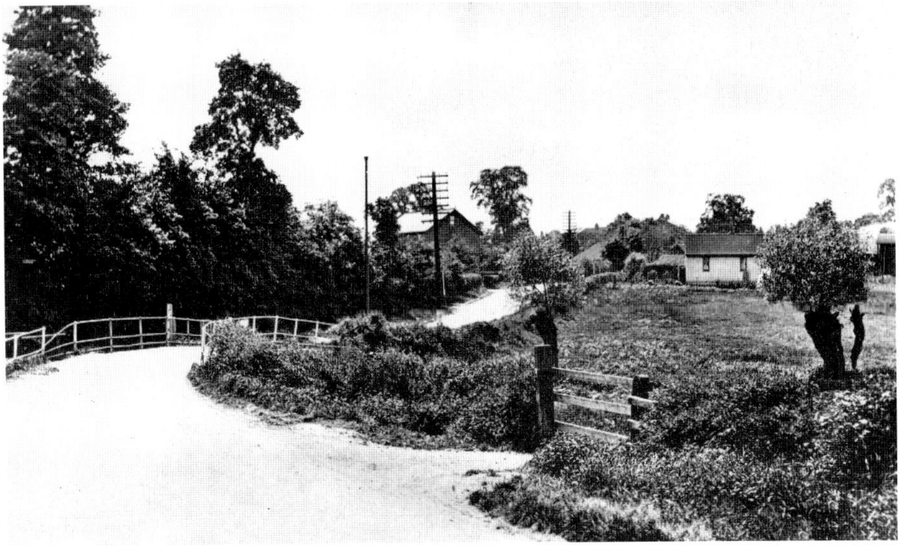

Preston Road, *c.* 1900. A postcard view indicative of the condition of Preston before its development this century. Preston was another rural hamlet that developed in the space of just a couple of decades, the population expanding from just a few hundred in the 1920s to 12,408 in 1951. Preston means 'the farm belonging to a priest'. It may have been granted to Abbot Stidberht by Offa in 767 but if this was the case its connection with the Church was lost before 1086.

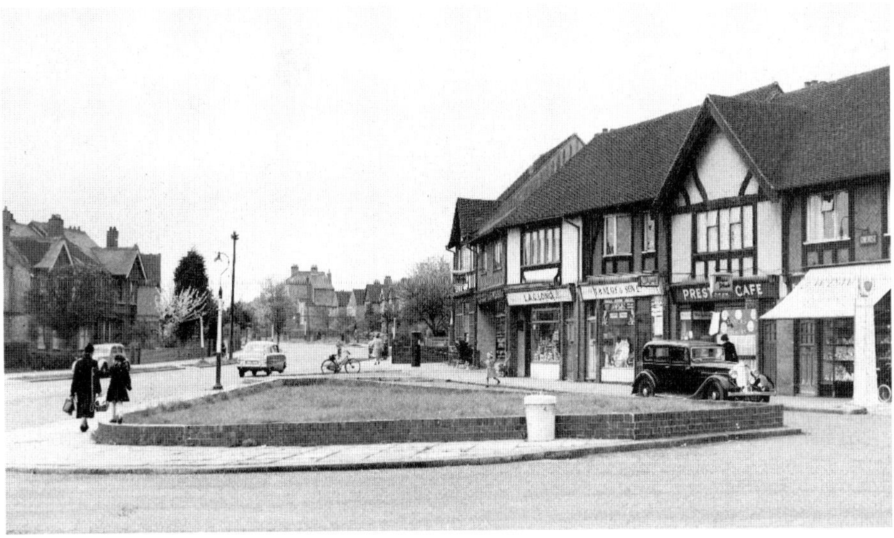

The small shopping parade at the junction of Preston Road and The Avenue, early 1950s. We are looking north towards the junction with Toley Avenue (named after the builder Albert Toley who obtained a development permit for the street in 1924). No. 340, the large house on the corner (centre left, middle distance) was the address, in 1956, of Dr R.E. Perth, Physician and Surgeon.

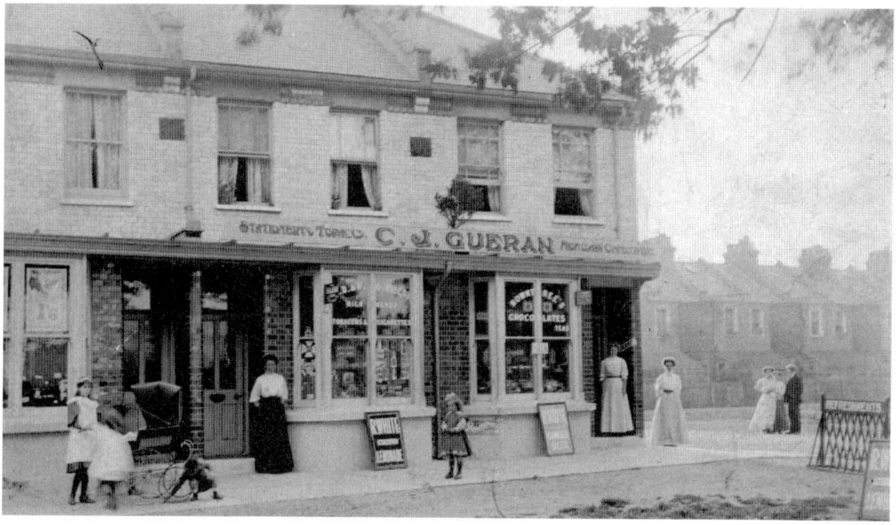

Gueran's confectioner's in Ealing Road on the corner of Burns Road, *c.* 1910. Burns Road was an estate of working men's cottages developed by Henry Haynes, the dominant entrepreneur in Alperton until his death in 1910. His main business activity was brick and tile manufacture but on his business card he described himself as 'a boat builder, wheel wright, wharfinger, supplier of building materials, coal and coke'. At one stage he owned seventy of the hundred buildings in Alperton, employed nearly the entire workforce and issued his own coinage.

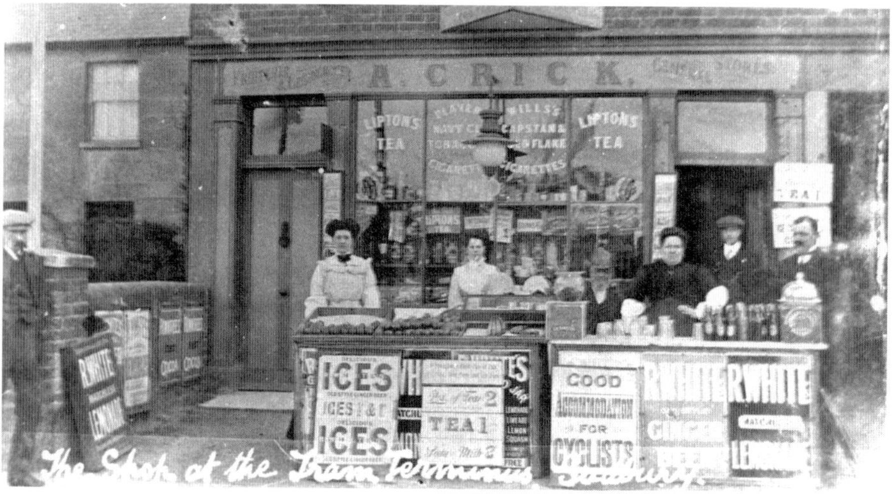

Arthur Crick's general store in Canterbury Place, Harrow Road. Crick moved to Wembley from his native Huntingdonshire around 1889 and was employed by his uncle Ruben Williams as the hansom cab driver for Sudbury. Williams, who had been a Wembley resident since 1850, also ran the general store and Arthur moved in with the Williams family above their shop, eventually taking over the business. The photograph was taken in 1912, and among other things being advertised is 'Good accommodation for cyclists'.

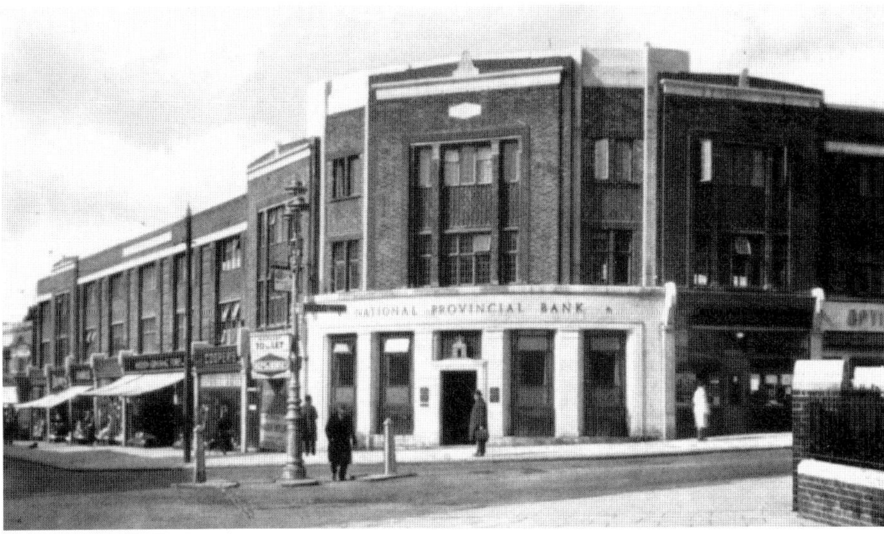

Park Lane Parade, High Road, Wembley, *c.* 1934. One of the many photos of Wembley taken by Kuno Reitz. Reitz was a German immigrant, having been born in Munich in 1876. He moved to England in 1911 and quickly established himself as an apprentice with Meisen Bach, a company pioneering the half-tone process for newspaper illustration. During the First World War he was engaged in roadmaking in Northumberland, presumably due to his nationality. By the 1930s he was a successful freelance photographer. Tragically he was blinded by a stroke towards the end of his life and died in 1958.

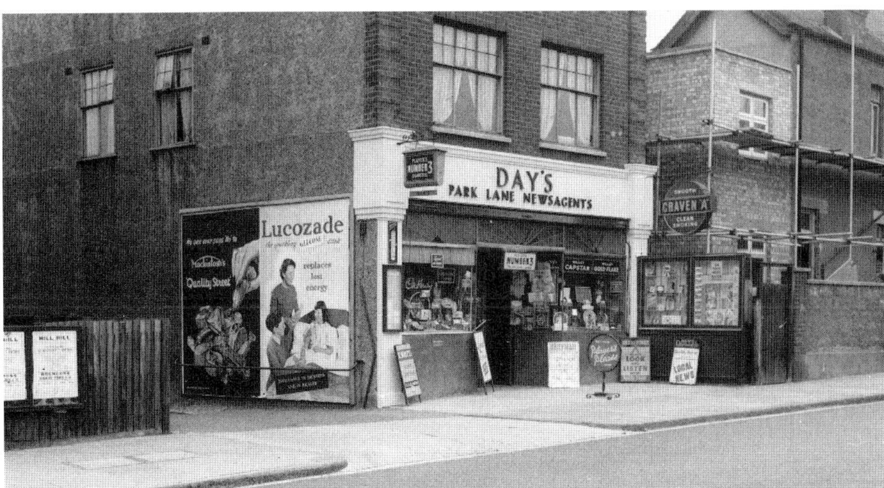

Day's newsagent's in Park Lane, 1951. Notice the adverts: the large posters on the side of the building for Mackintosh's Quality Street and Lucozade, the advertising boards outside for R. White's Soft Drinks, the *Daily Mail* (headline 'Dawson in the Box: Full Story') and the *Radio Times*. In the shop there appears to be a large display of Cadbury's products.

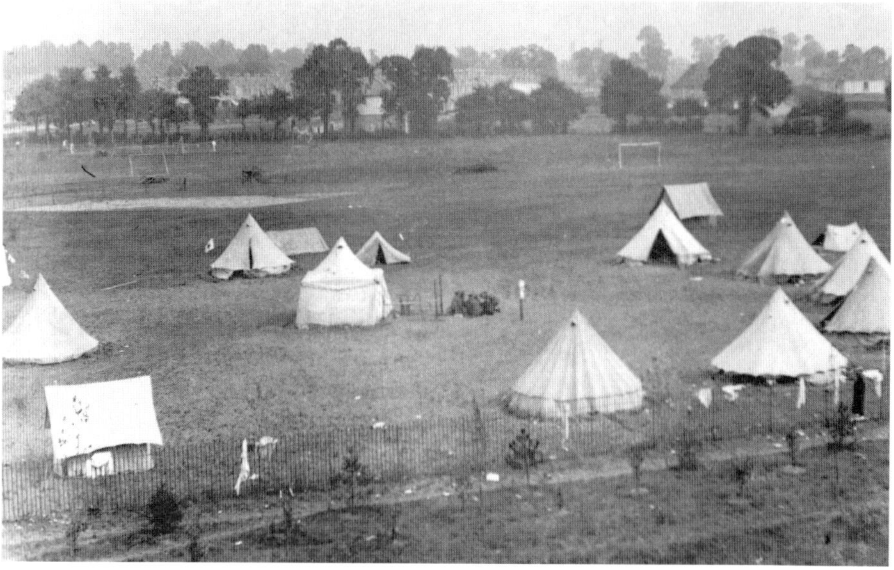

The Foreign Legion camping on East Lane in 1914. A group of soldiers can be seen outside the large tent in the centre of the field. The camp was sited on the London and Midland Railway Sports Ground.

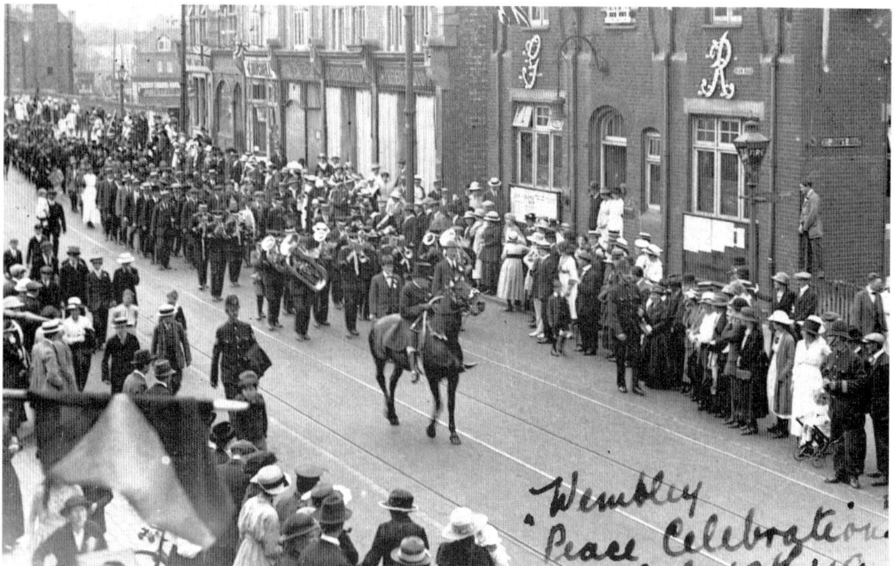

The peace celebrations passing the council offices in Wembley High Road on 19 July 1919. They are led by Councillor George Titus Barham, who was also responsible for the setting up of the committee to organize a memorial to the fallen of the First World War in King Edward VII Park. See also pp. 1 and 61.

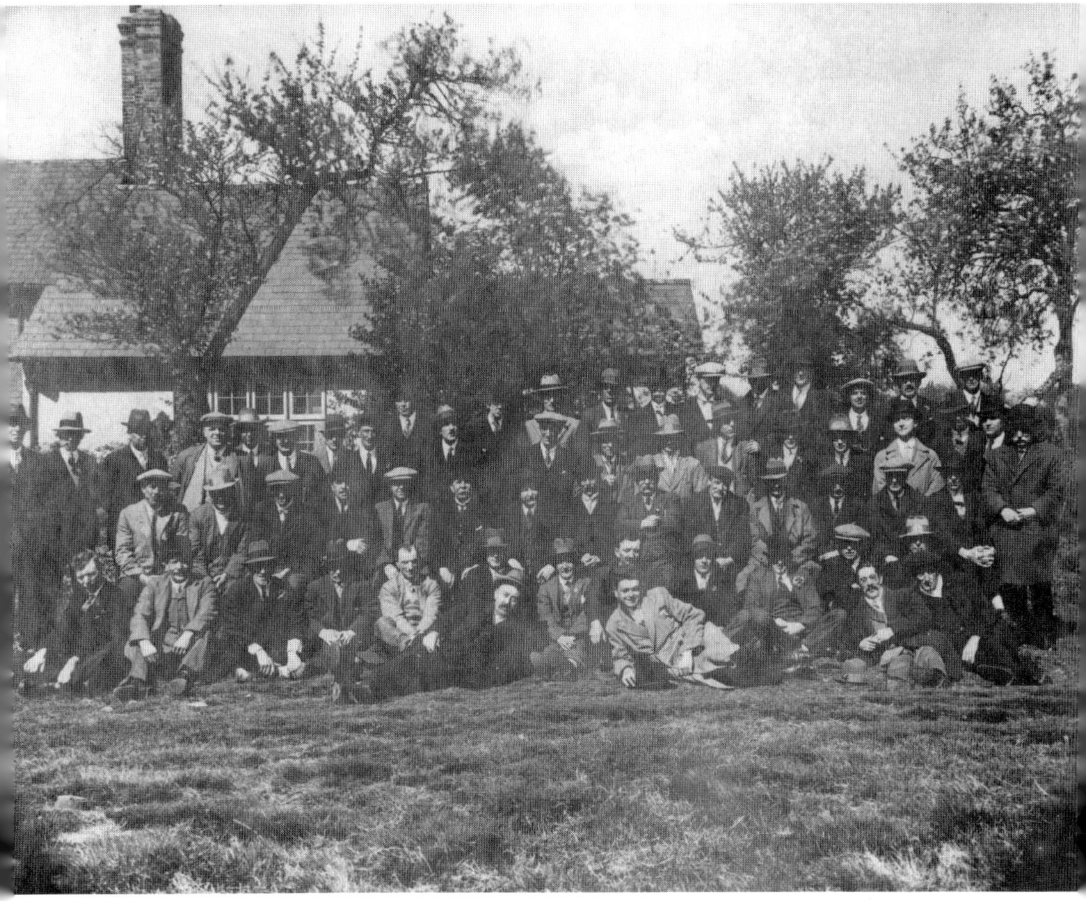

A group of Royal British Legion members posing for a photograph in 1922. This may be the British Legion, Wembley and Sudbury Branch, possibly in the grounds of their hall in Union Road. The organization was established to assist needy ex-servicemen and women and their families, their most obvious operation being the poppy appeal. The picture comes from the same source as the photo on p. 79 (upper).

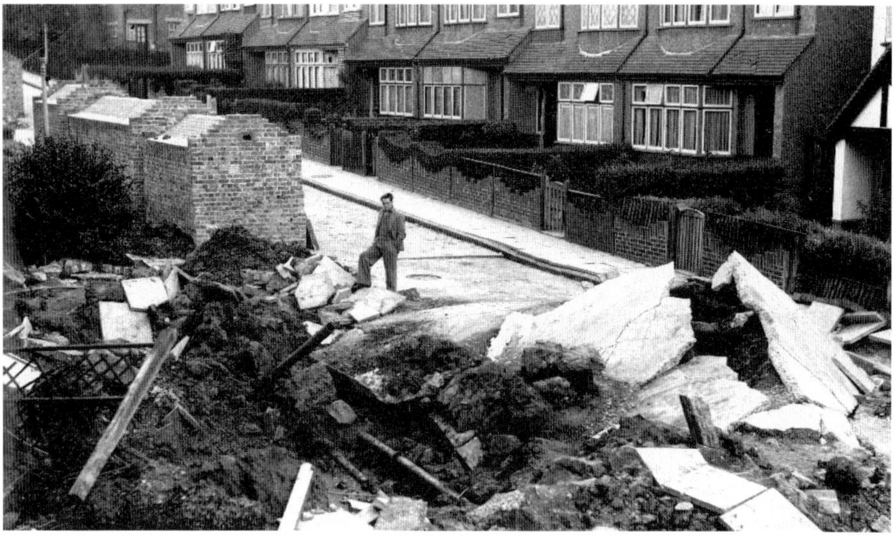

Two photos of bomb damage in Wembley during the Second World War. For reasons of security photos such as these were rarely annotated with an accurate location. The first raid on Wembley was carried out on 27 August 1940, and between then and 11 May 1941 numerous raids occurred. There were RAF depots in the British Empire Exhibition grounds and these obviously provided recurrent targets. In the later stages of the war fourteen V weapons fell on Wembley, the first on 19 June 1944. It is thought some 9,000 bombs fell on the area during the war, resulting in around 149 fatalities and 801 injuries. A total of 18,136 buildings were damaged, including 558 houses demolished or damaged beyond repair.

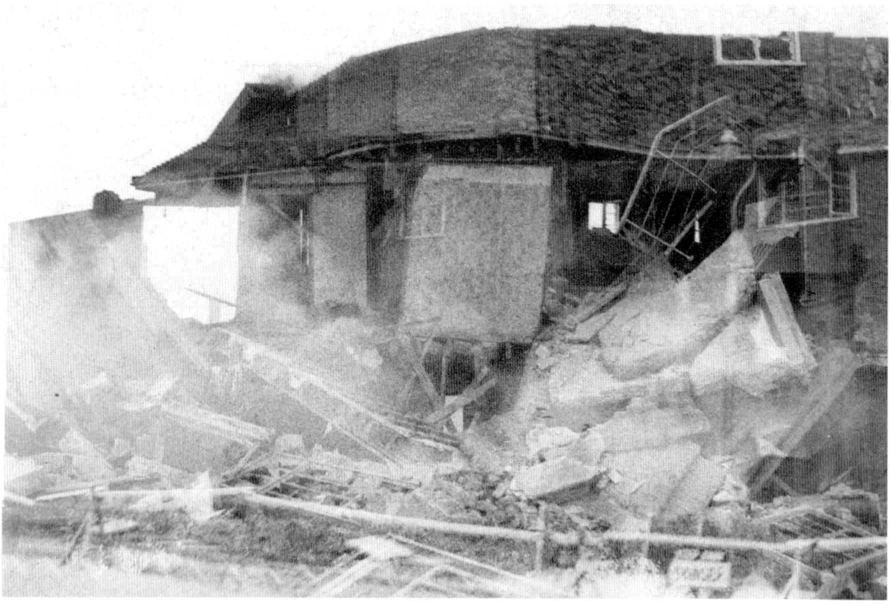

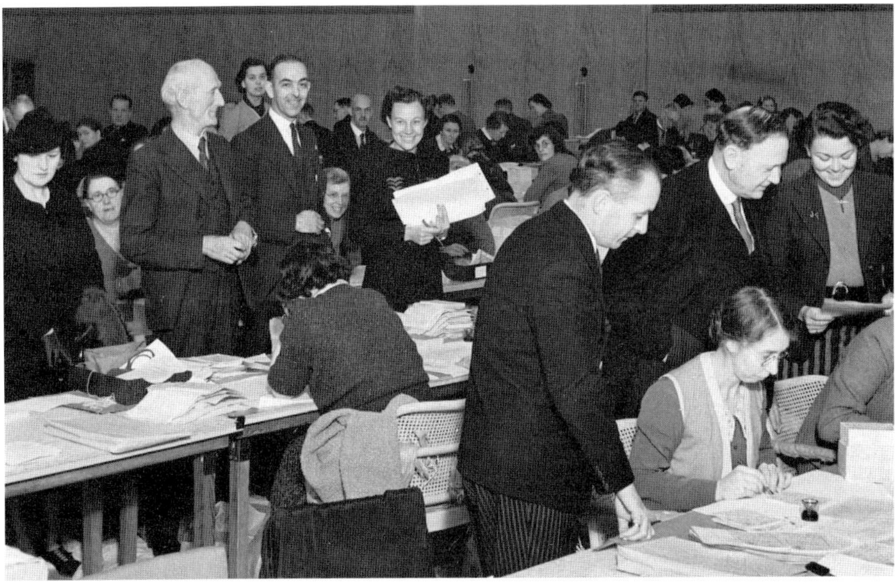

The assembly hall at the town hall, September 1939. This photo records the first time it was used for the writing out of ration books prior to their distribution.

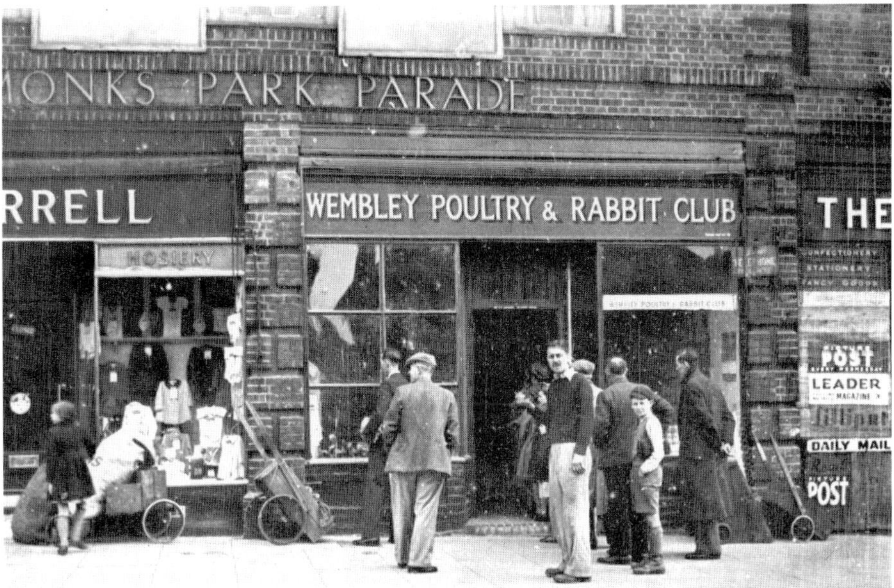

The Wembley Poultry and Rabbit Club shop on Monks Park Parade in Tokyngton, *c.* 1946. The club was originally called the Tokyngton Poultry and Rabbit Club. Essentially a part of the 'Dig for Victory' campaign, the rabbits and hens were of course bred to help meet the food needs of the civilian population.

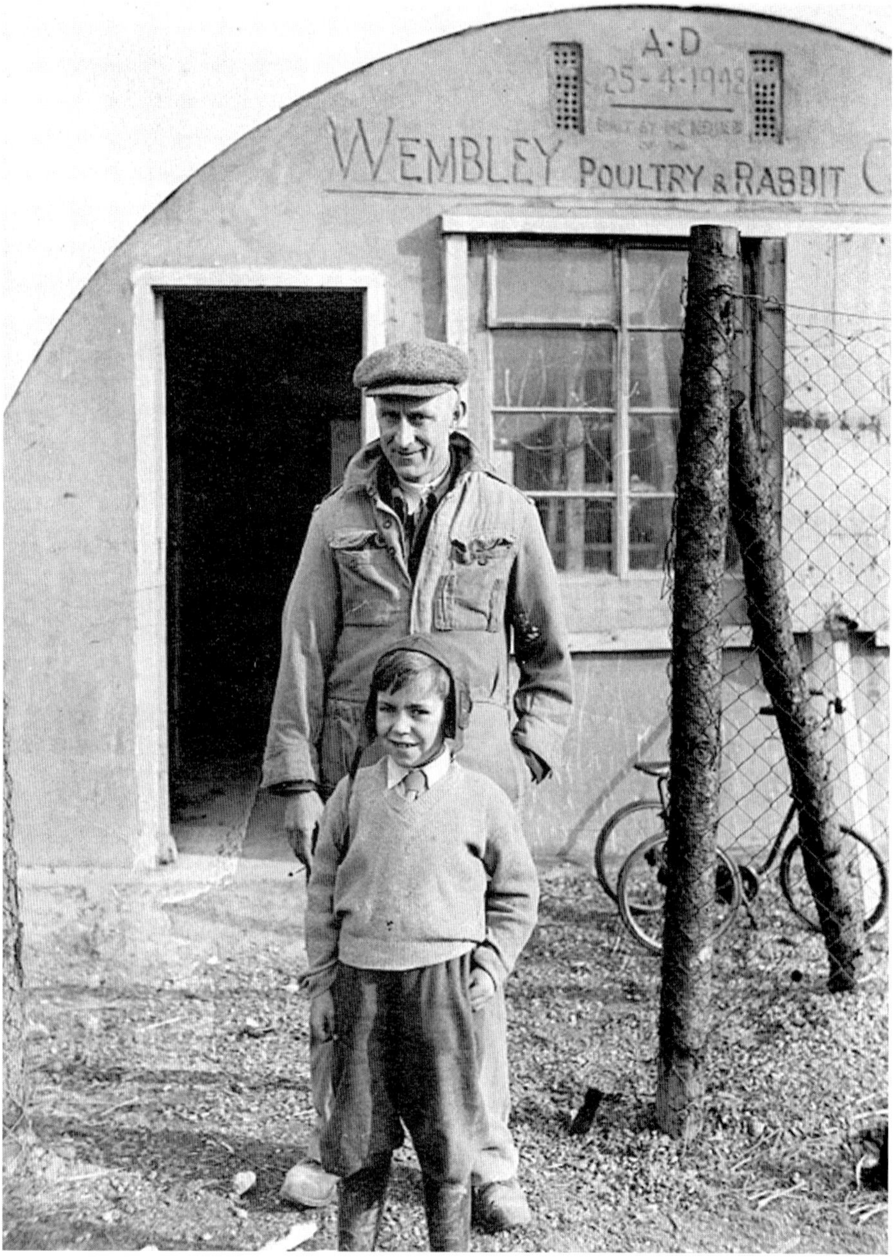

The Wembley Poultry and Rabbit Club Nissen hut, *c.* 1948. The date on the top of the hut is visible as 25.4.1942. By the early 1950s enthusiasm for the club began to wane and an agreement was reached for the 15th Wembley Scouts to use a hut that had been erected at Sherren's Farm in late 1948. The transfer of the premises was concluded early in 1955 with the official handing over of the keys.

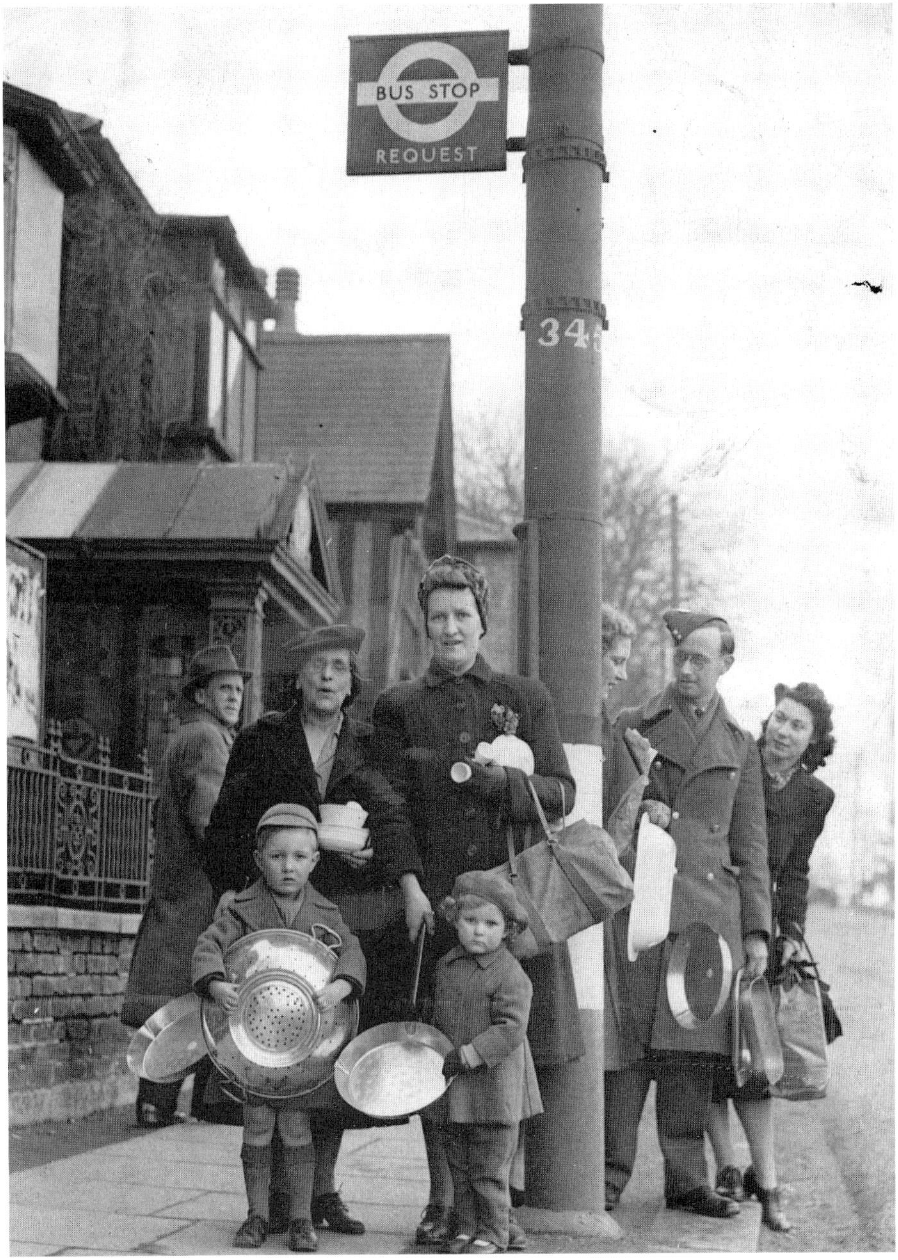

Londoners queueing for pots and pans, 19 February 1945. A group of delighted bargain hunters clutch their treasured possessions as they await the bus just outside what was to become Barham Park Library (see p. 61). The prospect of an end to the war led to the disposal of some £4,000 worth of surplus kitchen utensils, bought by Wembley Borough Council when invasion threatened.

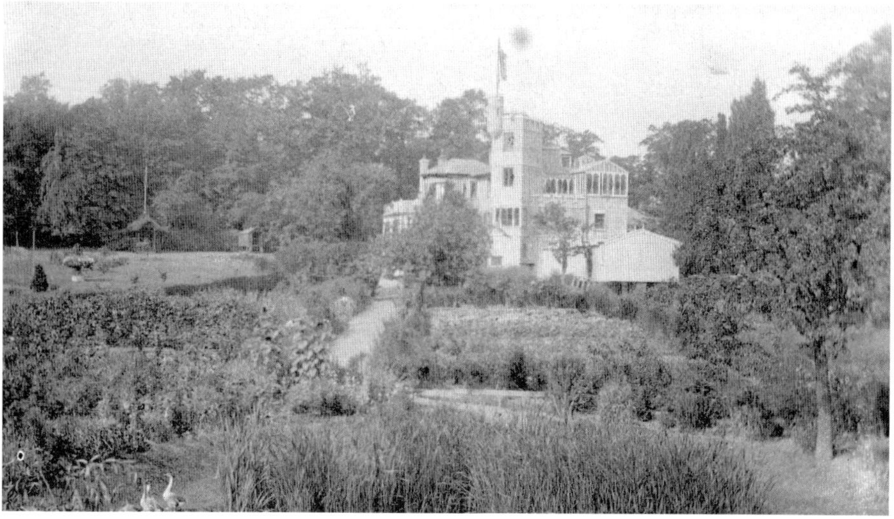

Wembley House in the early 1900s. A property here is marked on the map as early as 1510 when the Page family was in residence. A Georgian building appeared on the site in 1817, the succession of owners including Alperton farmer Thomas Withers. The house survived redevelopment in the early part of the twentieth century, but by 1915 the premises had become a school. The building was bombed during the Second World War and the site was ultimately used for Copland Community School.

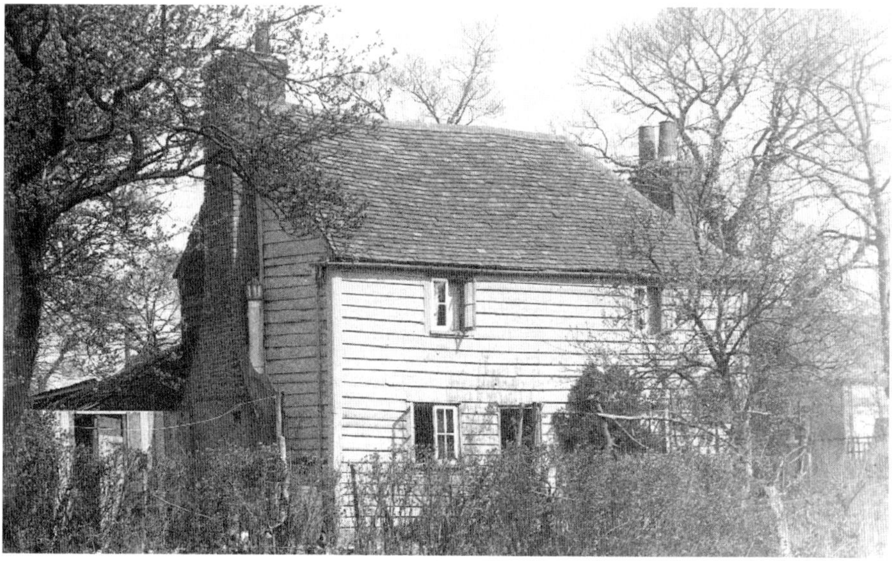

A cottage at Preston, 1933. The caption to this photograph gives us no further information, although we know the name of the photographer, Kuno Reitz (see p. 35). By the time of the 1935 revision of the Ordnance Survey map covering this area only Lyon Farm on Preston Hill remained. The cottage could have belonged to either one of the other farms in the area – Preston or Hillside.

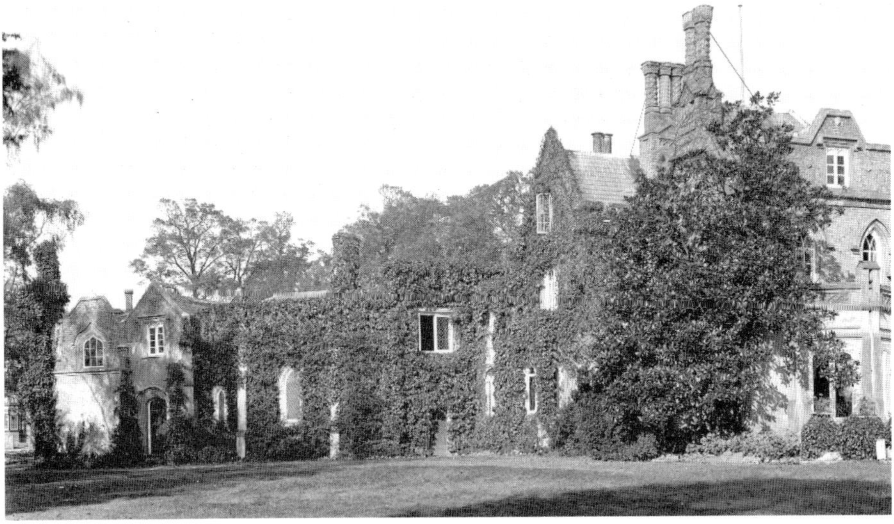

Sudbury Priory. Built in 1828, it is pictured here *c.* 1930, when Ernest G.W. Harmer had been in residence for about seven years. He had, by the mid-1930s, been secretary of the Sudbury Baptist Church for over twenty years. There had apparently been a property on the site since at least 1817 when Lady Sarah Fane of Osterley Park was living here.

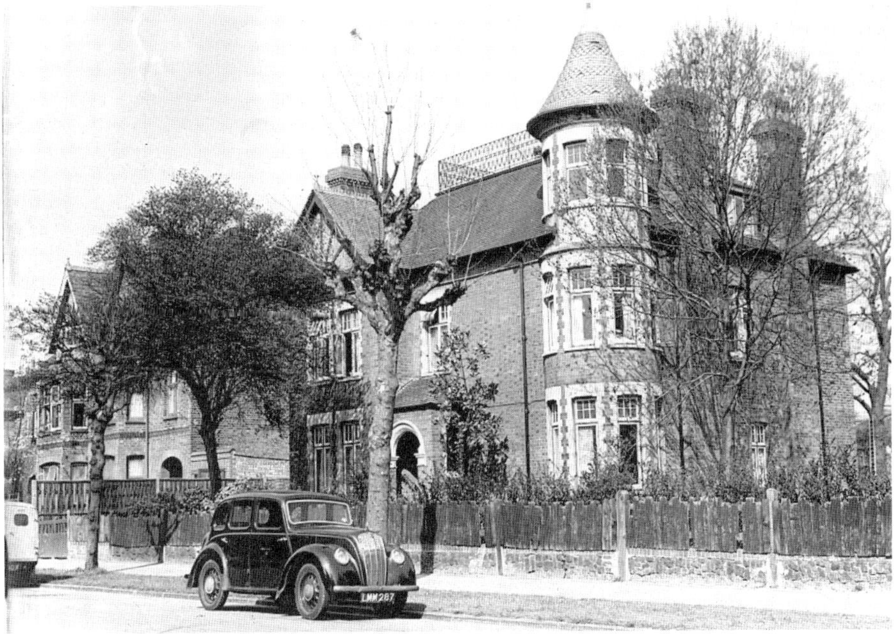

No. 88 Harrowdene Road in April 1958. J.T. Rossiter had this property built in 1899; he was certainly in residence by 1905 according to the Wembley directory, when the property was known as 'The Turret'. It is now an old people's home.

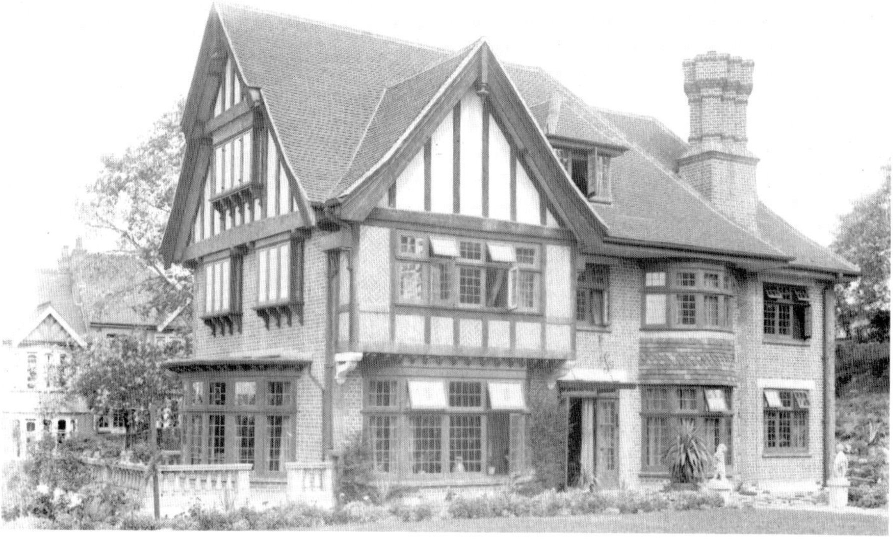

Tudor House, Dagmar Avenue, *c.* 1930. Comben and Wakeling were an active local building concern (see p. 54). They formed a partnership as early as 1891, which existed until the death of J.W. Comben in 1931. However by this time the sons Horace Comben and Eric Wakeling had joined the firm. Dagmar House, built around 1906, was acquired by the firm and became the home of the Comben family. This residence, Tudor House, was built in the back garden of Dagmar House for Wakeling and his family around 1926.

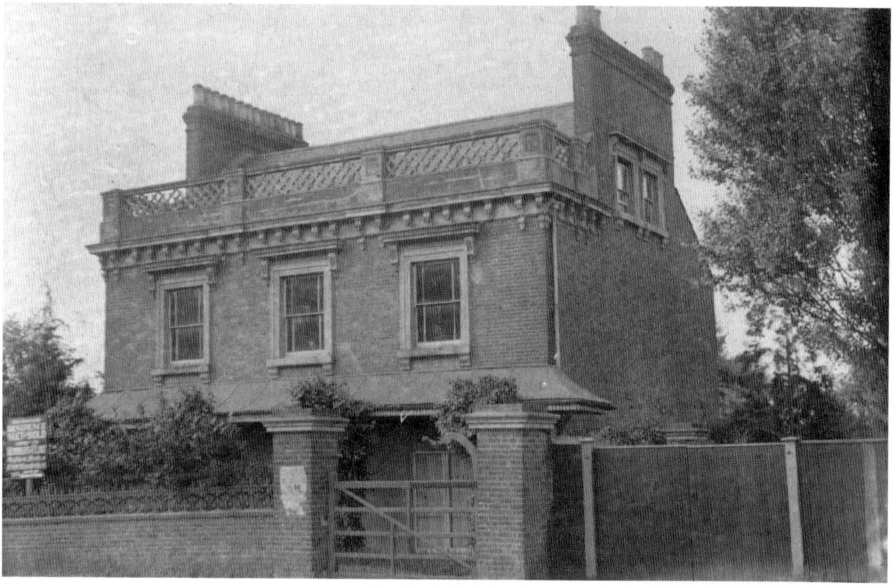

The Poplars, Harrow Road, Sudbury, before 1909. Now 773 Harrow Road, the property was once the home of the Epizootic Abortion Committee under the patronage of the resident, Dr Martin, a vivisectionist.

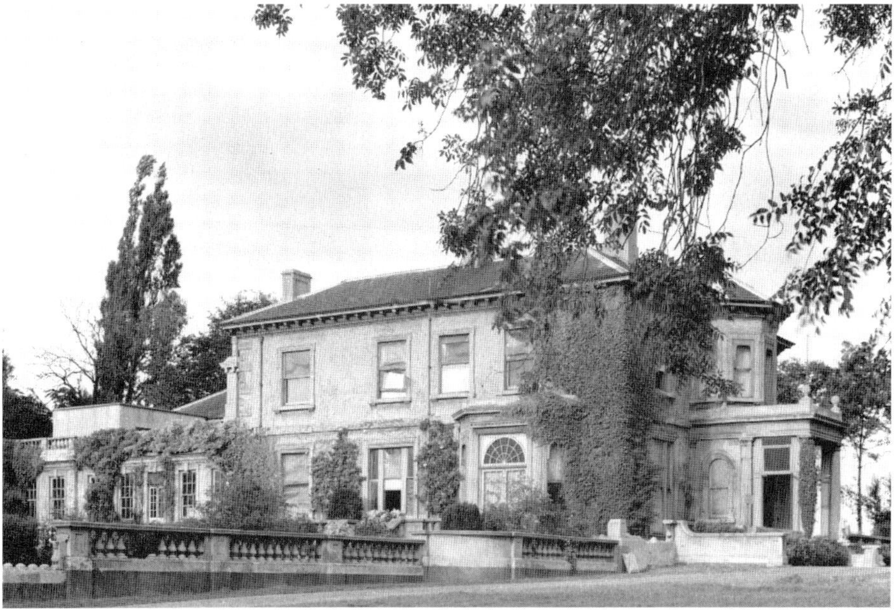

Barham Park Mansion in the early 1950s (above) and a view of the gardens, *c.* 1910 (below). Built by the Copland sisters in the 1850s, the property took its name from the family that founded Express Dairies. The conduct of the council throughout the twenty years following George Titus Barham's death in 1937 was little short of shameless. First they ignored the private museum collection the great man left to the people of Wembley, then they demolished the mansion itself (after leaving it to disintegrate) in 1956–7 – one of the greatest losses to the borough – and, adding insult to injury, the collection was disposed of piecemeal in 1952–4, some of it being sold, some finding its way to the Museum of Rural Life at Reading, while some, thankfully, found its way to the Grange Museum, Neasden, when it opened in 1977.

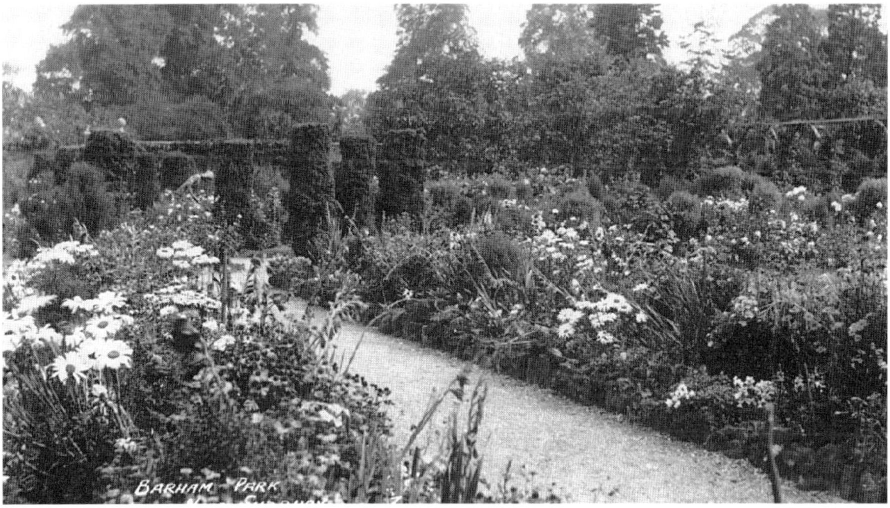

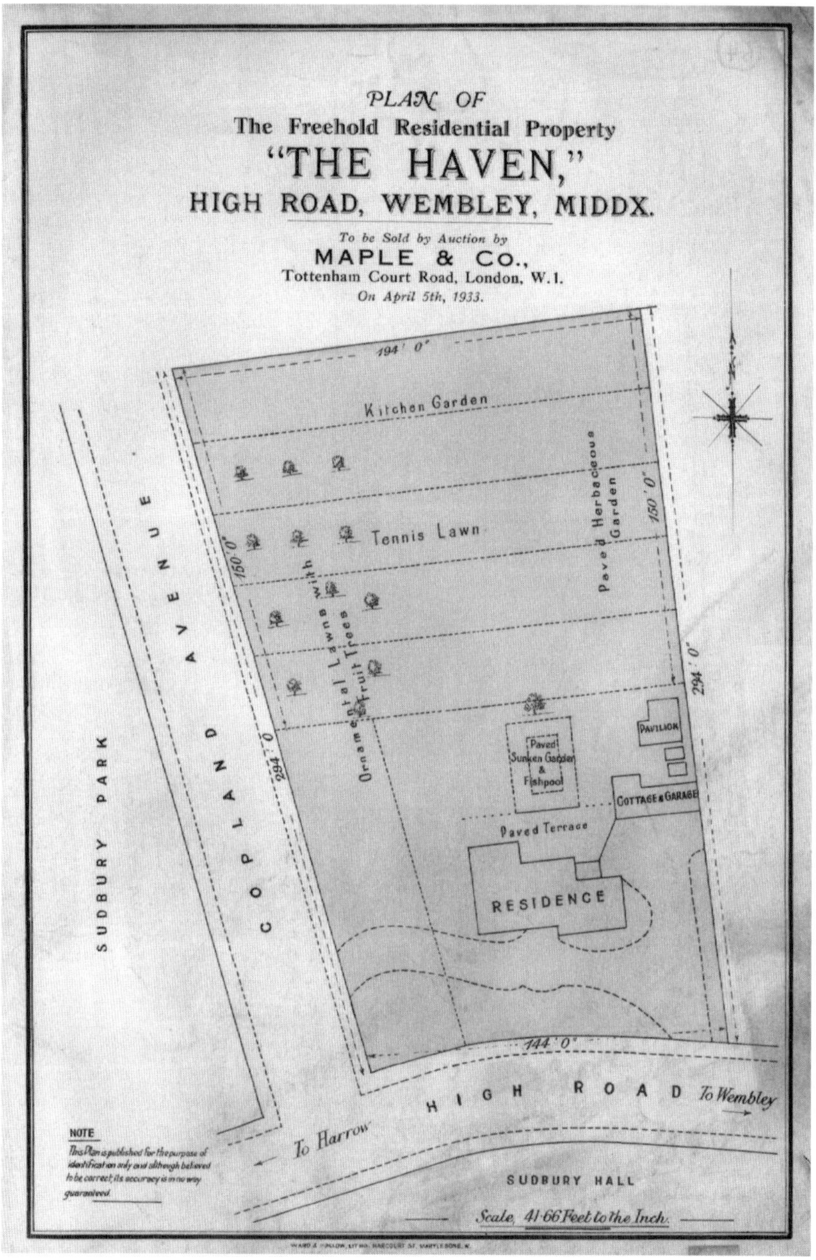

A plan of 'The Haven' from a sales brochure of 1933. The house was built for George Titus Barham, the plan being deposited with the Wembley Urban District Council on 7 January 1899 and gaining approval on the 16th. The property was to be sold by auction on 5 April and the details produced for the occasion were extensive, consisting of four photographs in addition to this plan.

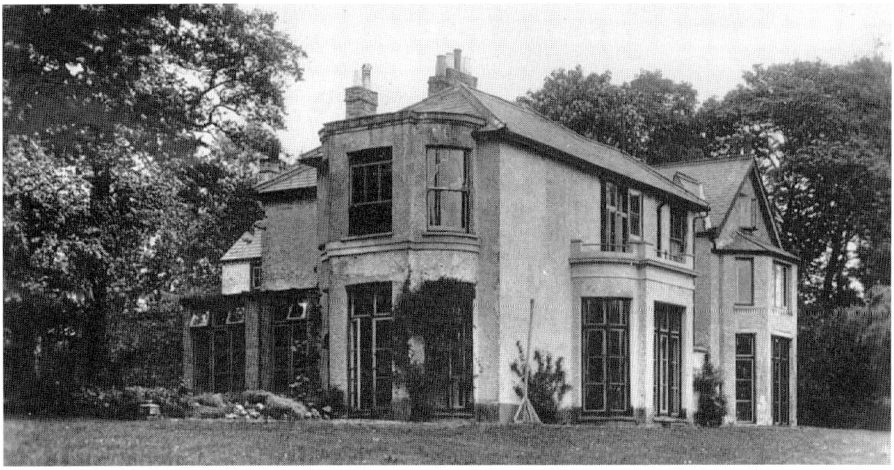

Chalkhill House, *c.* 1930, later to become Kingsgate Private School until its demolition in 1963. Chalkhill was historically part of Kingsbury, the estate centring on Chalkhill House, built in the seventeenth century. Development of the estate began after the First World War when, after some reservations, the Metropolitan Railway Board agreed to go into the field of property speculation. The results of the subsequent building works can be seen in the foreground on p. 59. These 'Metroland' houses were themselves the victims of further controversial development in the 1960s, Brent Council having to resort to compulsory purchase orders to gain some of the properties required for the new housing estate.

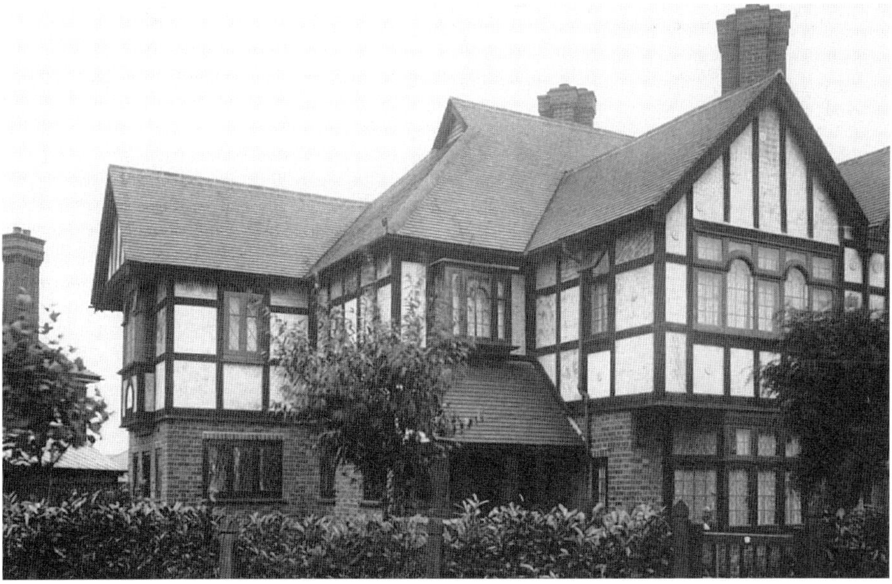

No. 2 The Fairway, North Wembley, 1932. From a sales brochure: 'Occupying a corner position just off East Lane, with an open view over private sports fields. The situation is most convenient for North Wembley Station (Bakerloo and LMS Lines) and the shopping centre.'

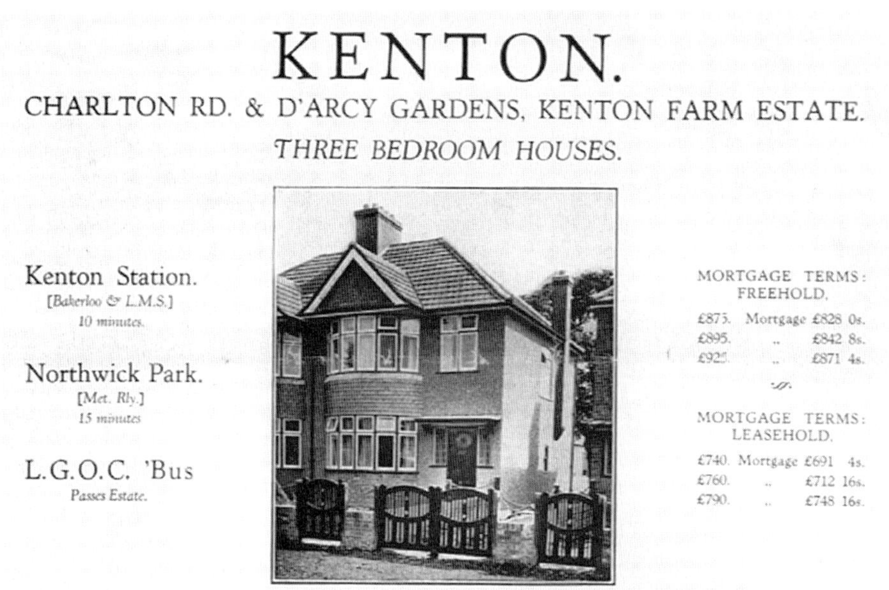

KENTON.

CHARLTON RD. & D'ARCY GARDENS, KENTON FARM ESTATE.

THREE BEDROOM HOUSES.

Kenton Station.
[Bakerloo & L.M.S.]
10 minutes.

Northwick Park.
[Met. Rly.]
15 minutes

L.G.O.C. 'Bus
Passes Estate.

MORTGAGE TERMS:
FREEHOLD.

£875.	Mortgage	£828	0s.
£895.	,,	£842	8s.
£925.	,,	£871	4s.

MORTGAGE TERMS:
LEASEHOLD.

£740.	Mortgage	£691	4s.
£760.	,,	£712	16s.
£790.	,,	£748	16s.

Sales brochure for properties in Kenton. Dating from the 1930s, this is an example of the kind of property produced during the building boom of the period. Although Charlton Road and D'Arcy Gardens are in the London Borough of Harrow, other properties were built in a similar style by the developers Thornborough in Wembley and Alperton. Prices ranged from £660 to £1,195.

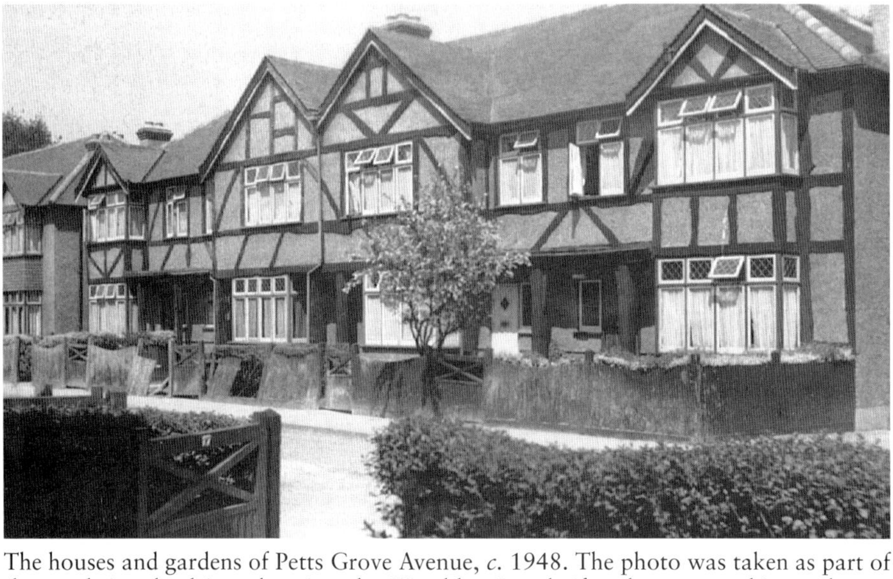

The houses and gardens of Petts Grove Avenue, *c.* 1948. The photo was taken as part of the work involved in culverting the Wembley Brook (for the reason this work was undertaken, see p. 18). Here we see Nos 14–16 on a bright summer day, the photograph being taken from the garden of No. 17.

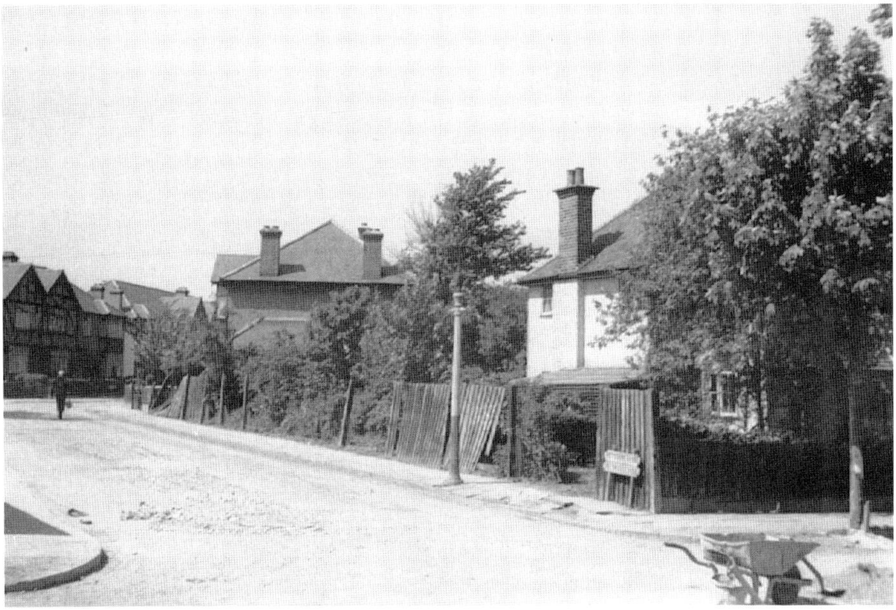

The entrance to Petts Grove Avenue from Sylvester Road, *c.* 1948 (above). The gardens of the properties (below) at the same date look very lush and green and are another reminder of the agricultural past of Wembley. The small bridges over the brook are very picturesque but were unlikely to survive the culverting scheme in this form.

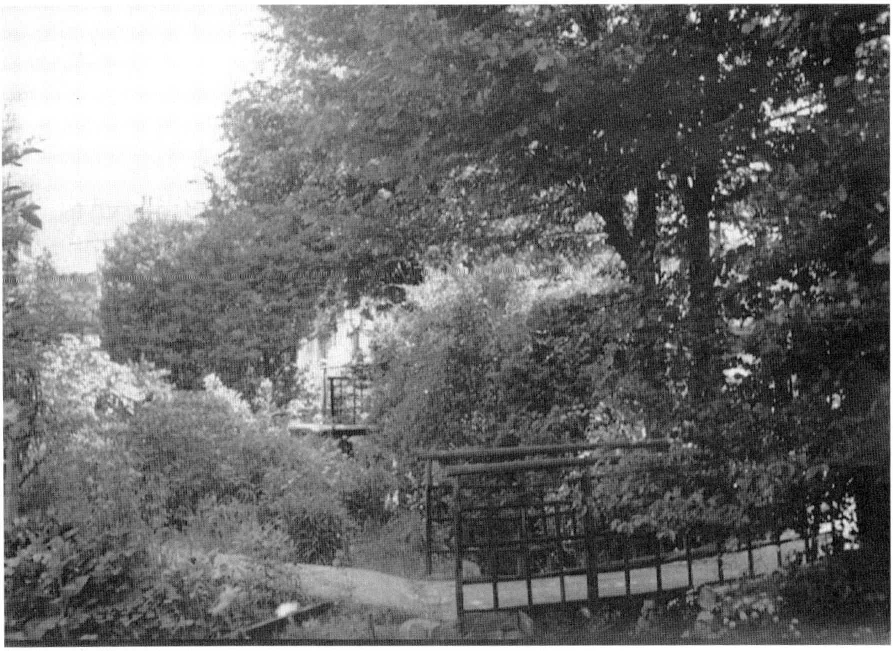

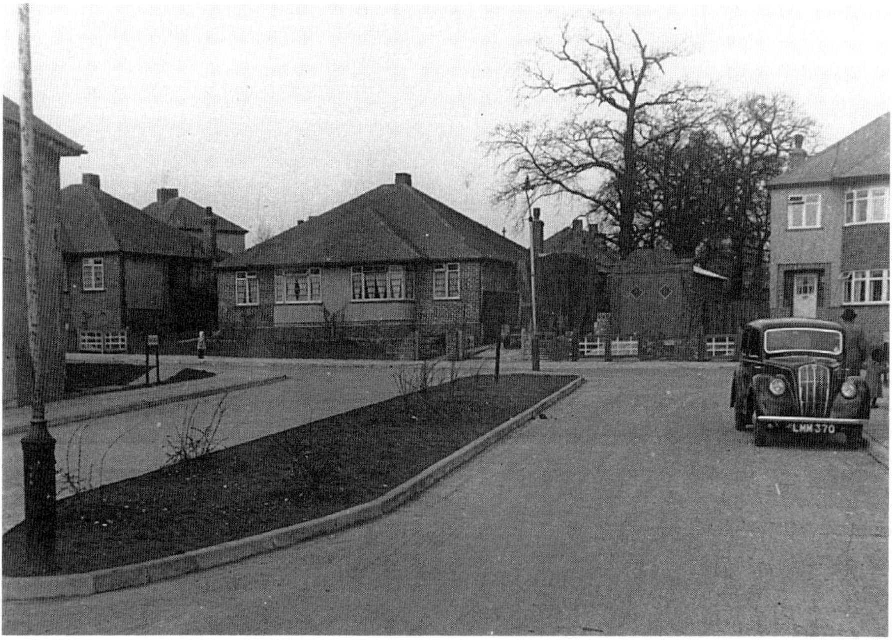

Farm Avenue, Wembley, *c.* 1948. The name comes from Sudbury Park Farm on which estate the road was built.

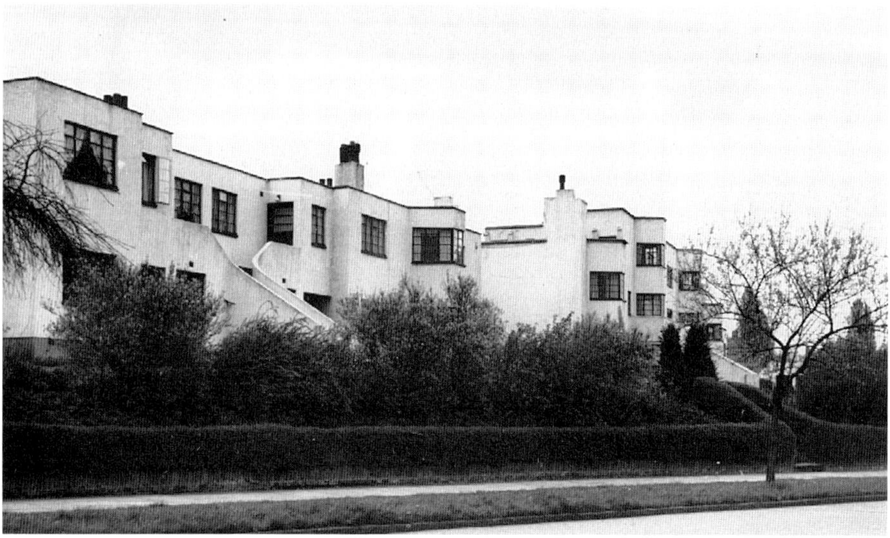

Lawns Court Flats, *c.* 1950, built in 1933–4 by Haymills. This property developer built other two-storey flats – called South Gardens – also on the Holland Estate in The Avenue. Other developments in Wembley were detached and semi-detached houses at Mayfields and East Hill. In 1934 the company made the decision to end its involvement in the Holland Estate and disposed of its interest to George Wimpey & Co.

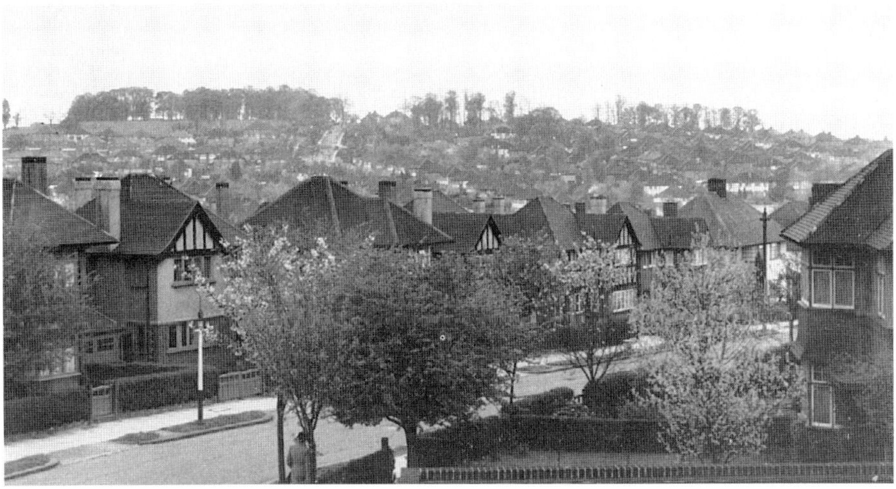

Uxendon Crescent, Wembley Park in the 1950s. Another example of the quality of the images from the Frith archive. The Francis Frith Collection contacted London Borough of Brent archive in November last year concerning the de-acquisition of a number of photos. Others can be seen on pp. 12, 21, 30 and 33. These are an excellent addition to the archive.

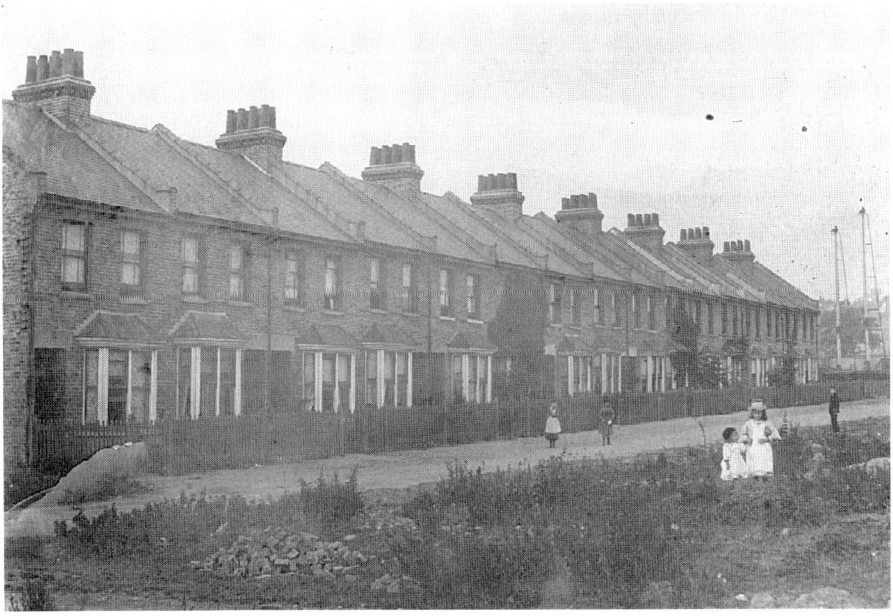

Turton Road, off Lancelot Road, after 1896. The view is of the road near the junction with Ealing Road, another street built by Henry Haynes (see p. 34).

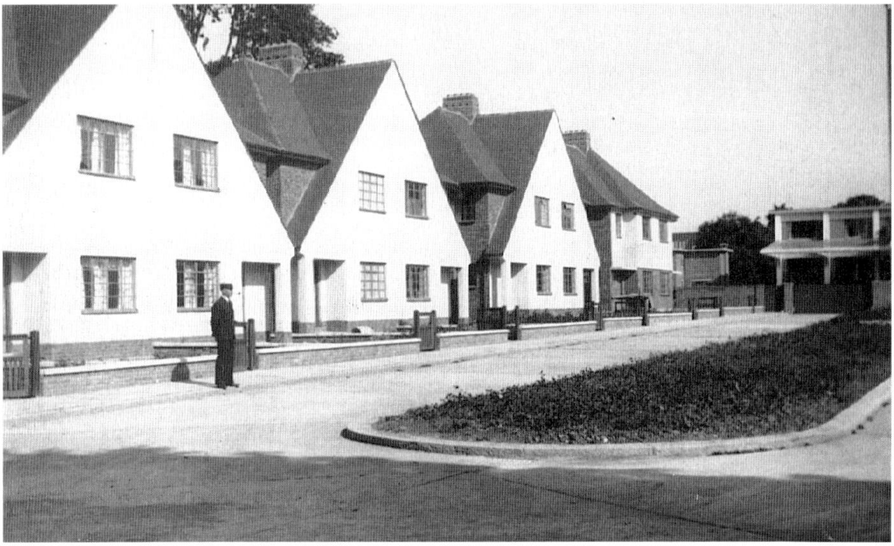

Harley Close, Wembley, *c.* 1939. These houses are the purpose-built quarters for officers of the Wembley Fire Service. The site had initially been acquired for the building of a new town hall but the amalgamation of Wembley and Kingsbury councils led to the purchase of a more central site at Forty Lane for this purpose (see p. 59). The building of this row of houses was an integral part of the scheme to build new fire stations at Fair View, off Harrow Road and the Mall, Kingsbury.

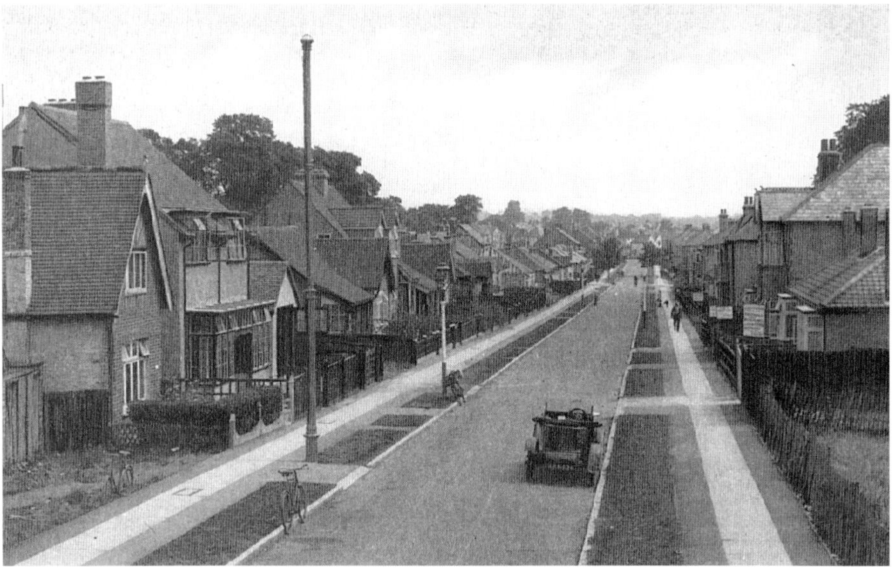

Rugby Avenue, Sudbury, probably *c.* 1920. The theme for a series of streets on the All Souls College Estate was that of public schools, such as Repton Avenue and, as here, Rugby Avenue.

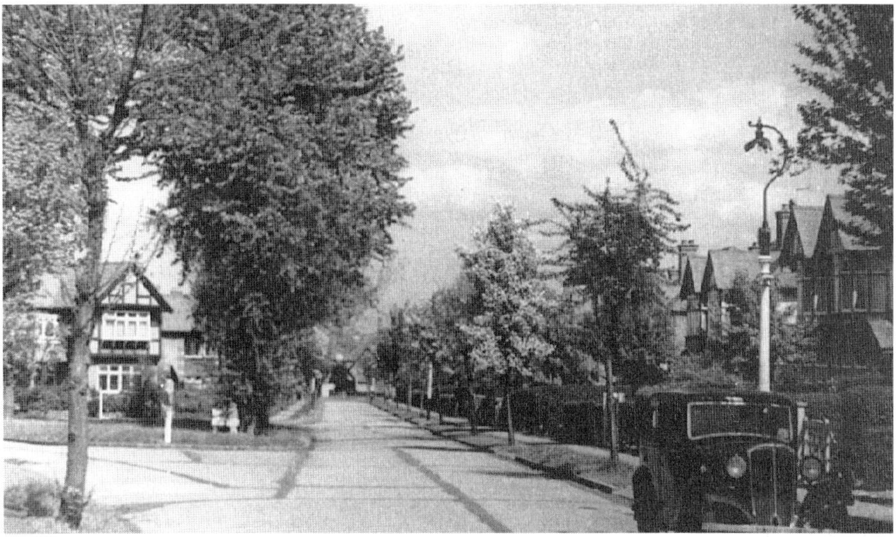

Holt Road, Sudbury Court Estate, in the late 1940s. Holt Road derives its name from Holt Farm, Sudbury; it was farmed by Thomas Anthony Trollope, father of the novelist, who leased the 157 acres of Ilotts Farm from Lord Northwick for a term of twenty-one years. He spent more than £3,000 rebuilding the farm, which was used by Anthony as a model for 'Orley Farm'. However, the expense of this remodelling and the agricultural depression caused Thomas to default on his rents and the family fled to Belgium.

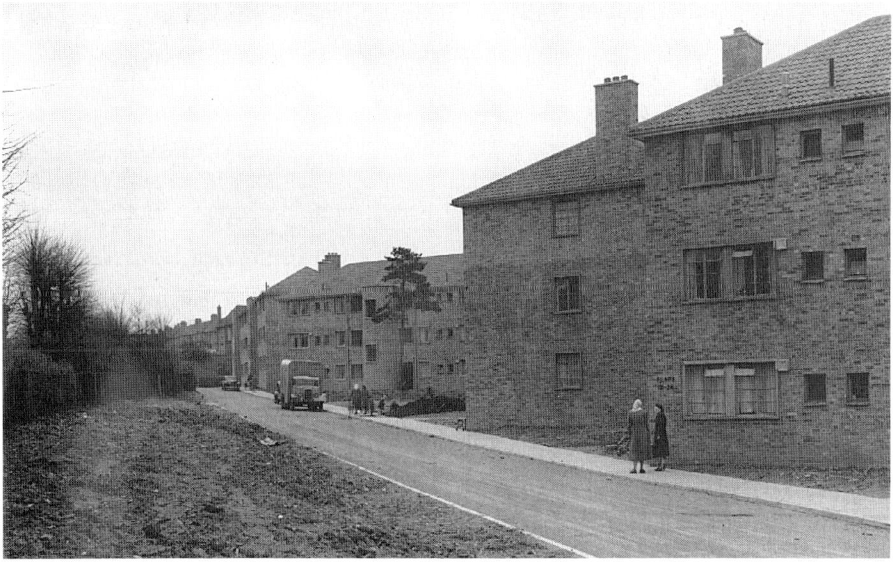

Newland Court, *c.* 1949. This was built on the site of the farm that had sprung up prior to 1882, known as North Forty Farm. A fine pine tree from the former farm garden and a field maple probably from the former farm hedge survived the redevelopment of the 1950s.

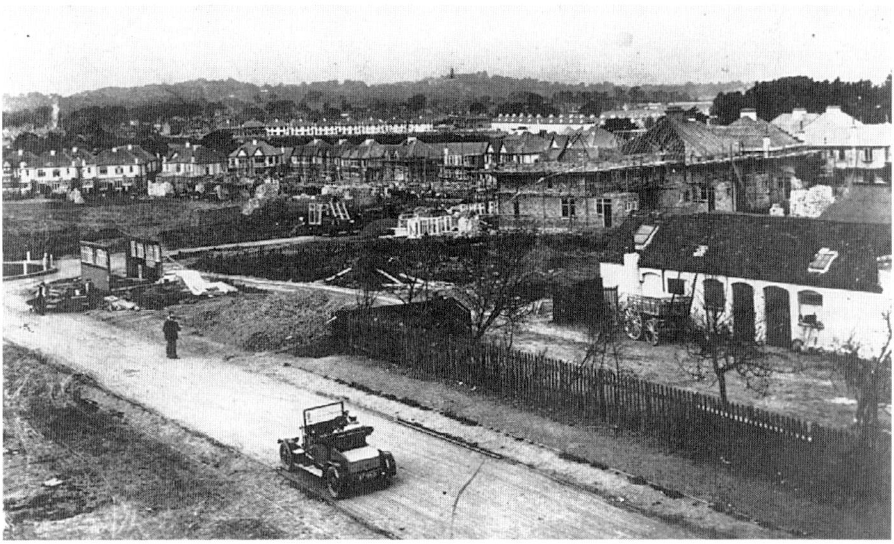

Building North Wembley Estate, between 1920 and 1930. This view gives a good impression of the vast amount of development that was undertaken between these years, much of it by the firm Comben and Wakeling (see p. 44). Such was the apparent quality of their work that fifty years later their houses, when offered for sale, were advertised as 'Comben and Wakeling built', implying that this was all the proposed purchaser needed to know.

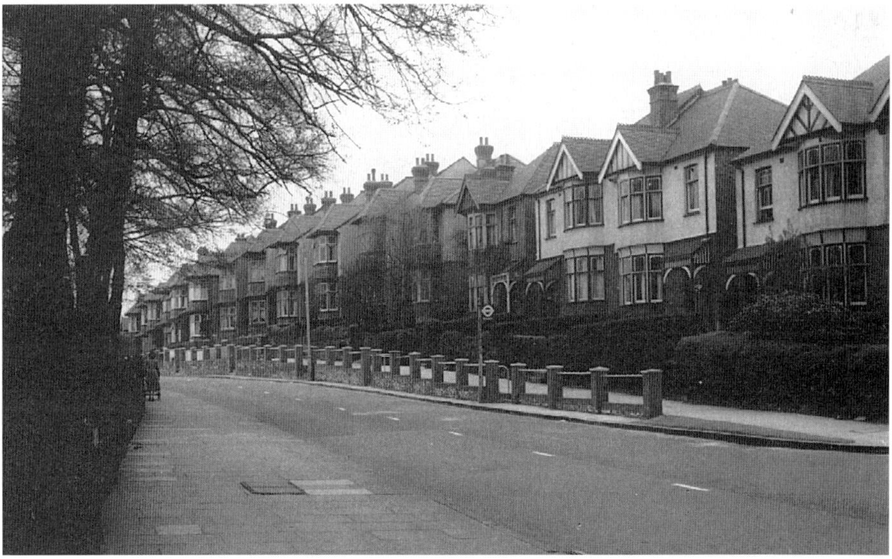

Park Lane, October 1951. The road leads from the High Road up past King Edward VII Park, ending at the junction with Wembley Hill Road. Originally known as Blind Lane (see p. 18), the name was changed around 1912 and certainly before 1914 as it was the main route to Wembley Park (see pp. 68–71).

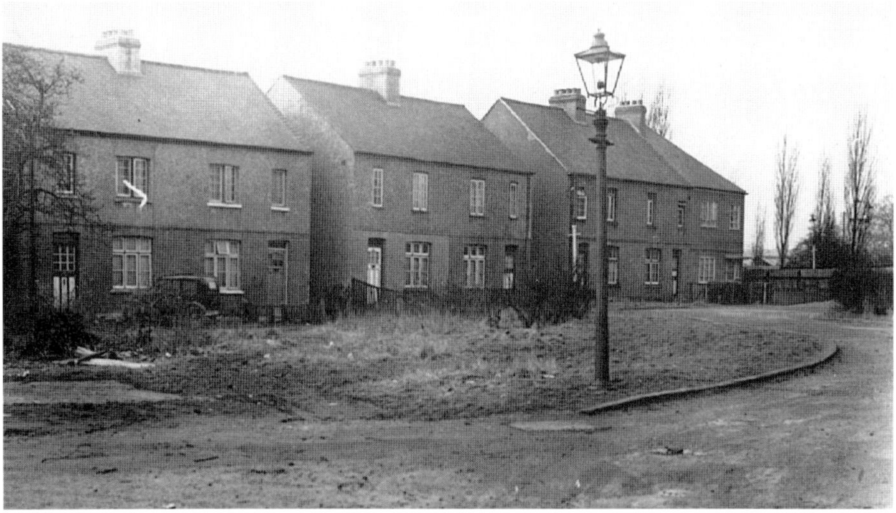

Sudbury Crescent, 1948. Built off Harrow Road behind the post office and near The Swan Inn, this image is one from a collection relating to the making up of the roads by Wembley Borough Council in the late 1940s. A tollgate was set up at The Swan in 1801 and its association with transport continued when it served as a tram terminus and then as a bus terminus. It continues to perform this function today.

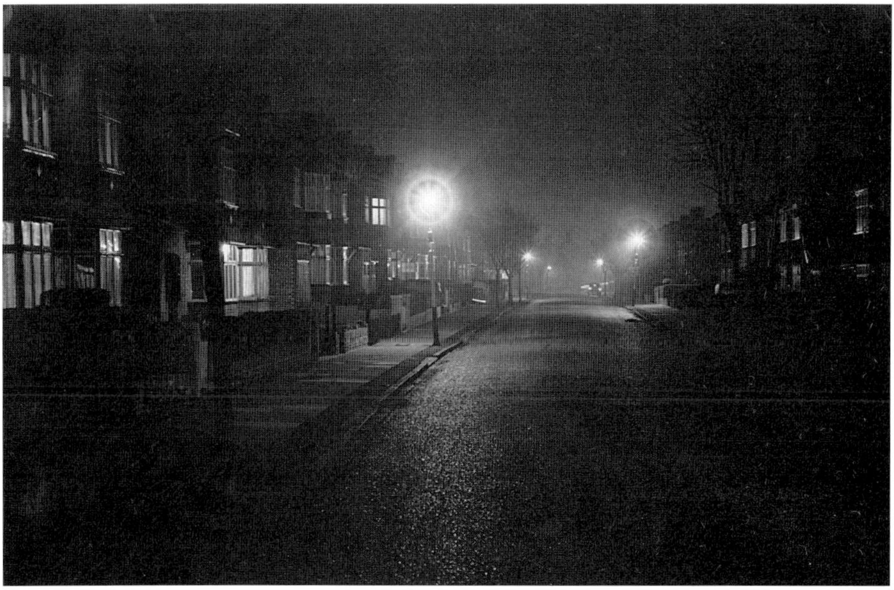

Elmstead Avenue photographed in November 1953 and showing the street lit by 100 watt tungsten lamps. Elmstead Avenue was close to the Wealdstone Brook (see p. 27), but it was not felt necessary to pursue flood control measures here until 1985 when the Greater London Council had to requisition parts of the gardens to ensure completion of the works.

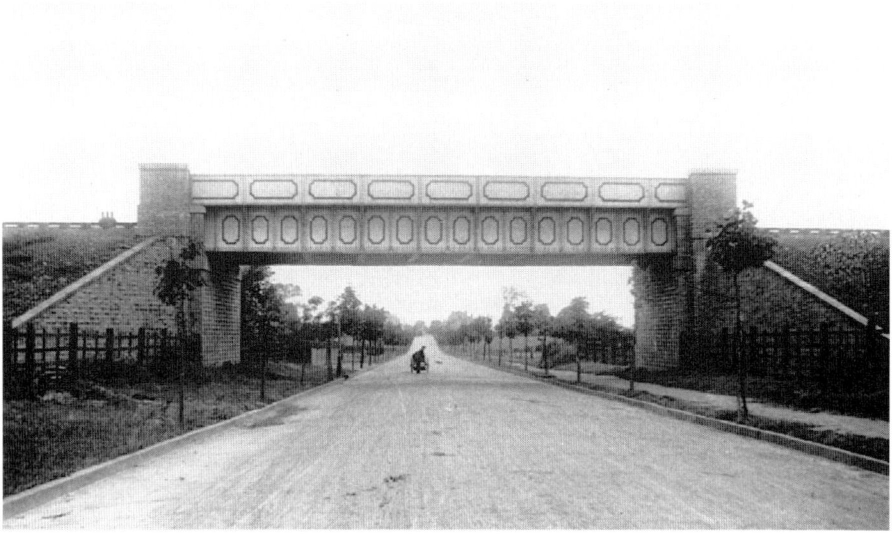

The Harrowdene Estate. The picture above shows the bridge over the estate in 1904–5. Clearly when the Neasden–Northolt section of the railway was built there was little development on the estate, apart from a few large residences such as The Turret (see p. 43), Harrowdene or The Red House. Constructed in 1895–6 across the Harrowdene Estate, the Harrowdene Road (see below, *c.* 1950) brought North Wembley within closer reach of St John's Church and thus put off the need to build the proposed mission church at the junction of Llanover Road and East Lane. Instead the churchwarden provided funds for an extension to St John's.

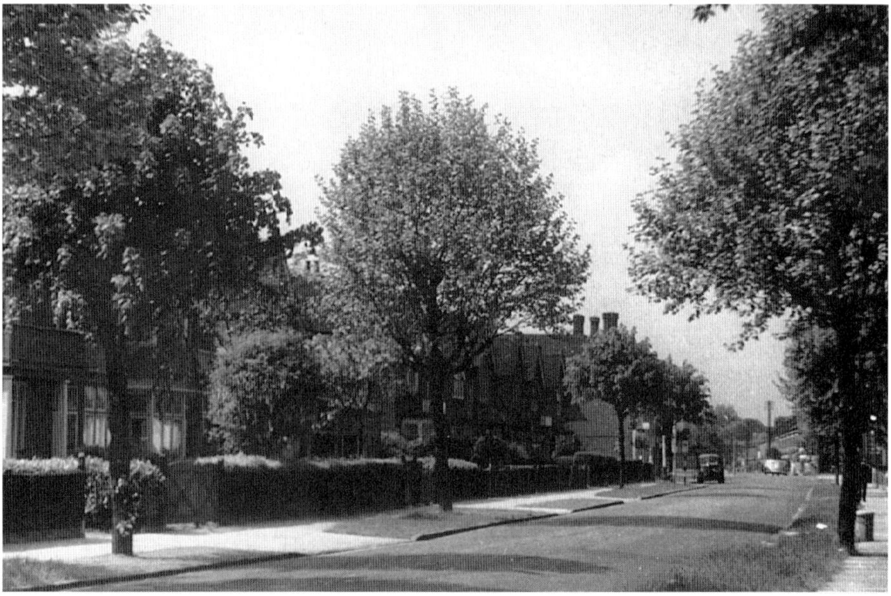

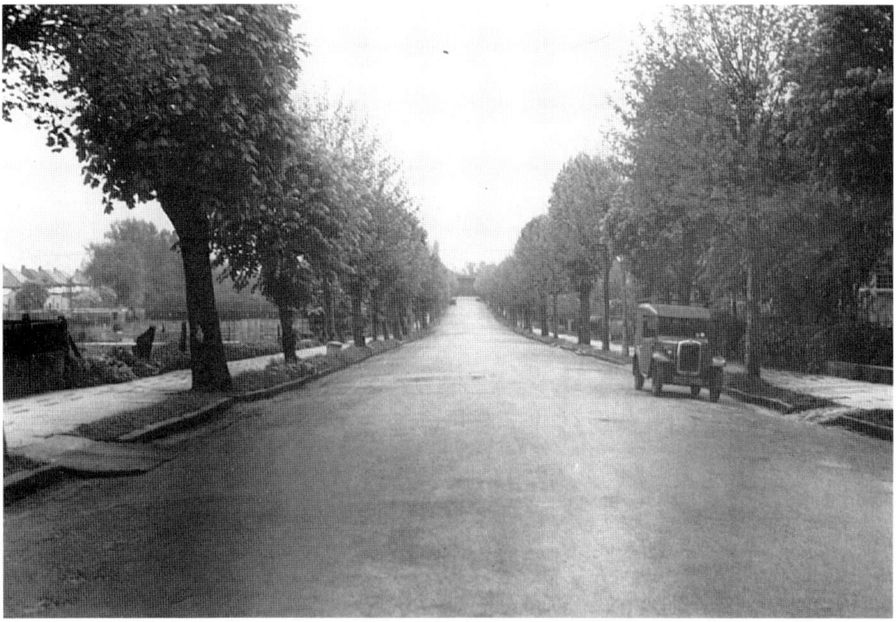

Harrowdene Road. Even by the early 1950s parts of Harrowdene Road looked remarkably rural. This photograph was taken prior to reconstruction in the mid-1950s, the open space to the left of the picture being grassland around the Wealdstone Brook.

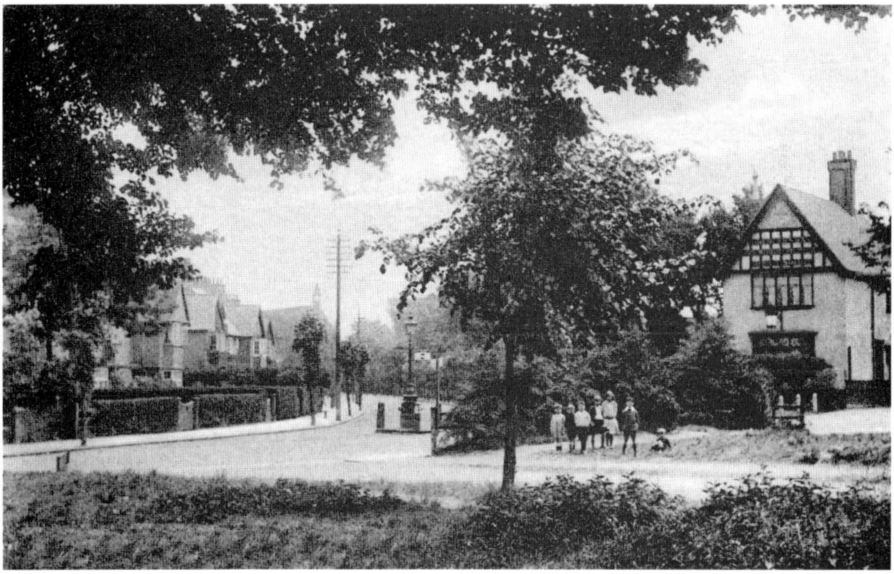

Stanley Avenue, Alperton, *c.* 1910. Apparently from the same series as other sepia images of Alperton in this book (see pp. 28 and 82). All were produced by J. Birch, Alperton and Wembley Library, 204 Ealing Road, Wembley.

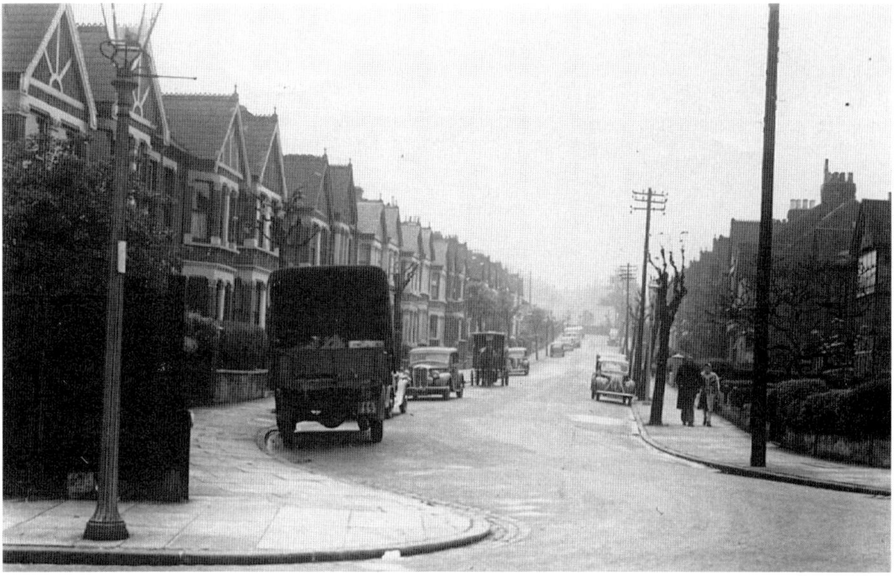

Elm Road, 6 May 1950. Note the continued presence of horse-drawn transport; in this case it is probably the rag-and-bone man.

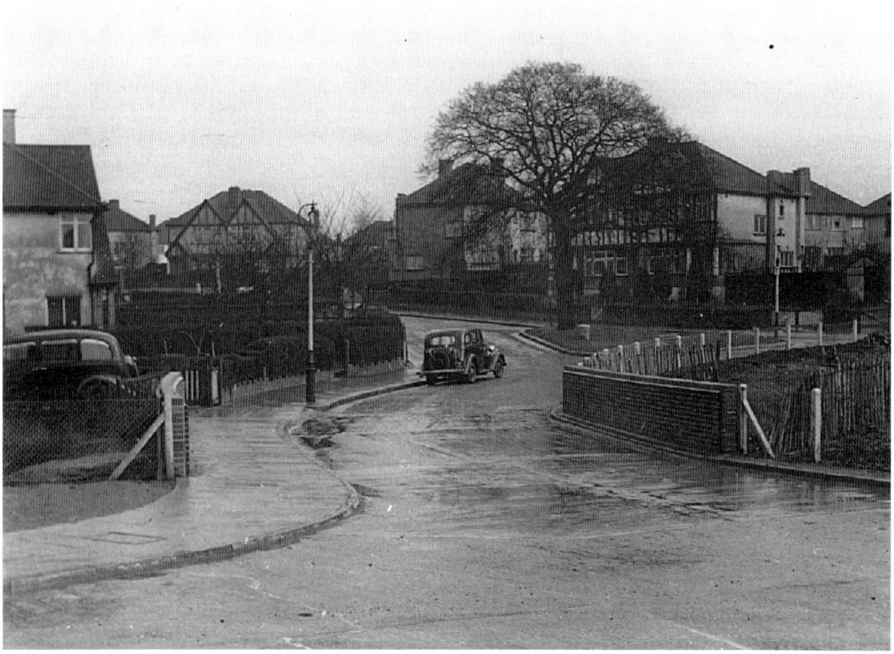

Lindsay Drive North Bridge, 1947–8. This photo comes from the record of the works undertaken on the Preston Estate by the Wembley Borough Engineer and Surveyor's Department.

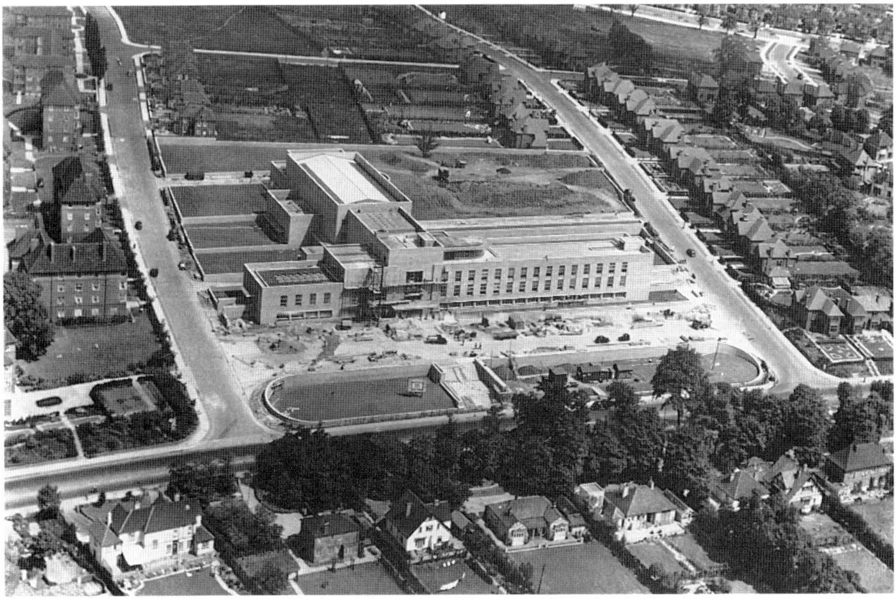

Wembley Town Hall, 2 June 1939. Building works were continuing and much of the area behind the town hall remained to be developed. See the two photos of Forty Lane (p. 20) for a 'worm's eye' view of the roads around the town hall.

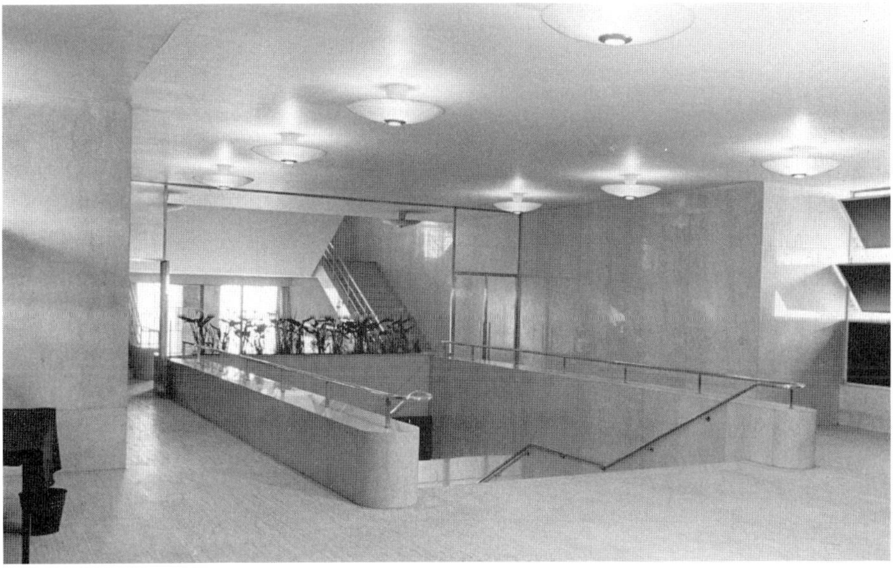

Interior of the town hall, *c.* 1939. This photo shows the main stairwell, looking towards the front of the building. Designed by architect Clifford Strange, who won the contract after the usual public competition, the building is a mixture of tradition and modernity. It is influenced by the art of the Dutch architect W.M. Dudok whose buildings appealed to those who shunned the functionalism and concrete of the Modern Movement.

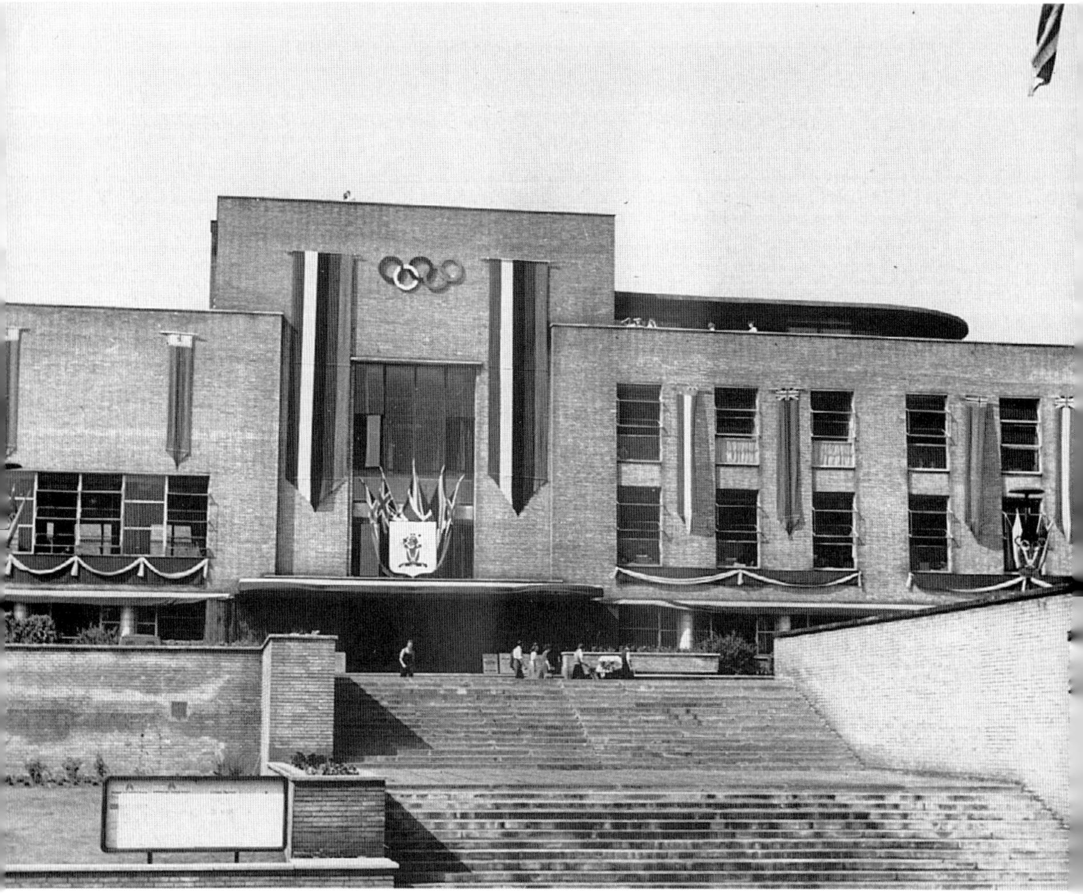

The town hall, decorated for the 1948 Olympics. The intention is clearly to portray the official buildings of the borough to their best advantage and to ensure that the image of Wembley Borough Council would be broadcast worldwide to the massive audience for the events.

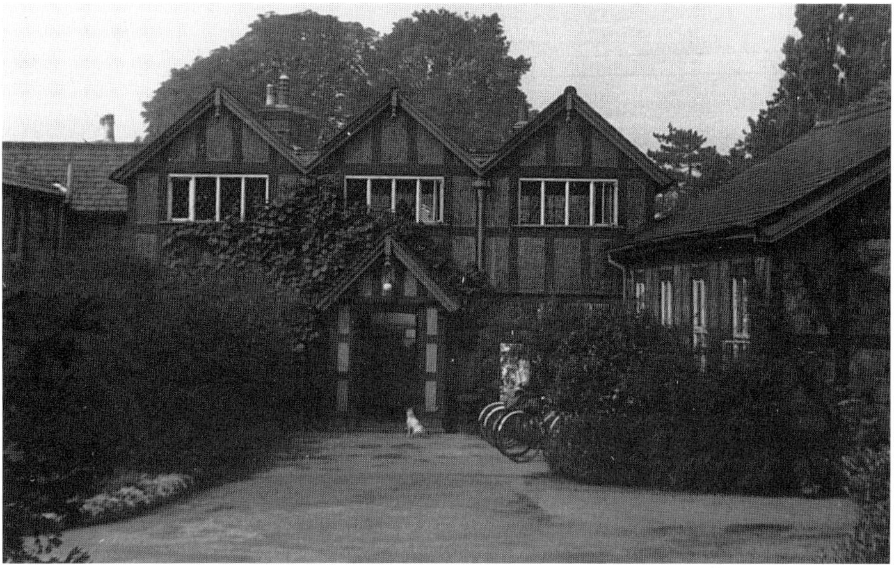

Barham Park Library as it looked in the 1950s. Originally named Crabs House after the family who lived there in the 1790s, and then called Old Court, it is one of the few surviving legacies of G.T. Barham. Converted into a 'Branch Library and Museum' by Middlesex County Council, the ceremonial opening took place on 30 May 1952. With an initial book stock of 10,000 volumes the county council hoped that 'the exhibits to be displayed in the Museum shall be of historical interest and of local significance, and that, by arrangement with the Wembley Borough Council, the Barham Collection of British Antiquities will be made available for display'. See pp. 1 and 45.

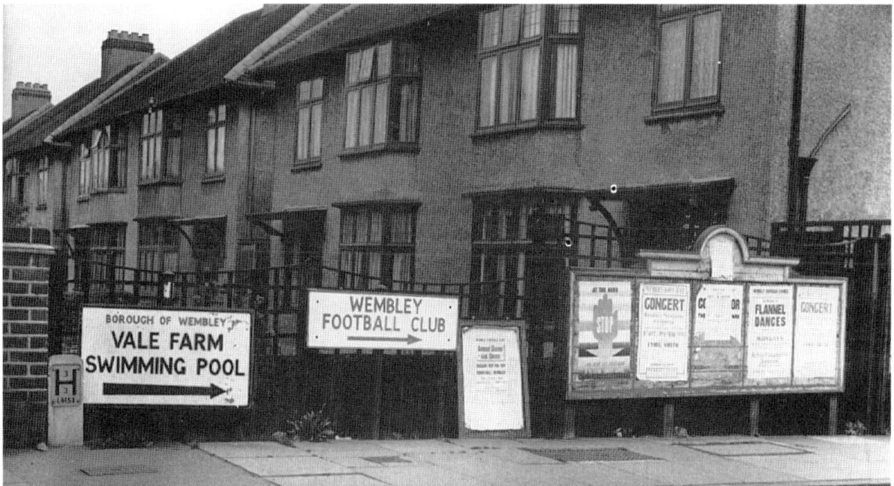

Notice boards at the entrance to Vale Farm Swimming Pool in Watford Road, *c.* 1950. This was also, of course, the home of Wembley Football Club. The England World Cup squad trained on their pitch prior to winning the Jules Rimet Trophy in 1966.

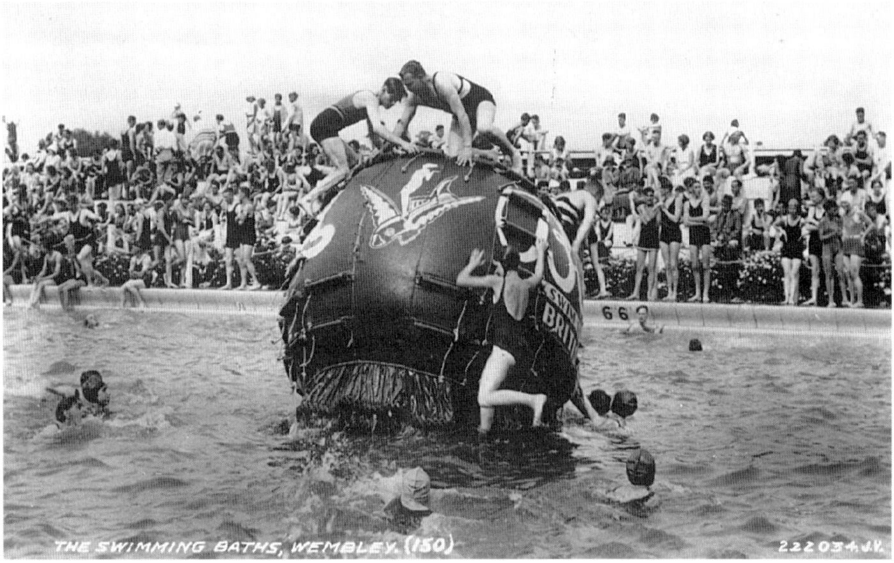

The Vale Farm Swimming Pool. A wonderful photograph of the pool early in its life (above), certainly in the 1930s. It is a good example of the 'Real Photograph' series of postcards, this one produced by Valentine & Sons Ltd, Dundee and London. The photograph below shows swimming by floodlight in the 1950s. The intention of the council to renovate the facilities was frustrated by lack of funds until 1979, when money was budgeted to build a new complex with two indoor pools.

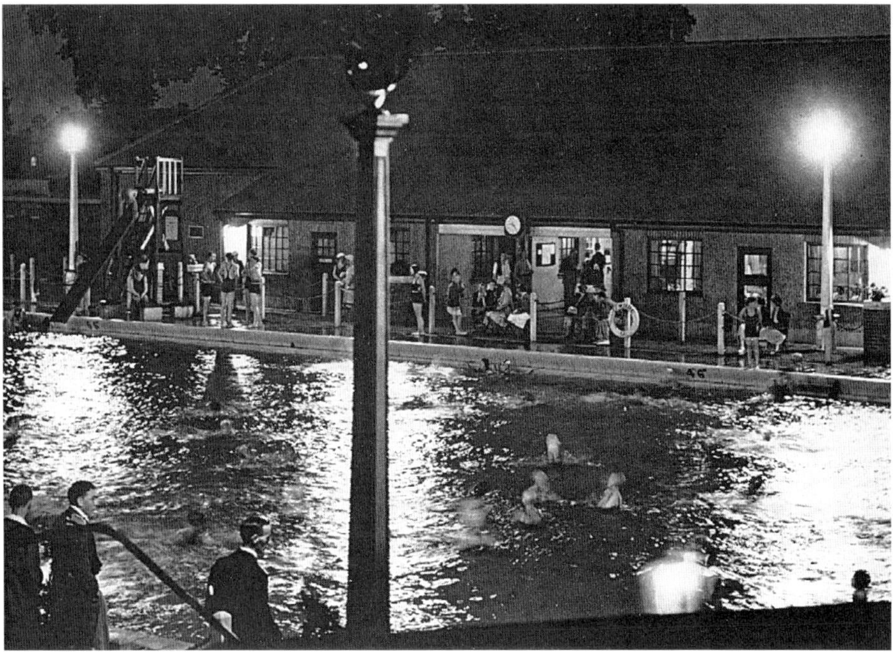

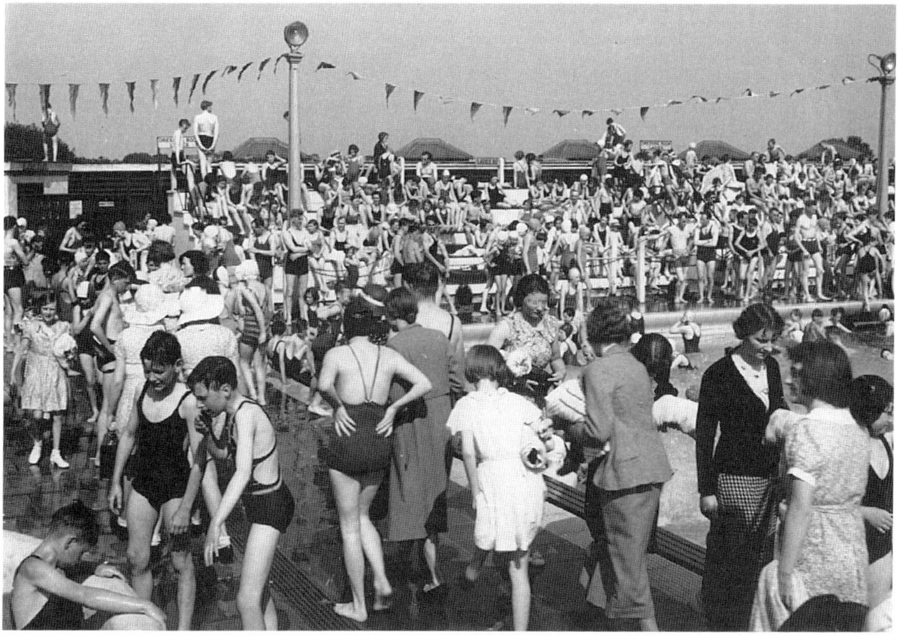

Residents of Wembley enjoying the open-air facilities at Vale Farm on a gorgeous summer day in the 1950s. The site for the swimming pool was purchased from E. and F. Toley in October 1928 by Wembley Urban District Council for open space purposes. The pool, the first in Wembley, was opened in April 1930 at a cost of £17,000.

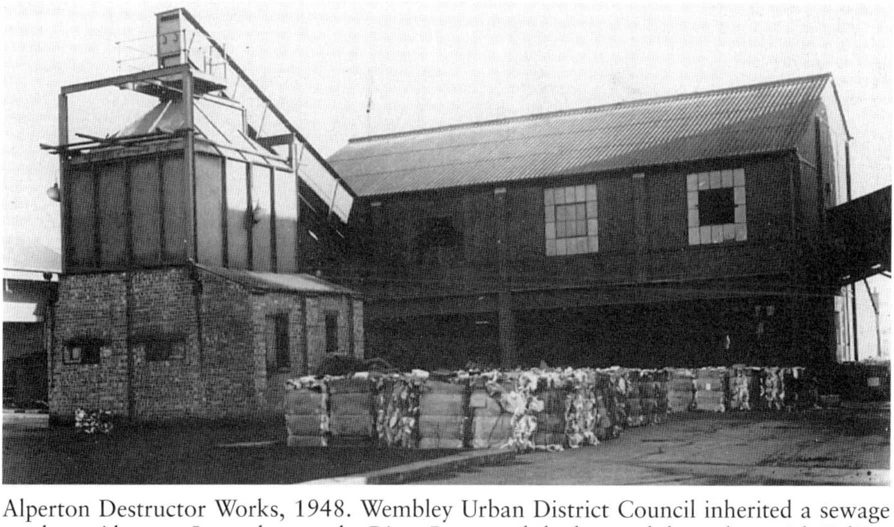

Alperton Destructor Works, 1948. Wembley Urban District Council inherited a sewage works at Alperton Lane close to the River Brent and the borough boundary with Ealing. However, the method of sewage treatment was altered in the 1920s, large sewers replacing the smaller treatment works. Alperton had become a refuse disposal site by the date of this photograph.

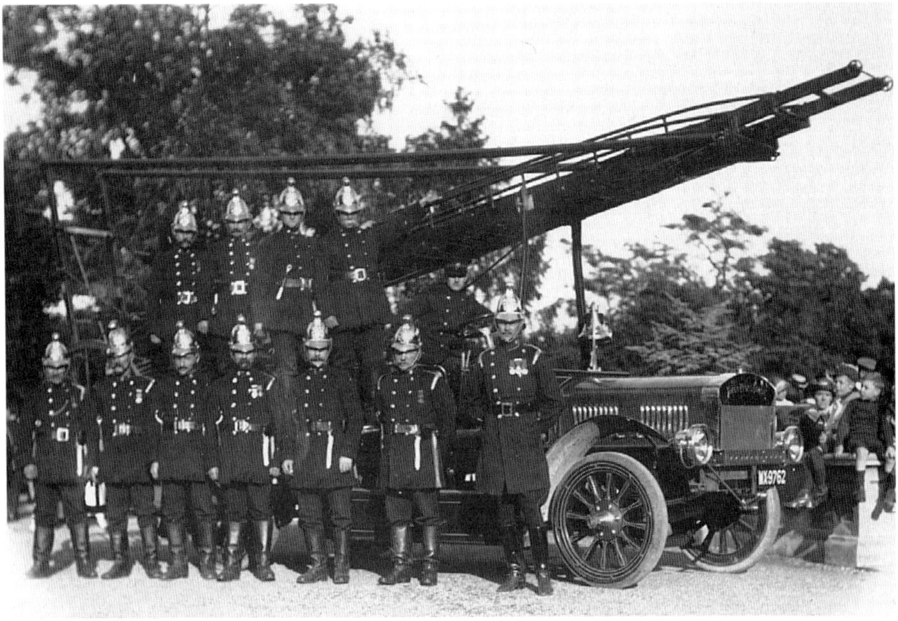

Wembley Fire Brigade posing with their Merryweather appliance in 1914. The first fire engine acquired by Wembley Urban District Council was an old manual engine from the neighbouring authorities at Harrow-on-the-Hill in 1895. The machine was already obsolete, and as there was no provision for providing ready access to the horsepower needed the engine was little used.

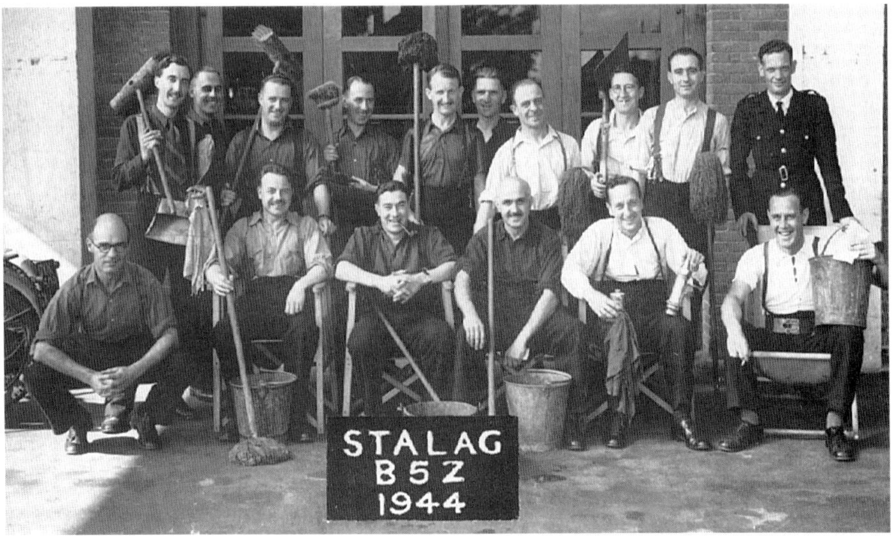

Wembley Fire Brigade in relaxed mood, 1944. Members of the fire service pose in this spoof photograph in the style of a prisoner-of-war camp. The men hold buckets and mops in front of the fire station.

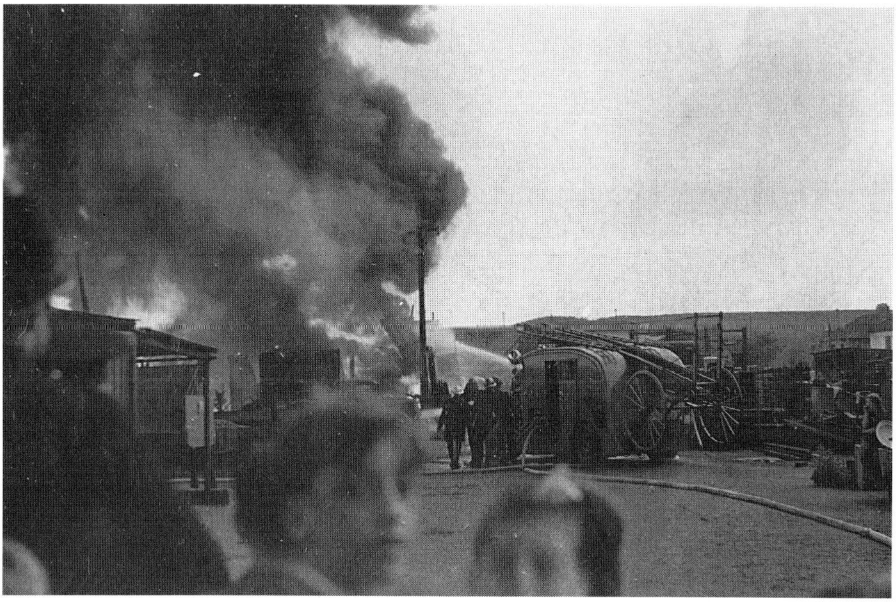

Fire at Herbert Boyer's builders' merchants in the 1940s. Complaints were made to Wembley Borough Council about the state of the site in October 1947. A number of problems were noted – fences were broken down, the sub-tenants, the Lime Free Water Co., caused a noise nuisance, and stacks of tyres, old wood and boxes were in the yard. The resulting fire should be seen in this context.

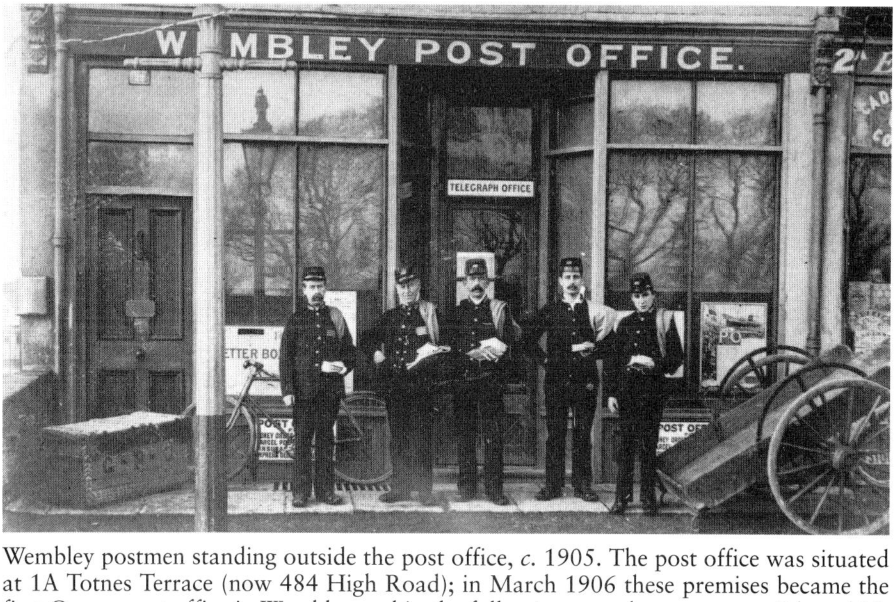

Wembley postmen standing outside the post office, *c.* 1905. The post office was situated at 1A Totnes Terrace (now 484 High Road); in March 1906 these premises became the first Crown post office in Wembley and in the following year the postmaster Edward M. Green received a civil service commission.

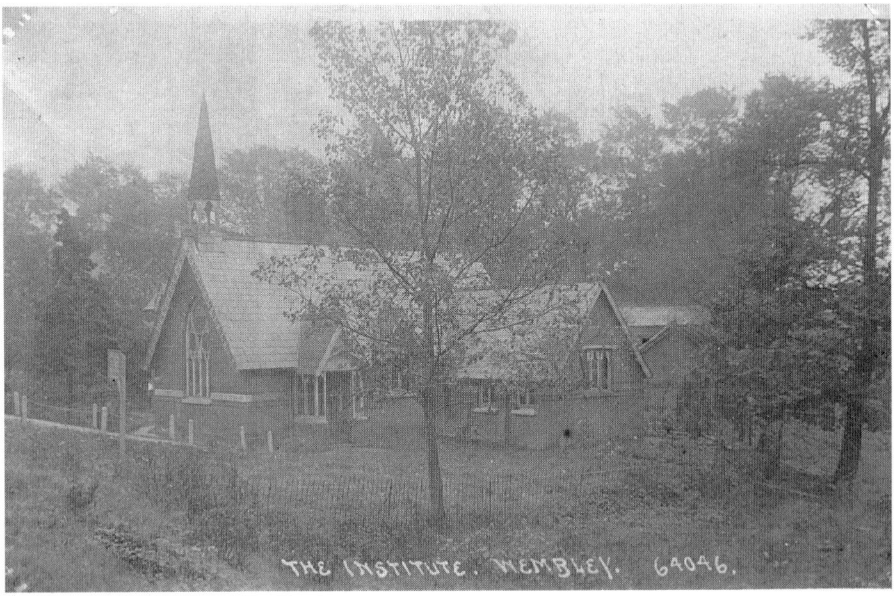

The Institute, Wembley, otherwise known as the Workmen's Hall, *c.* 1910. Frances Copland's indenture of 1869 gave land in Wembley for the building of a workmen's hall and this building gave the institute a home from 1869 to 1930, although the organization had been founded five years earlier in October 1864. Below we see the institute's soccer team for the season 1920–1.

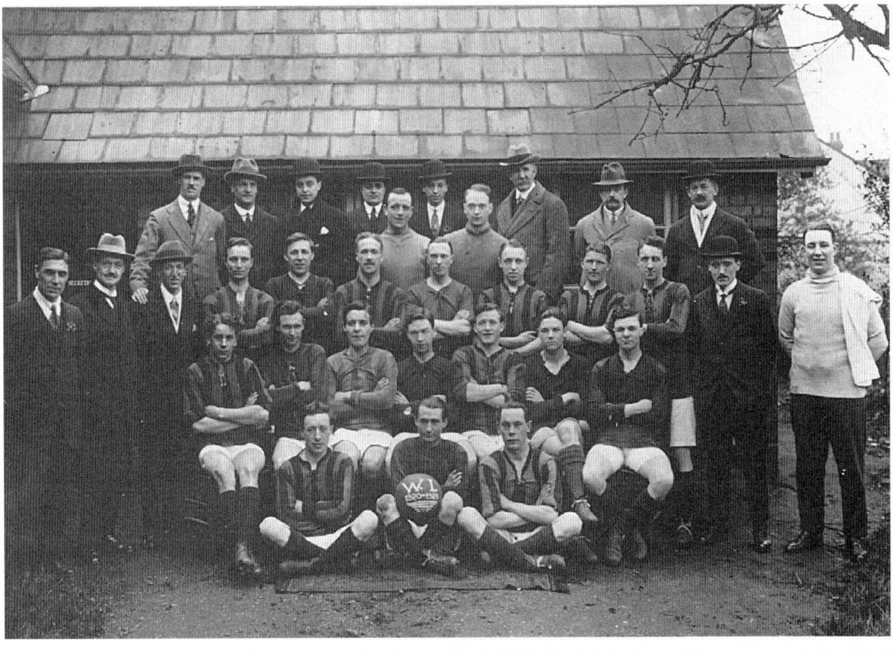

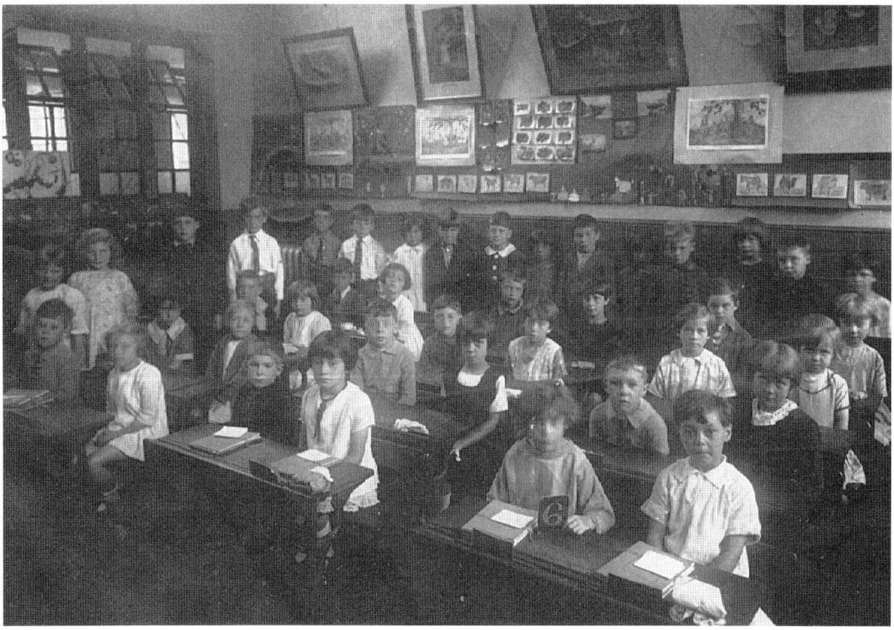

Alperton Infants' School, Ealing Road. Miss Musson's Class 6, *c.* 1910, is shown in the photo above. The first school provision for infants was provided by a short-lived schoolroom attached to Wembley parish school in 1876. A further temporary school was built before the permanent structure seen here was constructed by Harrow School Board in 1878. The building now hosts Brent Teachers' Centre. Below we see children of the school celebrating Mayday in 1934.

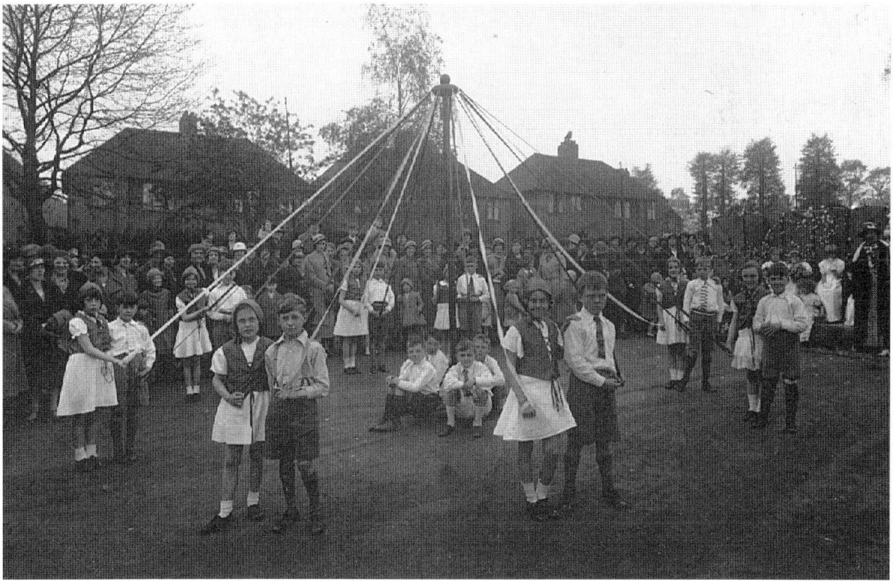

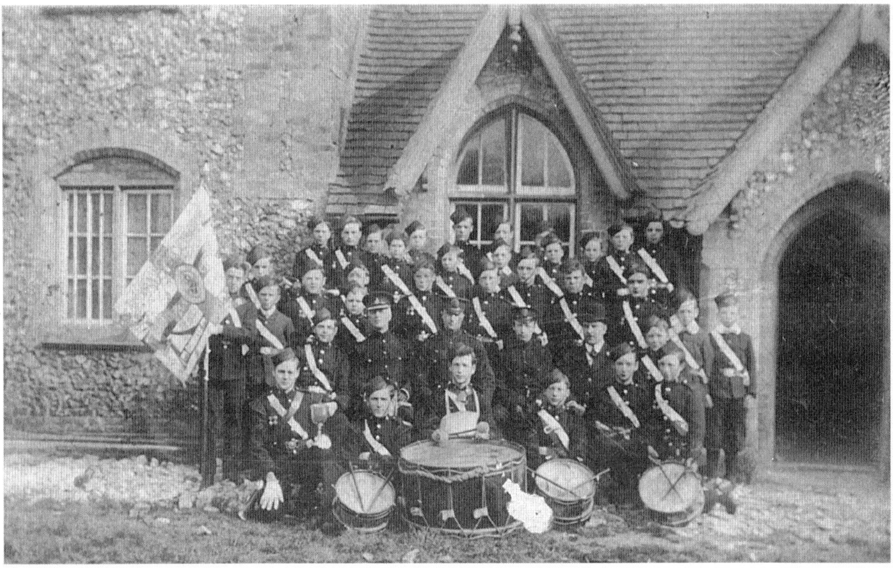

The Church Lads' Brigade, *c.* 1905. The brigade was formed in Wembley in 1901. This photo was probably taken outside the Drill or Brigade Hall built in 1912. The Lads' Brigade was wound up in 1931 when its aims and functions were taken over by scout and guide organizations.

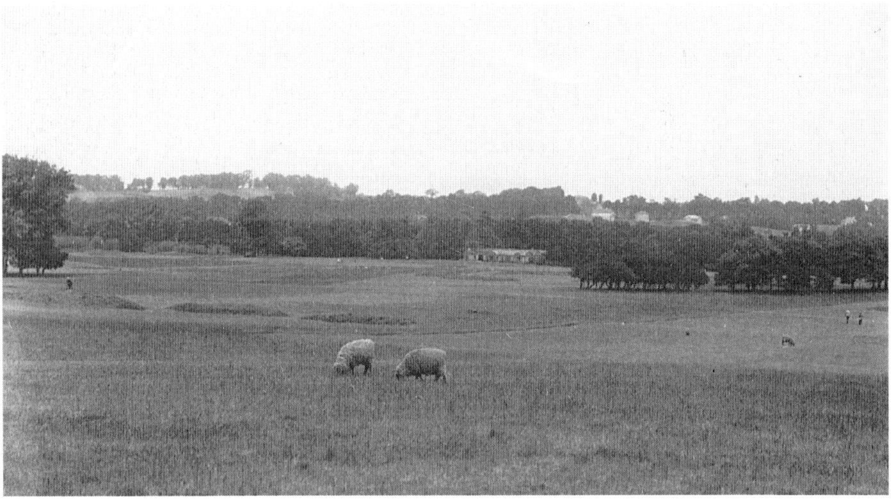

Wembley Park, *c.* 1905. Wembley Park was owned in the eighteenth century by the Page family; in the early 1790s Humphrey Repton worked on the landscaping of the park. The estate passed to the Gray family between 1804 and 1810, and by the 1880s the increasing proximity of the metropolis caused John Gray to sell forty-seven acres to the Metropolitan Railway Company. The death of Reverend Gray in 1887 led directly to the sale of the remainder of the estate to Sir Edward Watkin, the chair of the Metropolitan Railway Company.

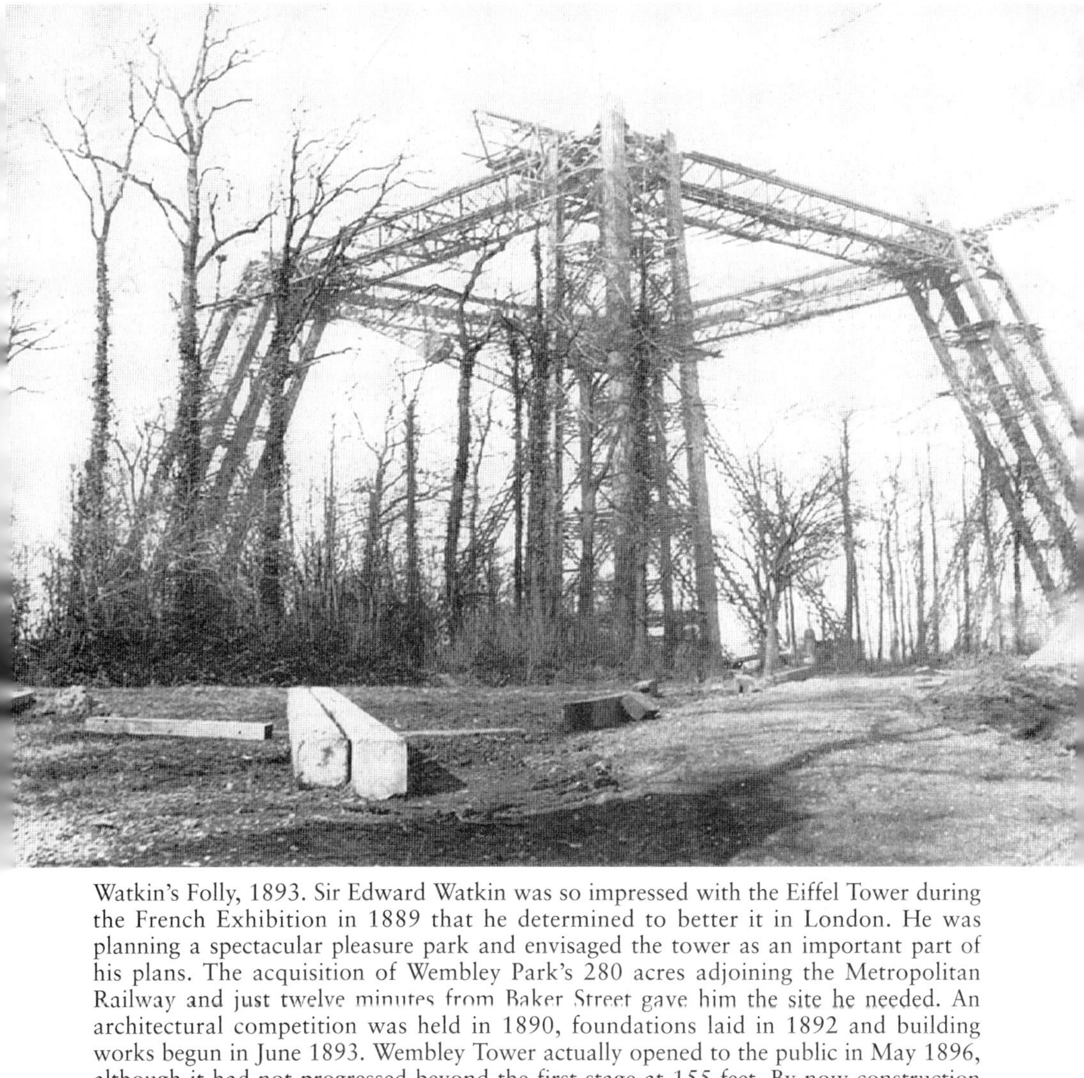

Watkin's Folly, 1893. Sir Edward Watkin was so impressed with the Eiffel Tower during the French Exhibition in 1889 that he determined to better it in London. He was planning a spectacular pleasure park and envisaged the tower as an important part of his plans. The acquisition of Wembley Park's 280 acres adjoining the Metropolitan Railway and just twelve minutes from Baker Street gave him the site he needed. An architectural competition was held in 1890, foundations laid in 1892 and building works begun in June 1893. Wembley Tower actually opened to the public in May 1896, although it had not progressed beyond the first stage at 155 feet. By now construction was behind schedule and the foundations had begun to move. The Metropolitan Tower Construction Company had difficulty in raising funds and went into voluntary liquidation in 1899. Even by this time the tower was almost certainly referred to as Watkin's Folly.

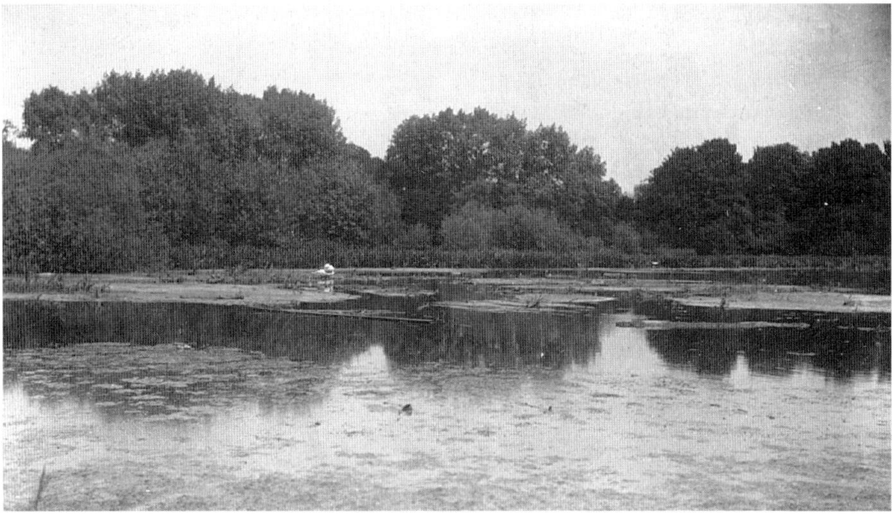

Wembley Park, *c.* 1920. As seen on the previous page, the ambitious Wembley Tower was never completed. The park itself, however, had opened to the public in May 1894. While problems had become apparent in the construction of the tower, the surrounding grounds had been laid out with cricket and football pitches, a large running track, a fountain, pavilions and, of course, the eight-acre lake (seen above, *c.* 1920) spanned by ornamental bridges and provided with a boat house. The end for the tower itself came in 1904. Although it remained open to the public until around 1902, the lift machinery was becoming unsafe due to neglect. In 1904 the decision was made to demolish it. The last leg was dismantled and the foundations demolished on 9 September 1907. Below (and on p. 71) are the resultant craters in around 1920.

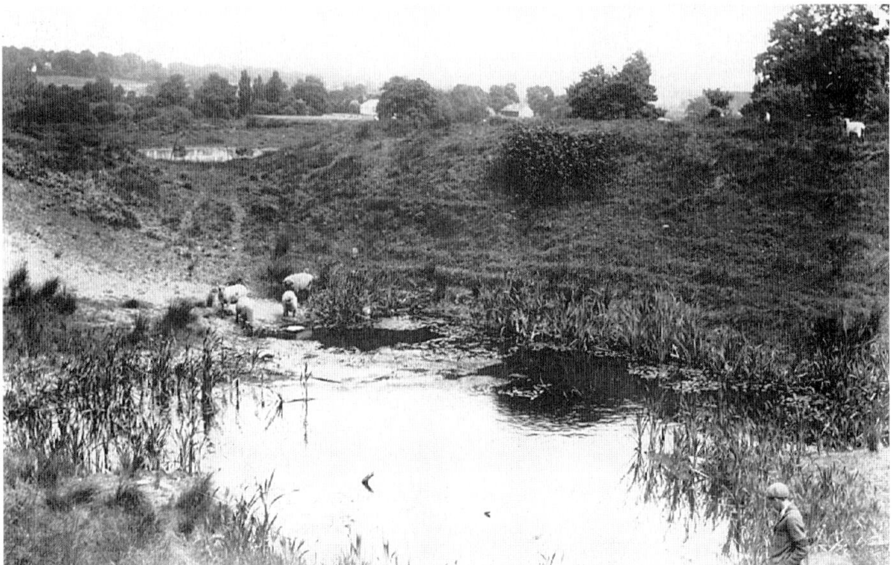

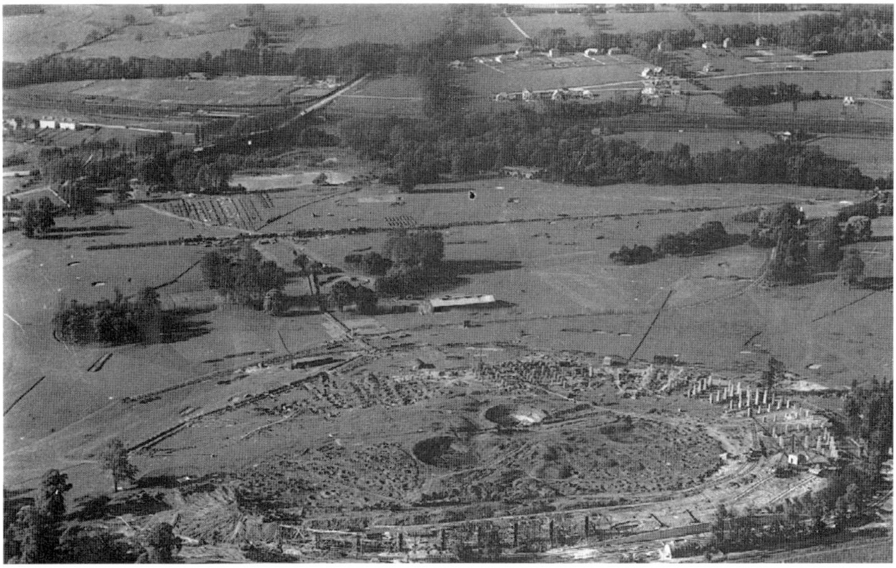

The building of Wembley Stadium, 1922. Above is an historic and touching photograph as one man's folly gives way to another's vision. The last visible remains of the unlucky Sir Edward Watkin's ill-fated Wembley Tower (the craters left after the demolition of the last of the structure) are enclosed by the foundations of the new stadium. The latter was in turn the brainchild of Maxwell Ayrton, the architect, and Sir Owen Williams, the engineer, in the comparatively new material of concrete. McAlpine's were also involved in the project as contractors; the picture below shows their workforce providing the final test for parts of the stadium before its opening to the public in around 1923.

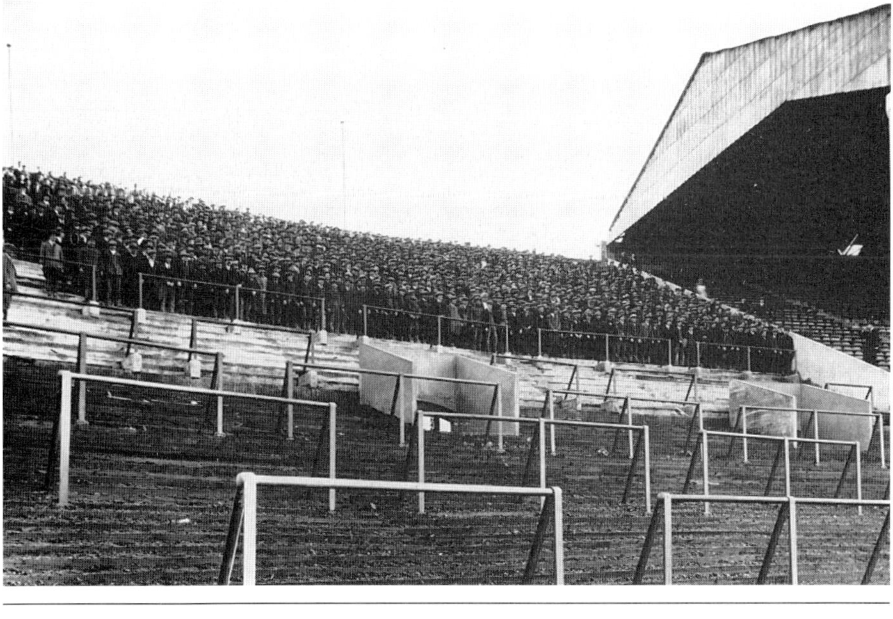

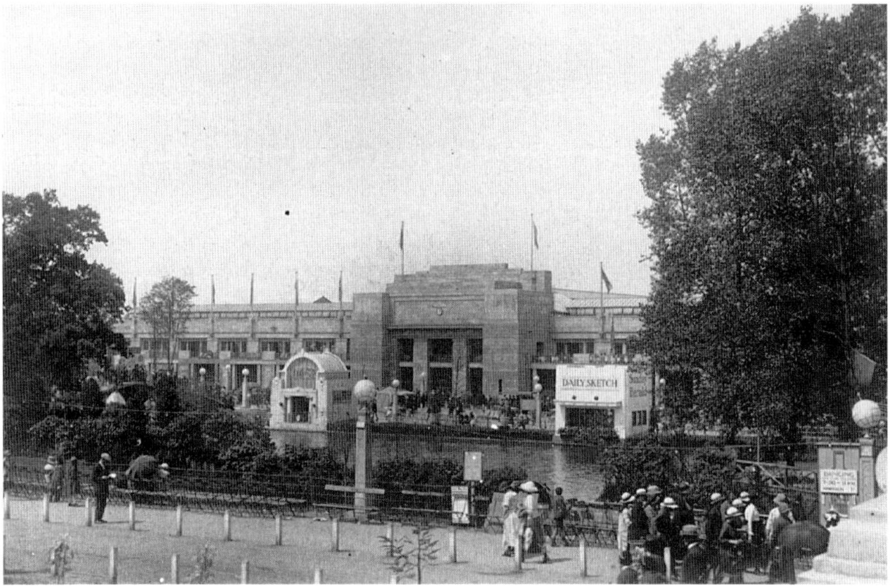

The British Empire Exhibition, 1924–5. On this and the next two pages are a small sample of the numerous photographs existing of the British Empire Exhibition. All six of these snapshots were in fact taken by the same gentleman, Stanley W. Martin. Above we have the Palace of Engineering, which was the largest concrete building at the time and hosted exhibitions from hundreds of British engineering firms. Below is the Indian Pavilion, looking eastwards over the lake. The building was not a copy of the Taj Mahal, though reminiscent of both that building and the Jama Masjid at Delhi.

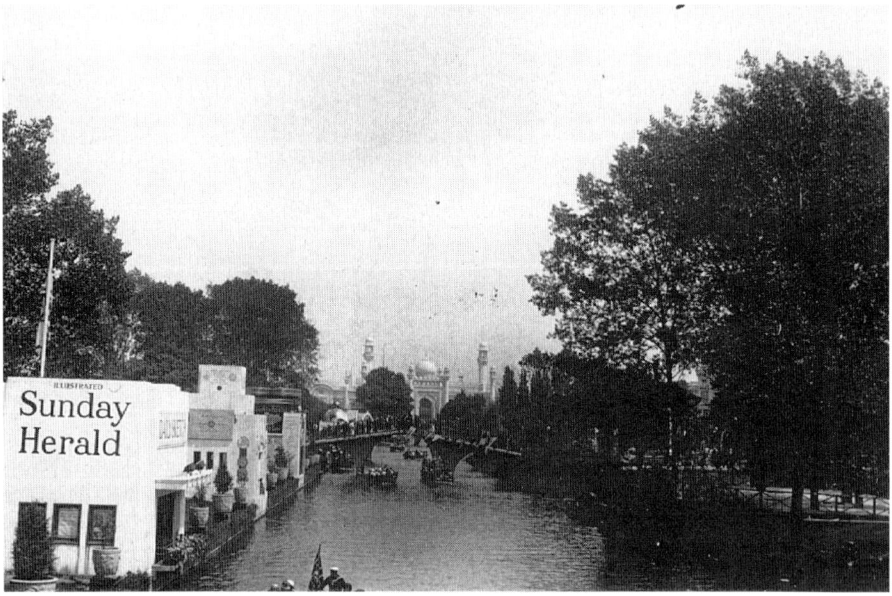

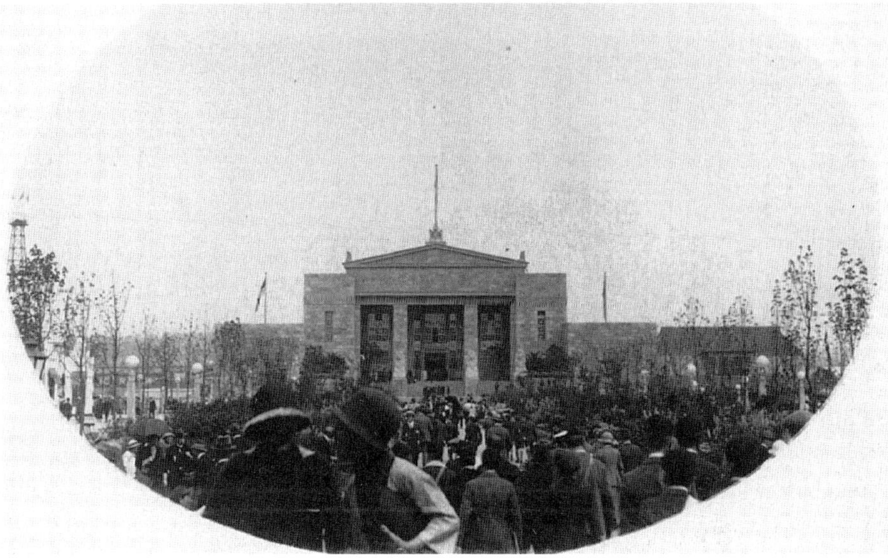

The British Empire Exhibition, 1924–5. Both of these photographs are of HM Government Building, which was designed to show 'what the Government is up to'. Beyond the six lions that guarded the building were employees of many government departments such as Whitehall, the Mint, Ordnance Survey and the Mines Department. There were also representatives from the three armed forces, and above the entrance to the building were special apartments for the king and queen and other members of the royal family when they visited the exhibition.

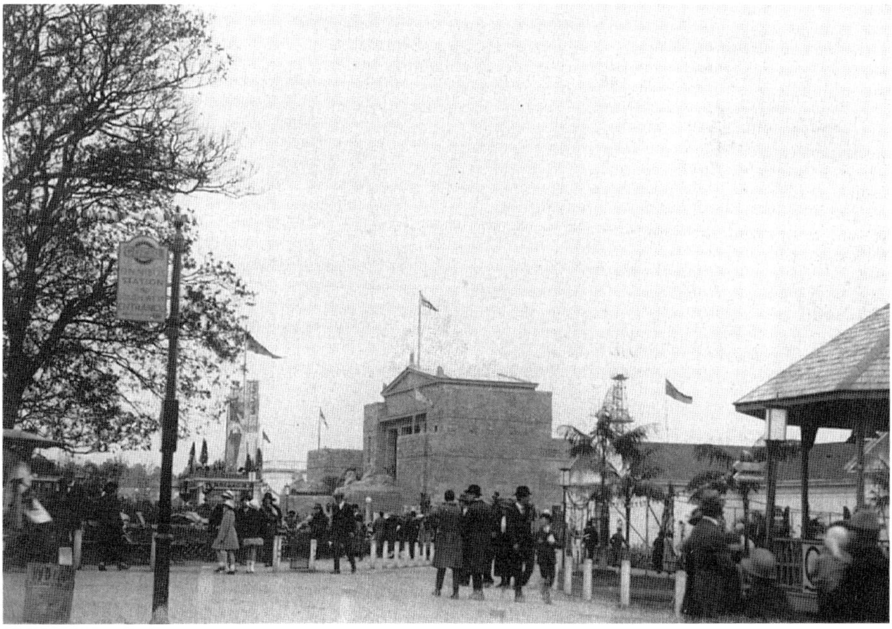

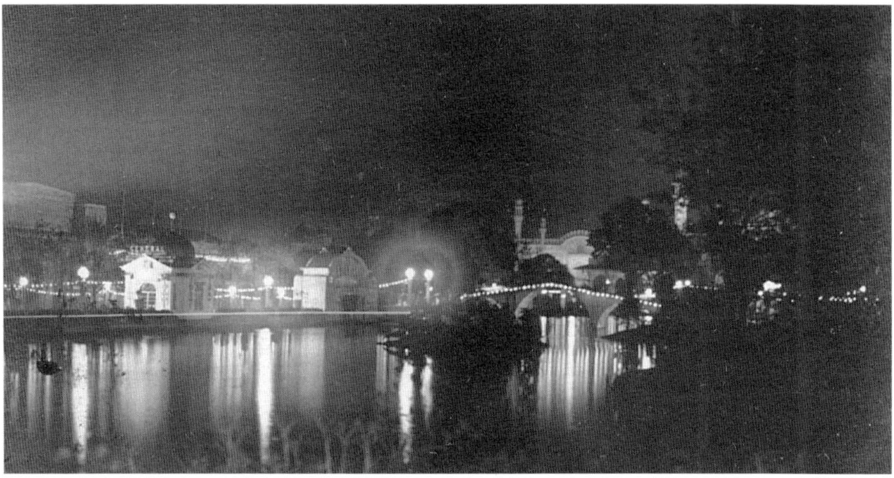

The British Empire Exhibition, 1924–5. Above is the Palace of Engineering and the Indian Pavilion at night, probably from the junction of Princes Path East and Dominion Way. According to the *Daily News* souvenir guide to the exhibition, one of the most popular attractions in the Palace of Engineering was the diver in a glass tank: 'The stall is always crowded with visitors who see him put on his weighted costume and descend into the sea water.' The main Canadian Pavilion seen at night from Engineers Way is shown below. The Canadians had three buildings at the exhibition, the two smaller ones housing the Canadian National Railway and the Canadian Pacific Railway. One of the most bizarre exhibits in the main pavilion was the Prince of Wales and his horse on his ranch, sculpted in solid butter.

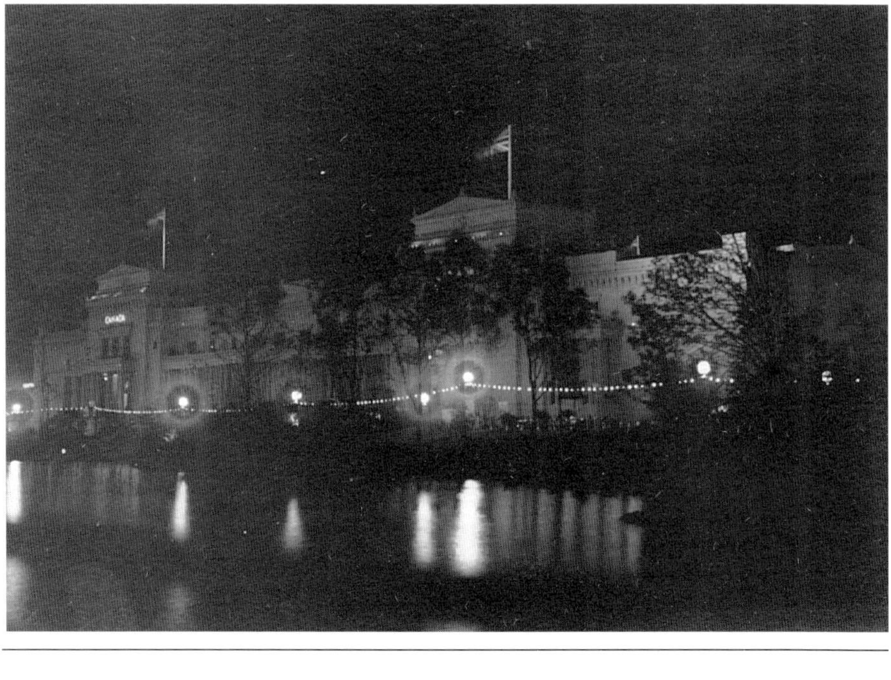

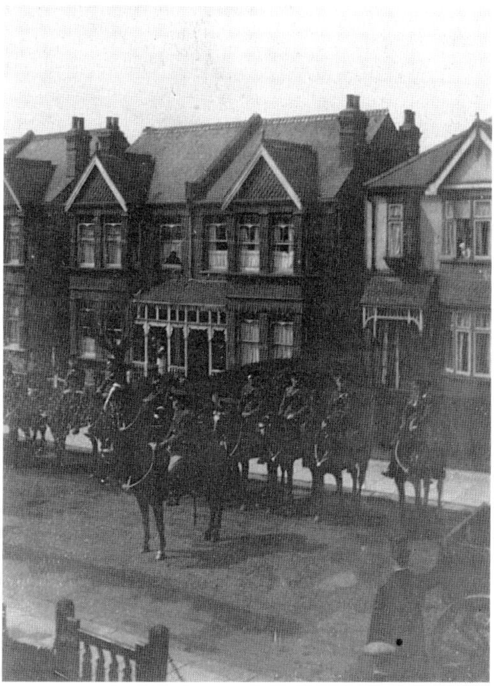

The royal party en route to the opening of the British Empire Exhibition in June 1925. Another rare and probably unique photograph, this was taken outside 120 Swinderby Road, not far from the High Road, and shows where the royal party changed from their motor cars, coming from Windsor, to the state coaches that were to relay them to the ceremonial opening.

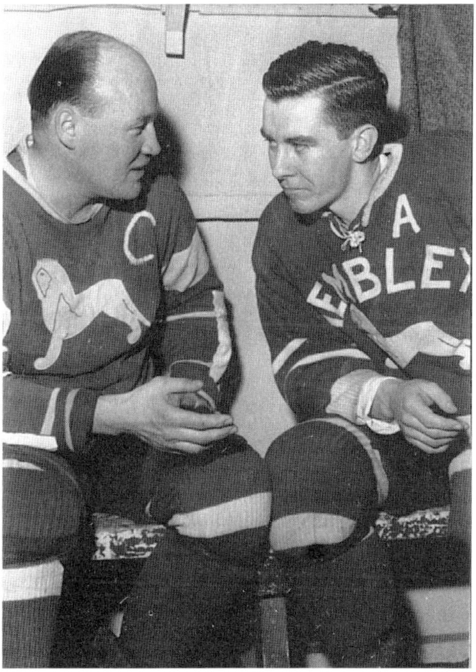

Two members of the Wembley Lions ice hockey team talking tactics, during the 1950s. Ice hockey dominated the sports scene at the Empire Pool in the years before the Second World War: 343,530 people watched matches there in 1936. There were in fact two Wembley teams, the Lions and the Monarchs, the two sides amalgamating in 1950. Ice hockey was a popular sport, even the war could not stop the 1939–40 season.

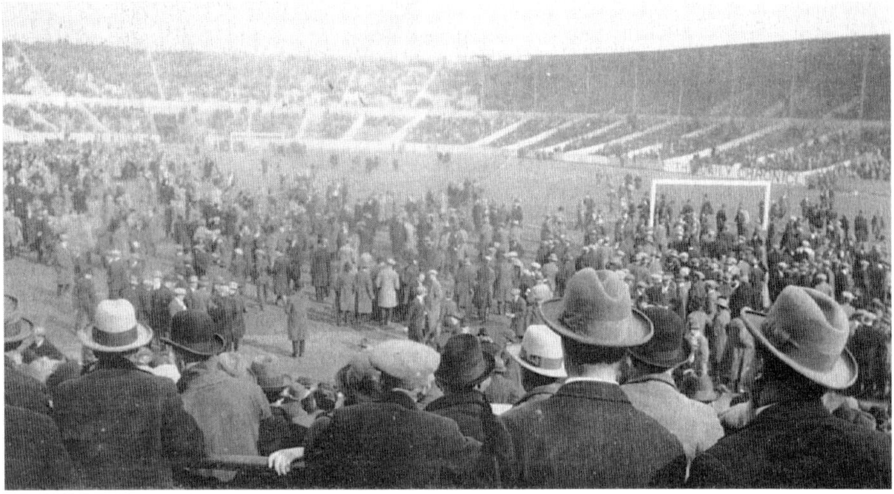

The first Wembley Cup Final, 1923 (in which Bolton Wanderers beat West Ham United 2–0). It was a truly massive event: 126,047 spectators gained admittance through the turnstiles and a further 75,000 rushed the gates or climbed the fences. This meant the total crowd of at least 200,000 was crammed into a stadium meant to cater for less than 100,000. In one of the most famous incidents, a mounted policeman, PC George Storey, on his white horse 'Billie', controlled the vast crowd which had surged on to the pitch and threatened the cancellation of the match. However, order was restored, the match began and David Jack had the honour of scoring the first goal in a Wembley Cup Final.

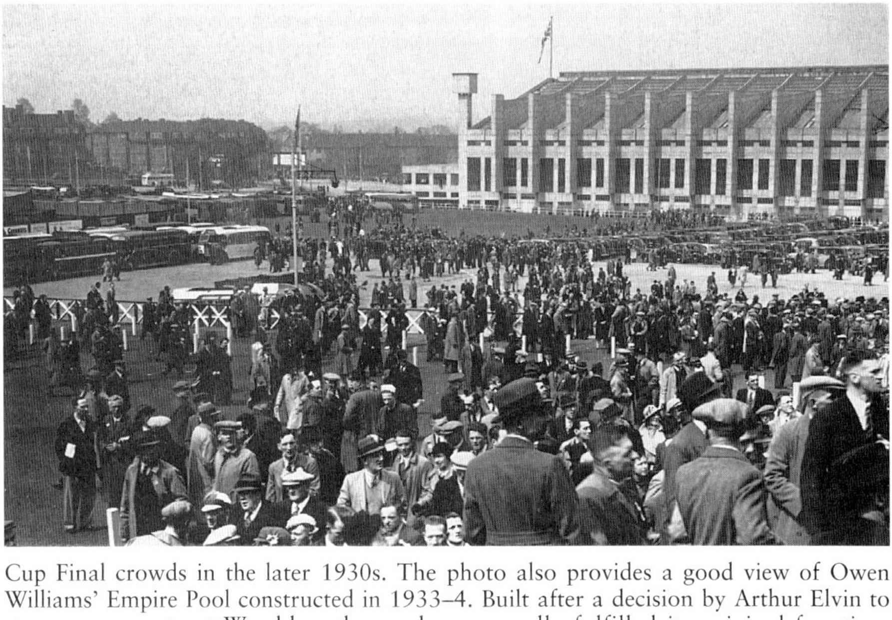

Cup Final crowds in the later 1930s. The photo also provides a good view of Owen Williams' Empire Pool constructed in 1933–4. Built after a decision by Arthur Elvin to stage new sports at Wembley, the pool never really fulfilled its original function, although it staged the swimming events at the 1948 Olympics.

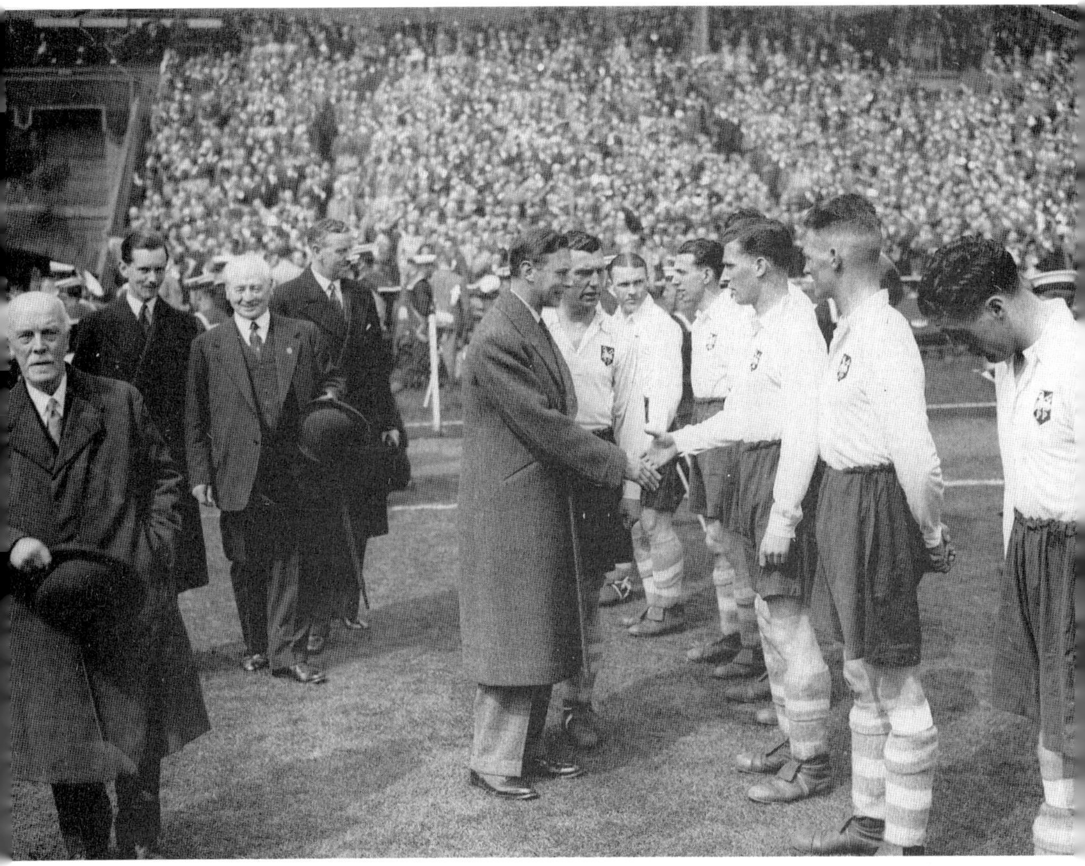

The 1937 FA Cup Final. Sunderland won the Cup for the first time, beating Preston North End 3–1 after going a goal down in the thirty-eighth minute. Second-half goals from Gurney, Carter and Burbanks secured the trophy for 'the Rokermen'. Here the Preston team meets King George VI before the kick-off. The player fifth from the right is the legendary Bill Shankly, here twenty-three years old. Interestingly, both teams refused to wear numbers on the backs of their shirts. Although there had been an experiment in the 1933 Everton v. Manchester City final and the Football Association had hoped it would assist spectators, the accepted wisdom declared 'that the game is so easy to follow owing to the standardised positions of players' that numbers were not necessary. Preston returned to Wembley the following year, this time beating Huddersfield 1–0 in extra time.

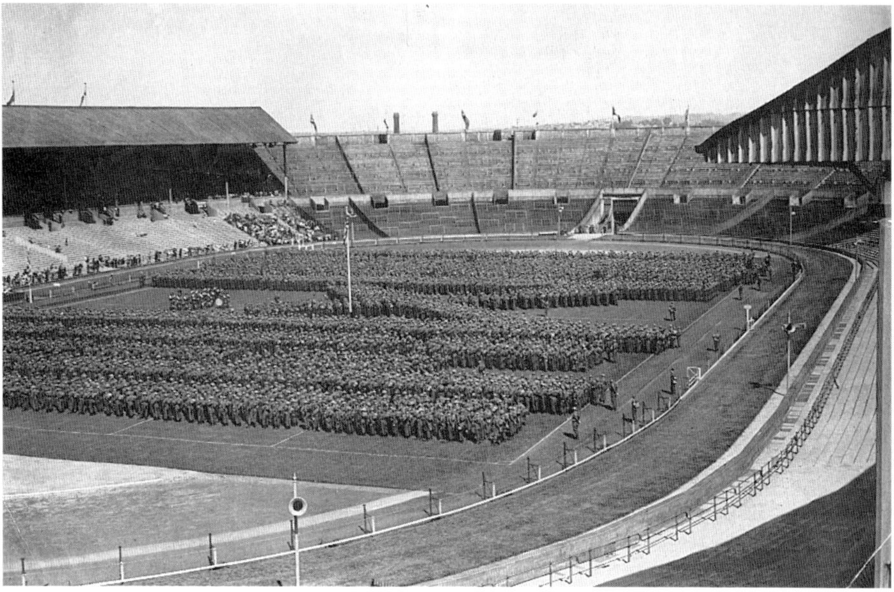

The army in Wembley Stadium, probably during the Second World War, when a number of reviews of different military forces, such as Civil Defence, the Home Guard and other local units, were undertaken.

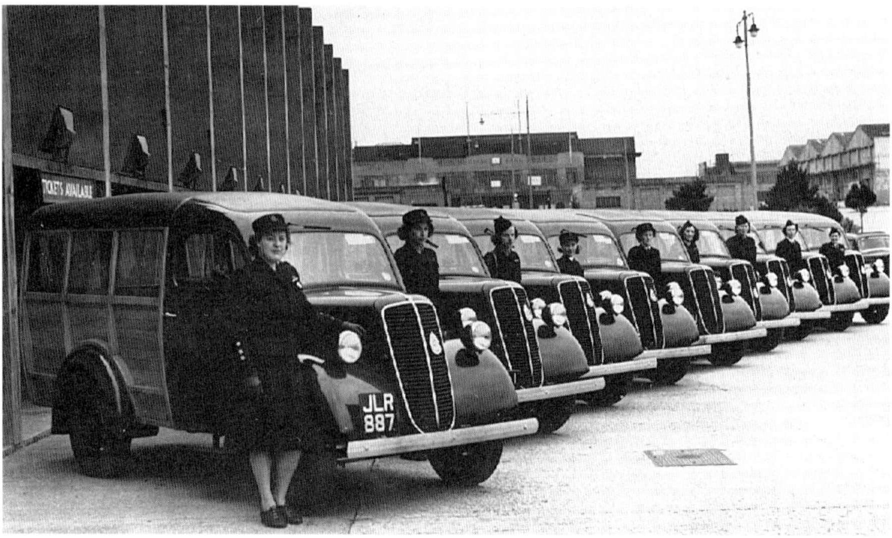

The array of drivers used to transport competitors and officials between sites during the 1948 Olympics. Their vehicles are parked outside the Empire Pool. The 1940 Games had been scheduled for Tokyo, offered hopefully to Helsinki and finally cancelled. The 1944 Games were offered to London but again cancelled. In 1948 London rose to the challenges of rationing, shortage and national austerity to stage the largest games thus far – with 4,700 competitors from fifty-nine countries.

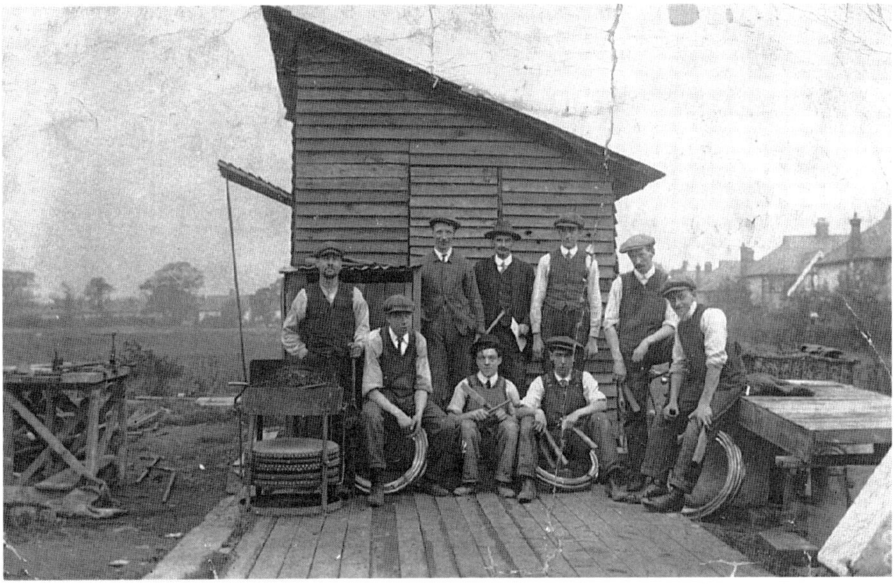

Wembley plumbers – possibly all of them, according to the donor of this photograph. The group is photographed in the yard of A.E. Howard & Sons (the donor's grandfather, who was also a member of the Volunteer Fire Brigade), London Road, Wembley, *c.* 1930. They are all equipped with the tools of their trade, posing beside a portable forge with round bellows.

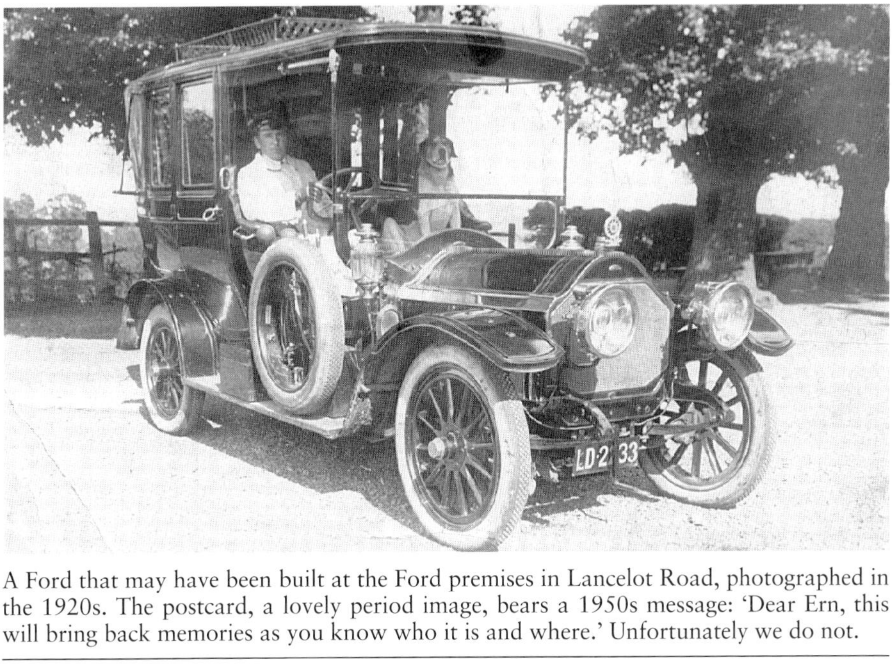

A Ford that may have been built at the Ford premises in Lancelot Road, photographed in the 1920s. The postcard, a lovely period image, bears a 1950s message: 'Dear Ern, this will bring back memories as you know who it is and where.' Unfortunately we do not.

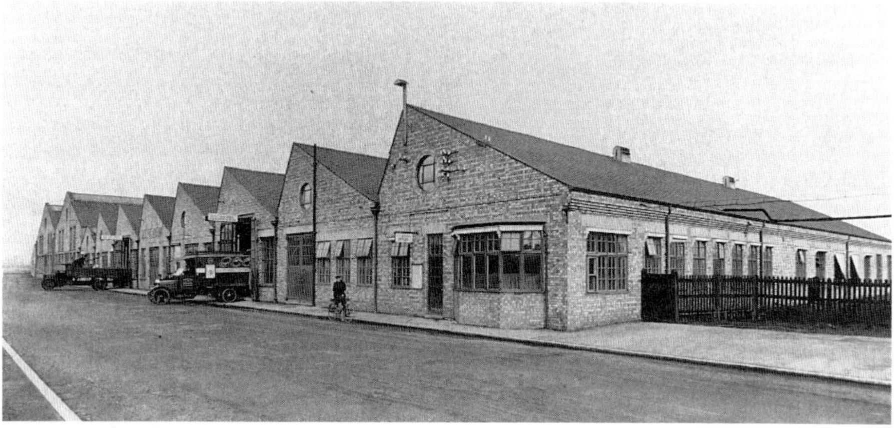

General Electric Company, formerly Hooper's, *c.* 1922 (above). F.W. Hooper & Co. came to North Wembley in 1917. As the production targets for aircraft being urged on the company by the Air Board could not be met by the company's main factory at Chelsea, a new factory was built on the site adjoining North Wembley station. By the end of the First World War Hooper's factory was making three complete aircraft per day. The last such vehicle was delivered in June 1919, when the factory went over to car production. Hooper's quit the site and it was taken over by the General Electric Company in 1922. They opened the Hirst Laboratories in February 1923 with further expansion on the site in 1925 and 1927. The photograph below shows GEC from the air, 22 April 1932.

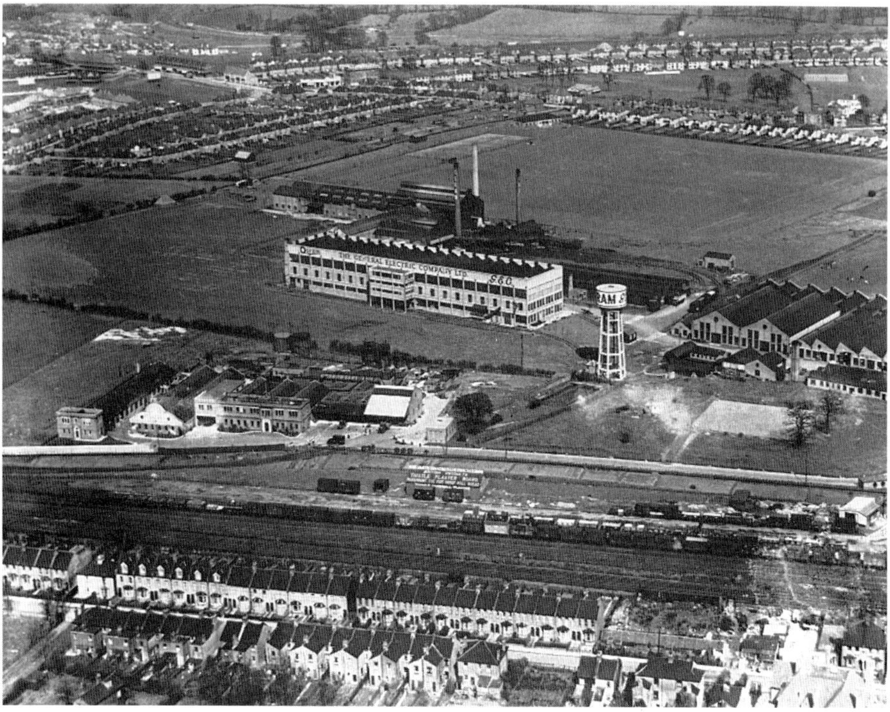

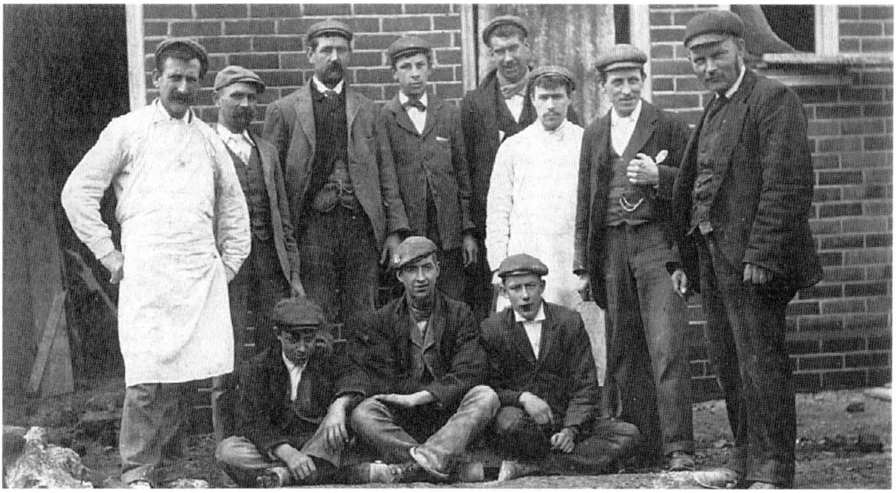

Building labourers and craftsmen posing in front of the fruit of their labours, possibly *c*. 1910. Unfortunately, neither building nor workers have thus far been positively identified. The name on the photograph's mount – perhaps Eames – would normally indicate the photographer but may just be a reference to the Eames family of Alperton who were builders.

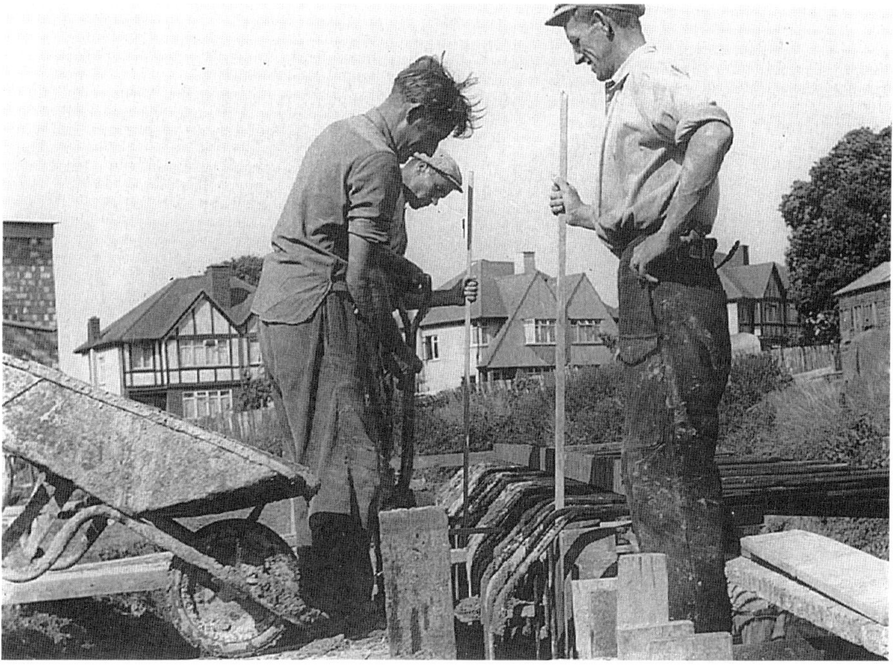

Work on the construction of the Preston Estate in 1947–8. This photo actually shows the Falcon Way bridge being built, while in the background can be seen the inter-war semis typical of this part of the borough.

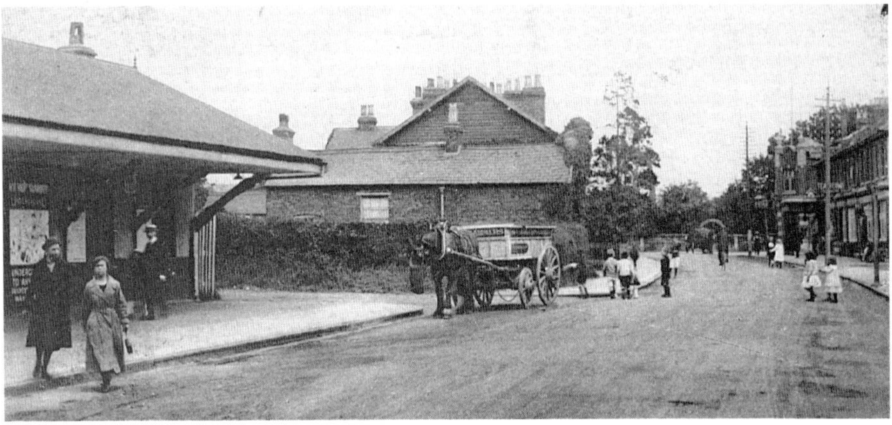

The Metropolitan District Line railway station, *c.* 1910. It opened in 1906 and was originally called 'Alperton and Perivale'. Things to notice include the Underground poster on the station and the horse and cart in the middle of the picture, which provides some amusement for a small group of children. On the right is the Alperton Park Hotel, the licensee in 1906 being I.J. Russell. Next door was Silvester Puddephat's butcher's shop. He died in 1962, aged ninety-five, having lived in Wembley for seventy-three years.

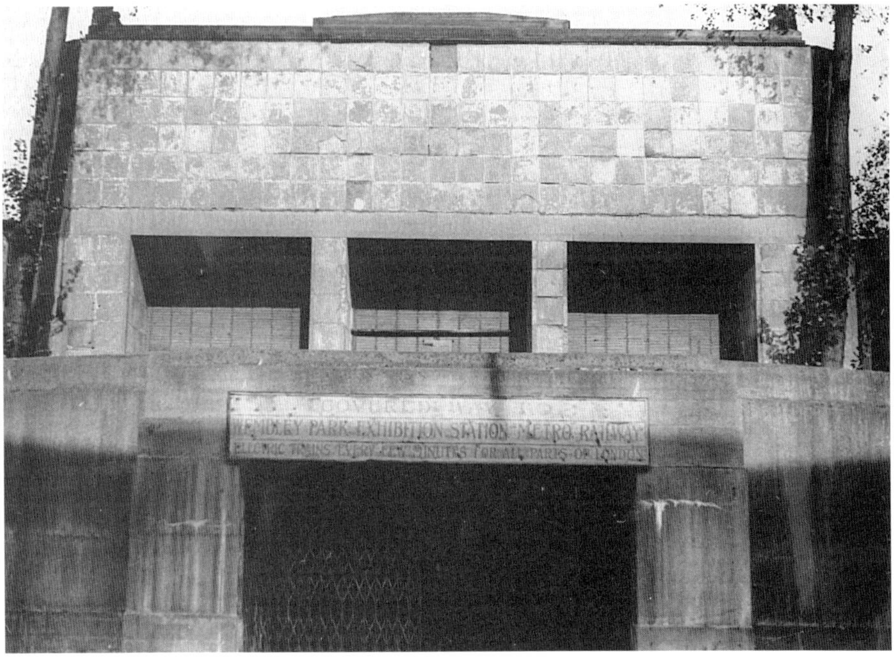

Wembley Park Exhibition station, late 1950s. This station was built especially for the British Empire Exhibition, the first sod of the requisite loop line being cut by the Duke of York in January 1922. Despite its extensive usage during the 1924–5 exhibition it was never again able to command sufficient passengers to warrant its long-term survival. Renamed Wembley Stadium station in 1927, it was last used for the 1968 FA Cup Final.

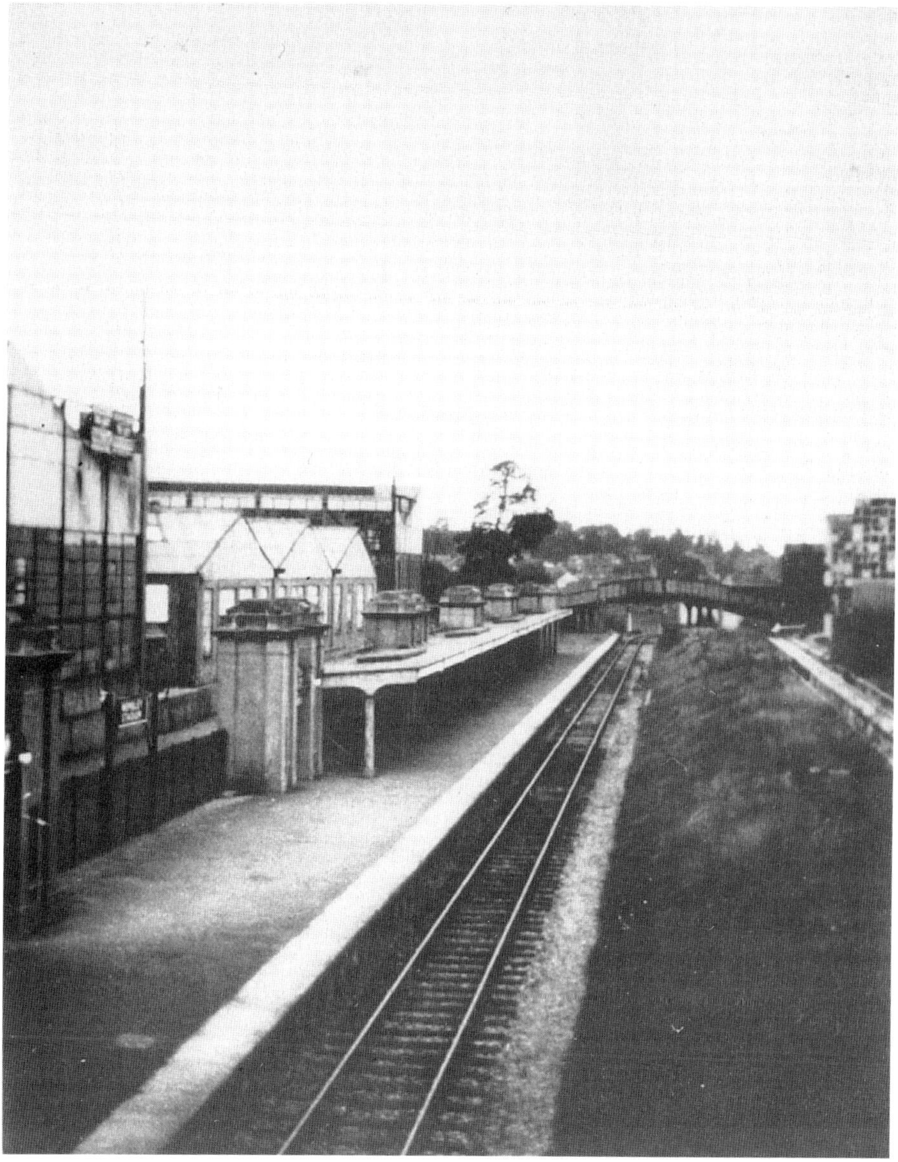

The somewhat derelict Stadium station in 1950. While the commercial success of the British Empire Exhibition is arguable, the economic power of Great Britain was probably already on the wane, particularly with the rise of the German and American economies. This photograph is somehow symbolic of the eclipse of Britain as a world power.

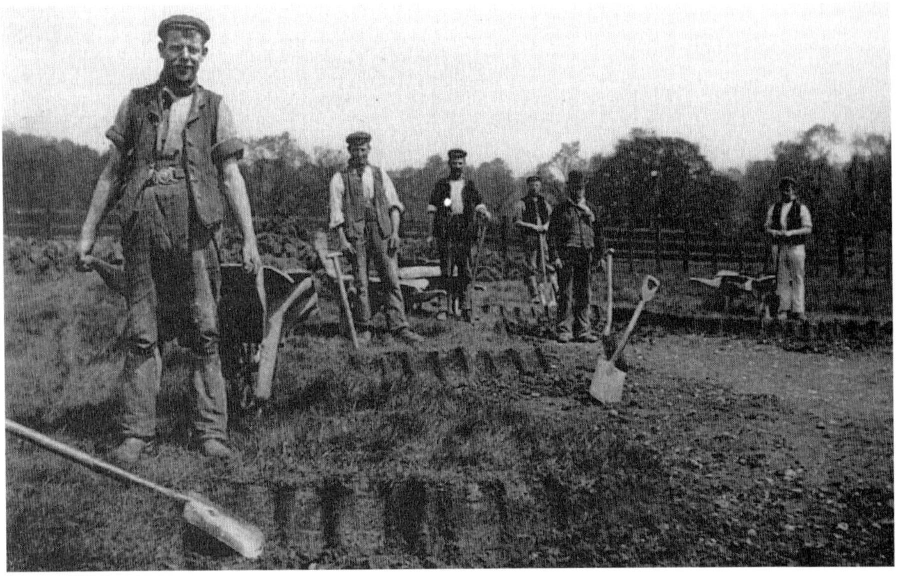

These photographs come from an album taken by Alfred Newton of 17 King Street, Leicester between the years 1902 and 1906. They show a turf-removing gang at Wembley Park (above) and a steam navvy working on the Great Central Railway, Wembley Cutting (below). The photos on pp. 9 and 13 have been selected from the same album. All the pictures were taken to show the construction of the link between Neasden and Northolt.

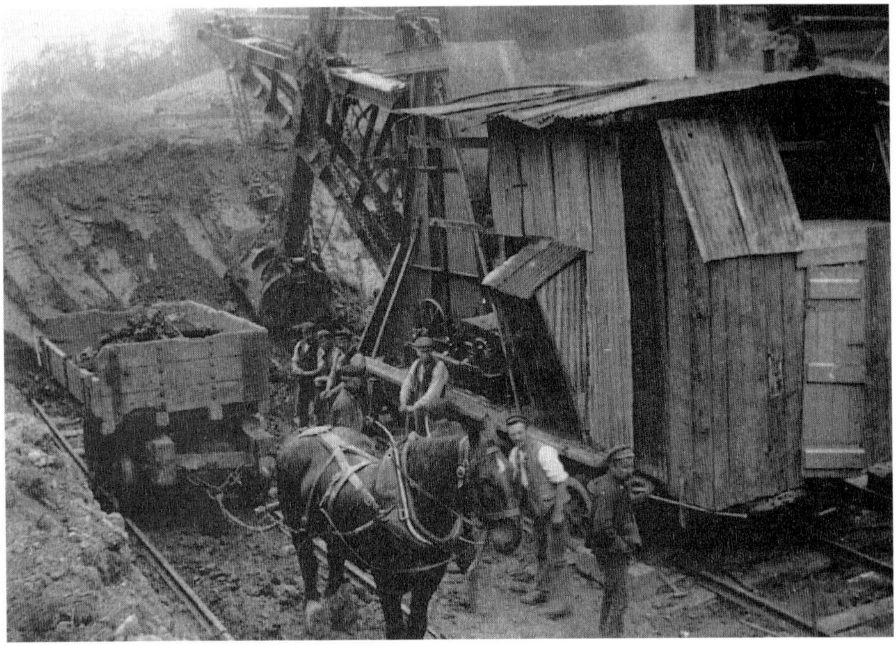

Section Two

KINGSBURY

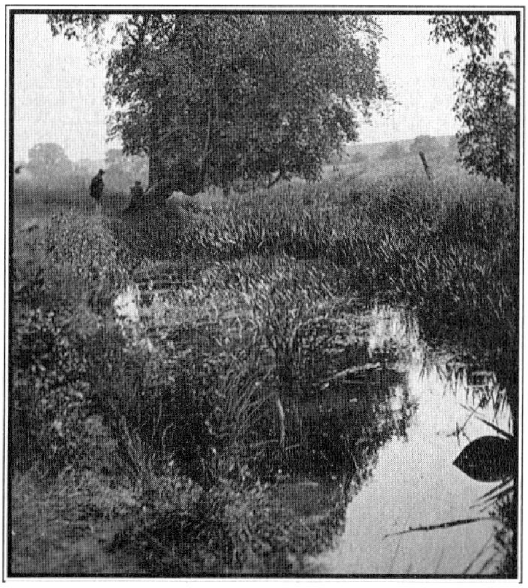

The River Brent at Kingsbury, 1927. This photograph conveys an image of rural tranquillity and unspoilt countryside that reflects the limited development at the time.

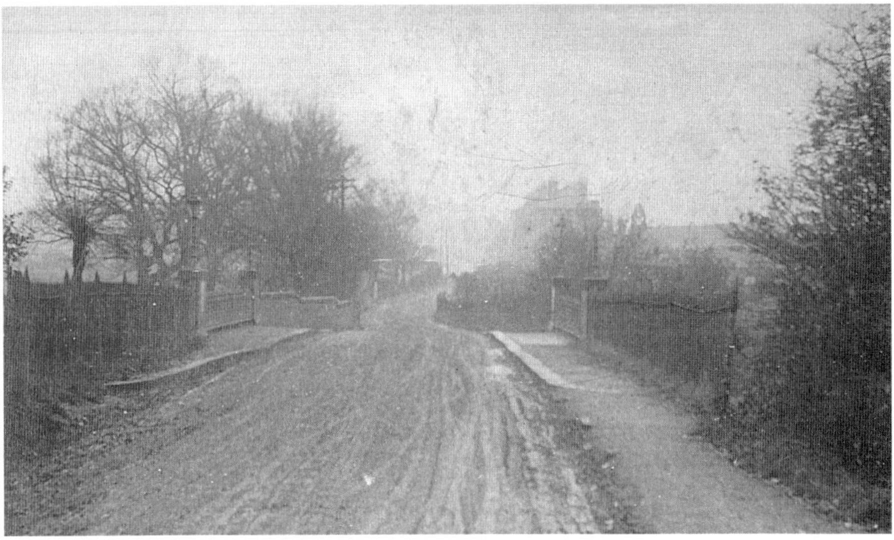

View of Kingsbury Lane (now Blackbird Hill to avoid confusion with Kingsbury Road) looking back towards Neasden. The bridge over the River Brent forms the parish boundary. This photo can be dated to around 1880 as other contemporaneous images show St Catherine's iron church (the movement of which in 1915 resulted in a number of newspaper stories).

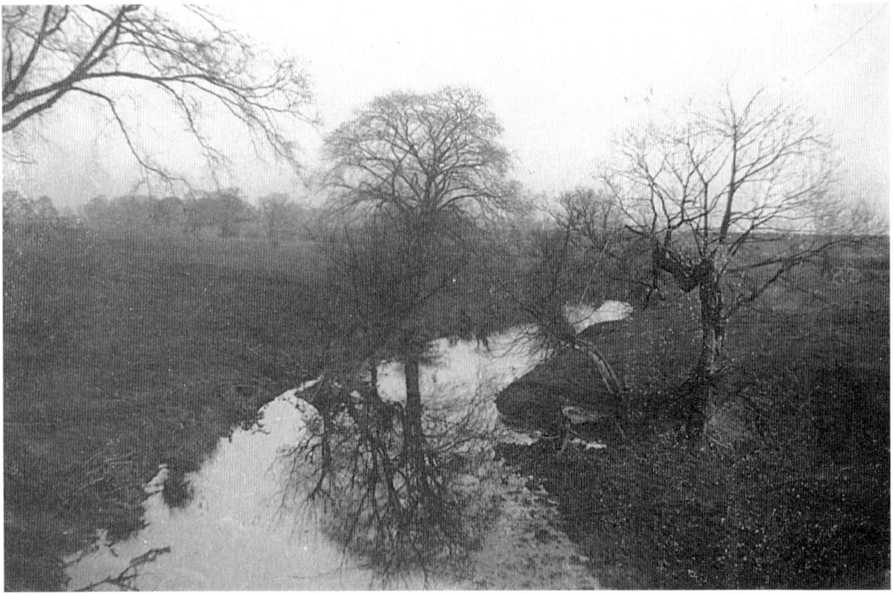

The Brent from Kingsbury Bridge, *c.* 1920. One of the few surviving Celtic place-names, Brent is probably derived from 'Brigantia' and means 'holy river'. The river originates as the Dollis Brook and flows down through North Finchley, Kingsbury, Wembley and Willesden to Ealing whence it reaches its confluence with the Thames, unsurprisingly, at Brentford.

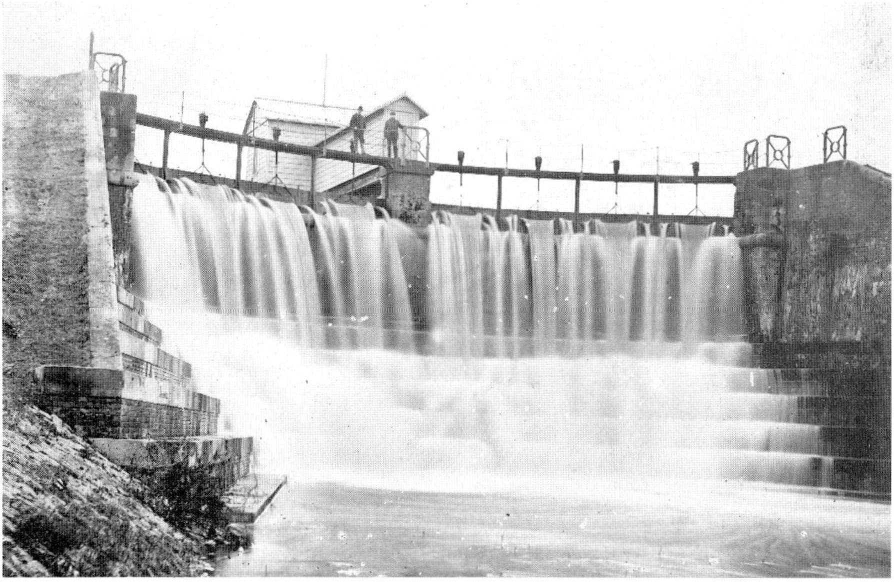

The Falls at Kingsbury, *c.* 1880 (above). Concern over the need for a dam was first voiced in 1803, in response to the urgent requirement for a more satisfactory water supply for the Grand Junction Canal. The canal feeder was built shortly after 1809 but this did not solve the problem. It was not until 1833 that real consideration was given to the construction of a reservoir; work began in late 1834 or early 1835, the ceremonial opening taking place in 1838. Since its construction the Welsh Harp, or Brent Reservoir, has provided many opportunities for recreation. Perhaps one of the most impressive was the Willesden (later Brent) Regatta (below) in the 1940s, a regular event until its abandonment in the 1960s.

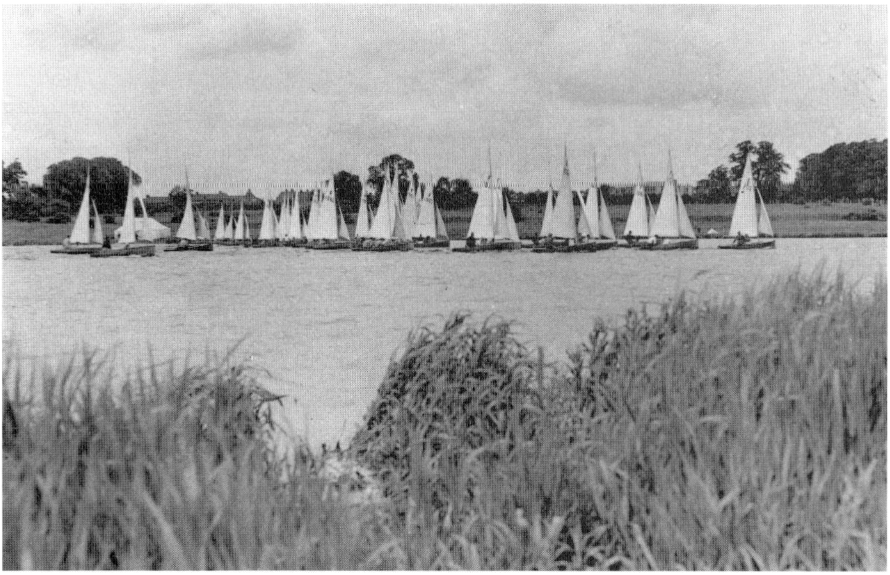

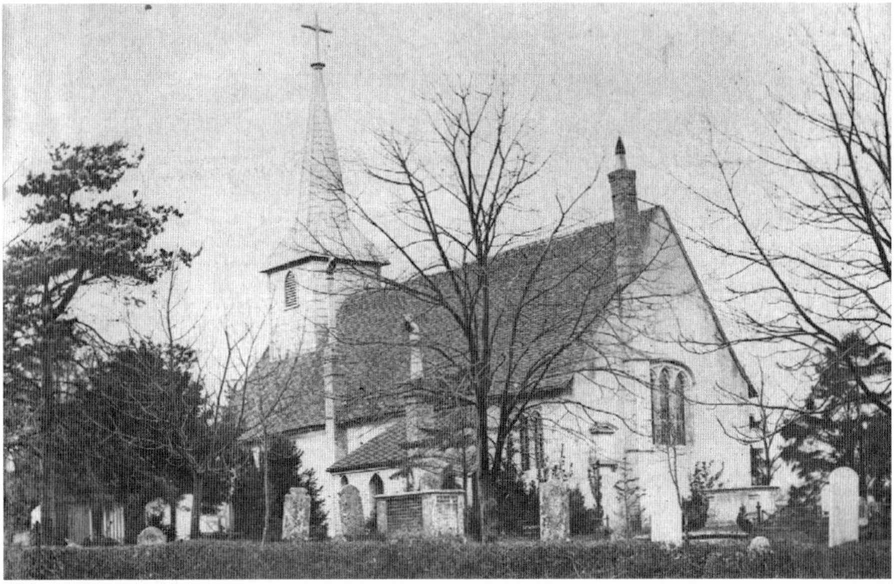

St Andrew's Church. Although there is disputed architectural evidence that St Andrew's pre-dates the Norman conquest, it now seems more likely that its flint and rubble walls were erected in the twelfth and thirteenth centuries. The photo above shows the church and churchyard from Old Church Lane; below is the interior of the church. Both photos are from F.A. Wood's collection and consequently date from around 1880.

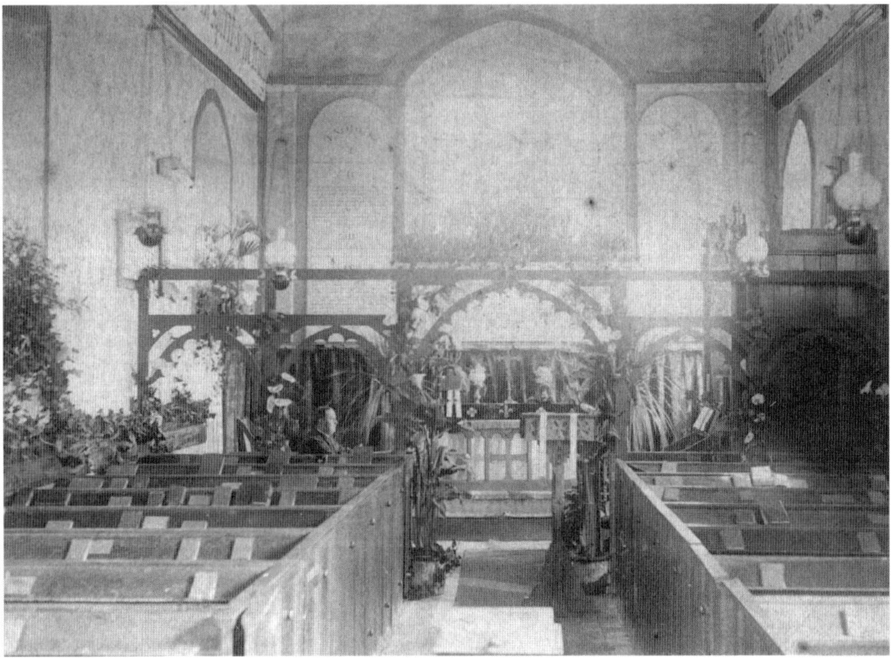

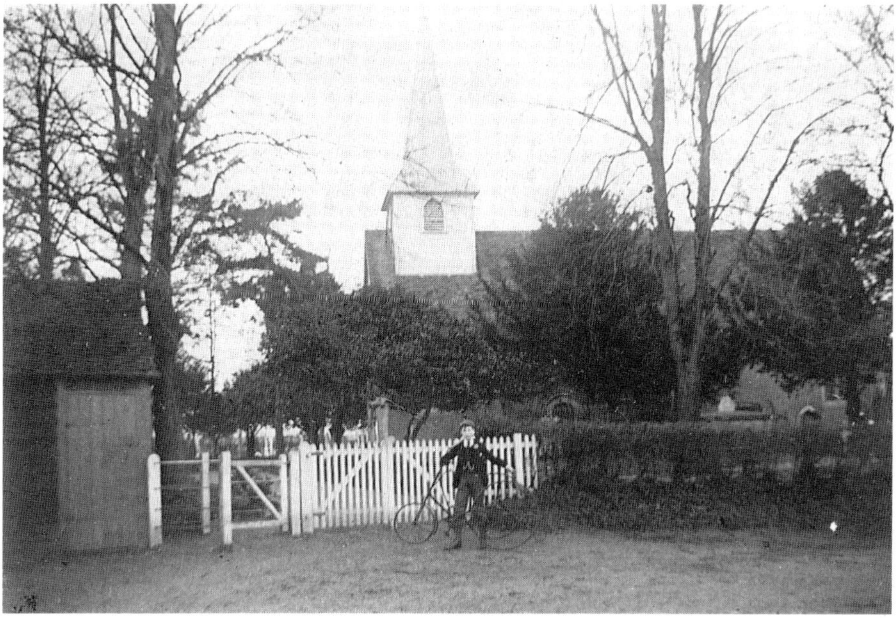

Old St Andrew's, photographed from Old Church Lane, *c.* 1910. A young man poses proudly with his tricycle: this is informal portraiture of the most appealing kind.

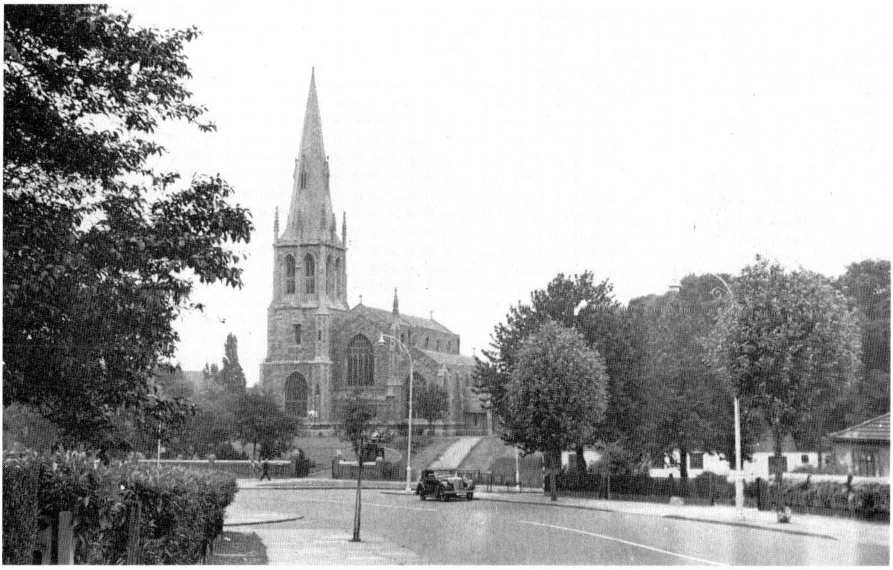

New St Andrew's, *c.* 1950. Previously sited in the City, this church was built by Dawkes and Hamilton in 1847. In 1933 it was disassembled, transported brick by brick to Kingsbury and then rebuilt with a few additions by W.A. Forsyth. As one of the earliest neo-Gothic churches and a centre for Anglo-Catholicism it was furnished with many interior embellishments.

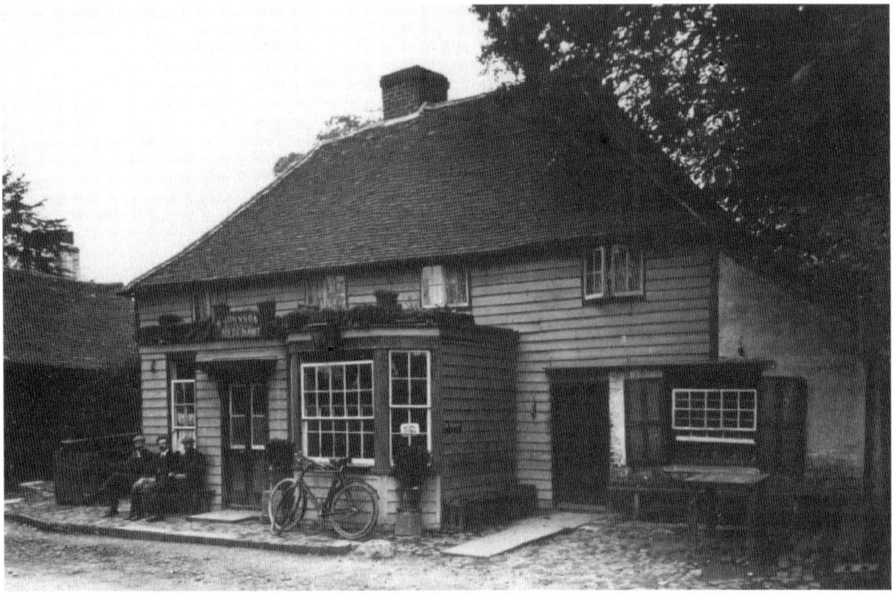

The Plough, Kingsbury Green, 1906 (above). There is no evidence of an inn on the site before 1748 despite the fact that as many as one in nine houses in eighteenth-century Kingsbury were inns. It was certainly on the site of a medieval tenement. The new pub (below), a two-storey building with attics, replaced the earlier weatherboarded structure in the early 1930s. Here, in the 1950s, the continued presence of the bicycle reminds us that at the turn of the century The Plough was the headquarters for thirteen cycling clubs, as well as an attractive destination for walkers.

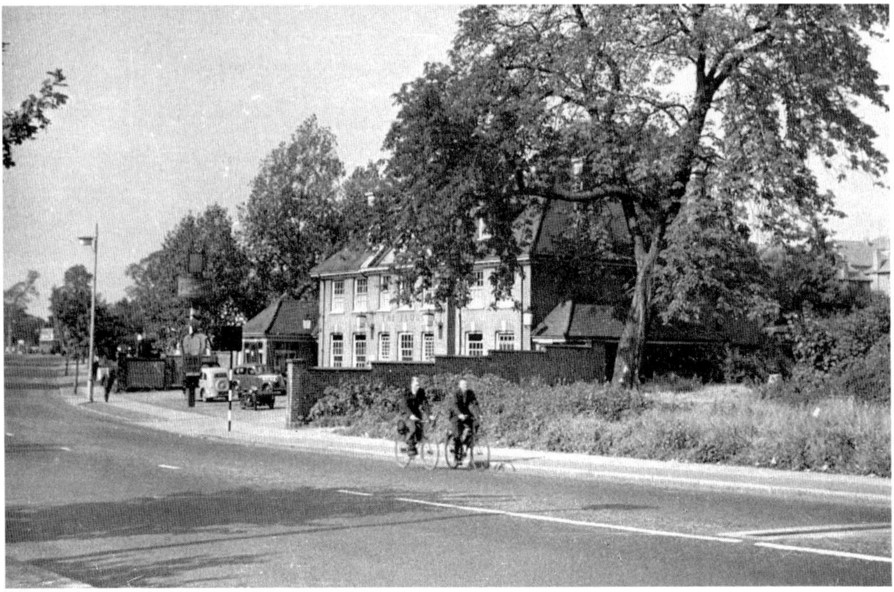

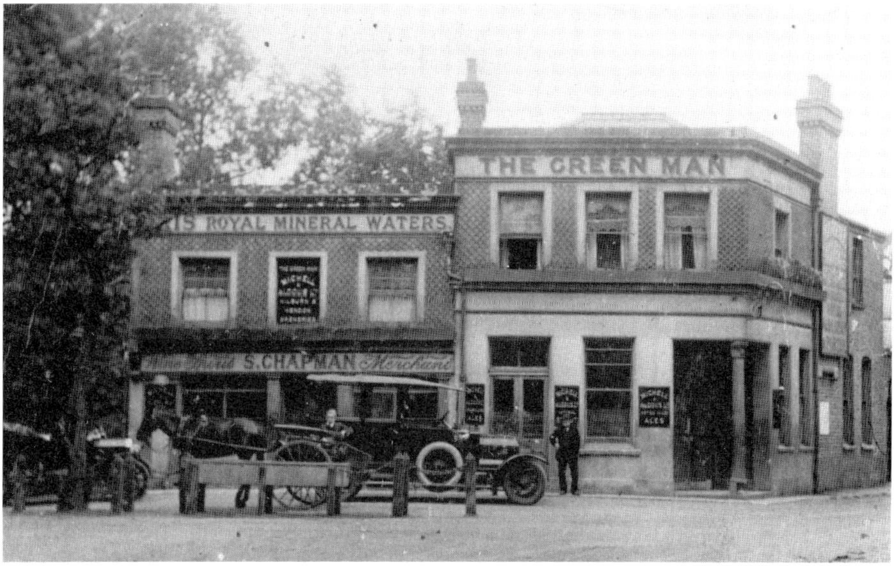

The Green Man at the junction of Old Kenton Lane and Slough Lane, *c*. 1920 (above). It was originally opened as a beerhouse in the late 1840s; the 1851 census returns tell us that the beerhouse keeper was a Mrs Emma Richardson, whose daughter Julia was also living on the premises. Before the building shown here was built, the premises consisted of a two-storeyed part brick, part rendered building tied to brewers Truman, Hanbury & Buxton. The photo below was taken around ten years later and is included for its unusual subject-matter: there are comparatively few photos taken at night within the archive collections of the London Borough of Brent.

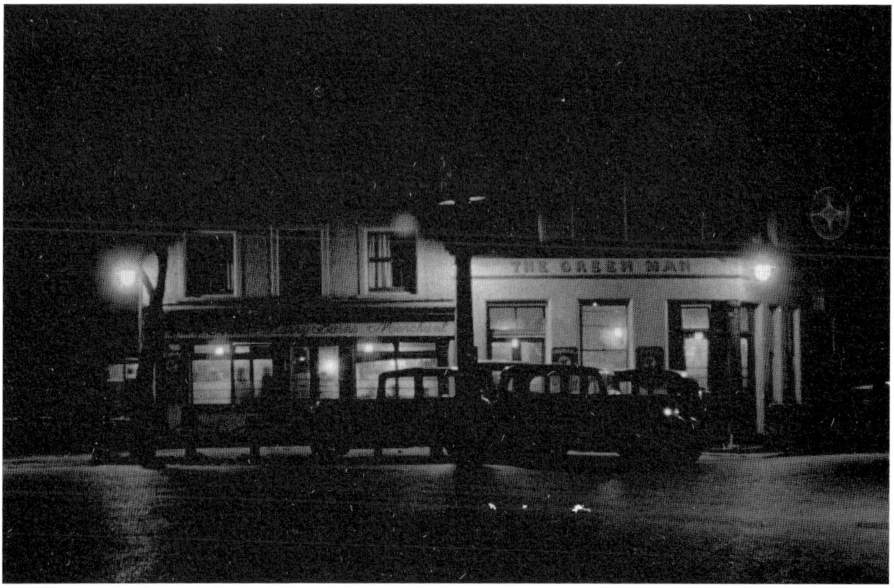

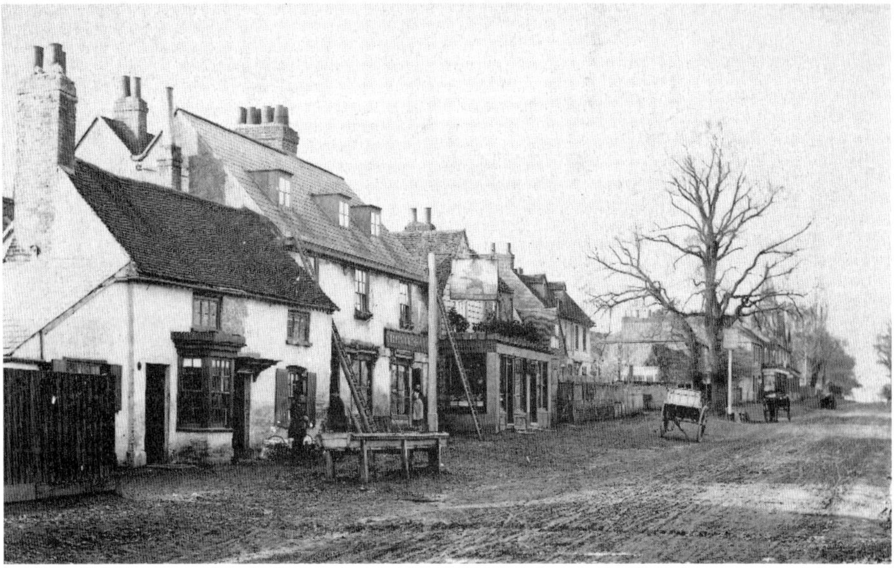

The Hyde, Kingsbury, looking north towards Colindale, *c.* 1880. The Red Lion public house on the left dates from around 1839 and is still in existence, although now a very different building. This pub was enlarged in 1921 and rebuilt in 1931. In 1918 the publican was Henry Johnson, formerly of The Plough at Kingsbury Green.

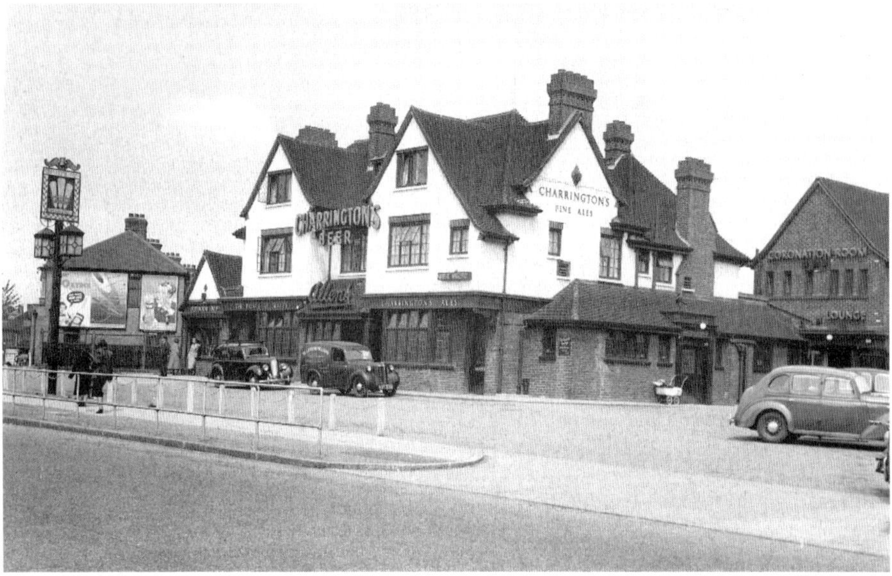

The Prince of Wales, *c.* 1933. A modern public house sited on Kingsbury Circle, or Circus, as it was referred to in the 1937 Kelly's Directory when J. Burdett was the landlord.

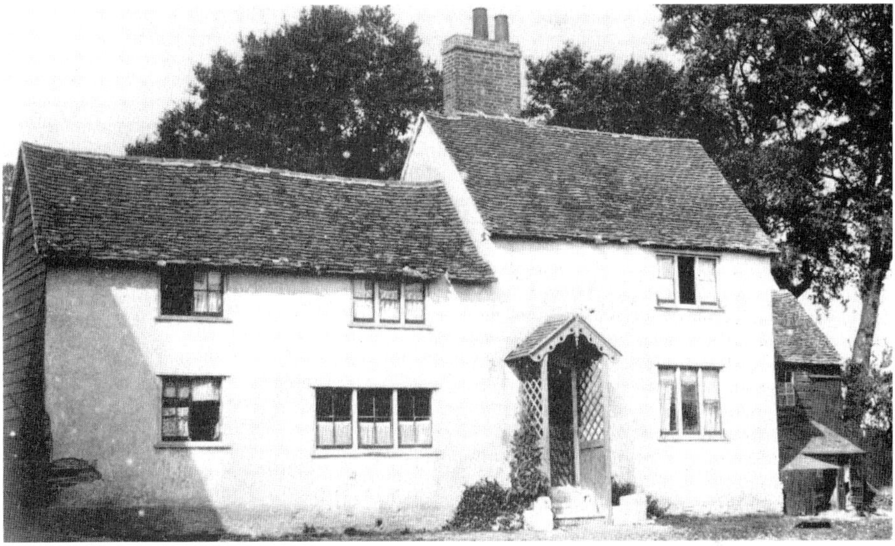

Blackbird Farm, *c.* 1880 (above) and in 1952 (below). Blackbird Farm was a dairy farm on the site of medieval Kingsbury; it has been traced back to 1442. It consisted of a cluster of buildings on both sides of Old Church Lane. Part of the farm was demolished in 1936, and the farmhouse was pulled down in 1955 despite dating from the mid-sixteenth century and being scheduled for preservation under the Town and Country Planning Act 1947. Protests by the Wembley History Society failed to save the building and Councillor Curley's suggestion that the brewers should incorporate the existing structure in the new 'Blackbirds' public house came to nought. As can be seen from the picture below, the building was also the victim of mock Tudorization.

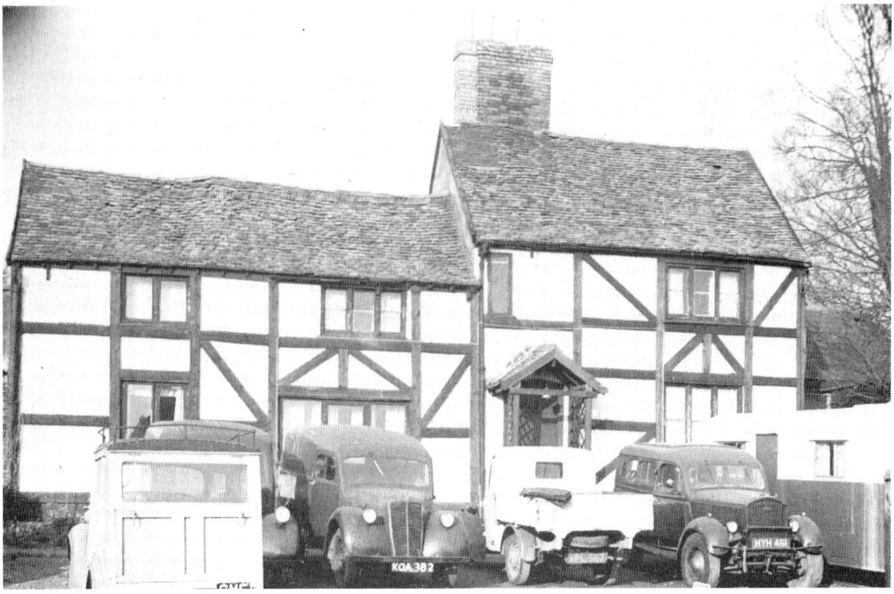

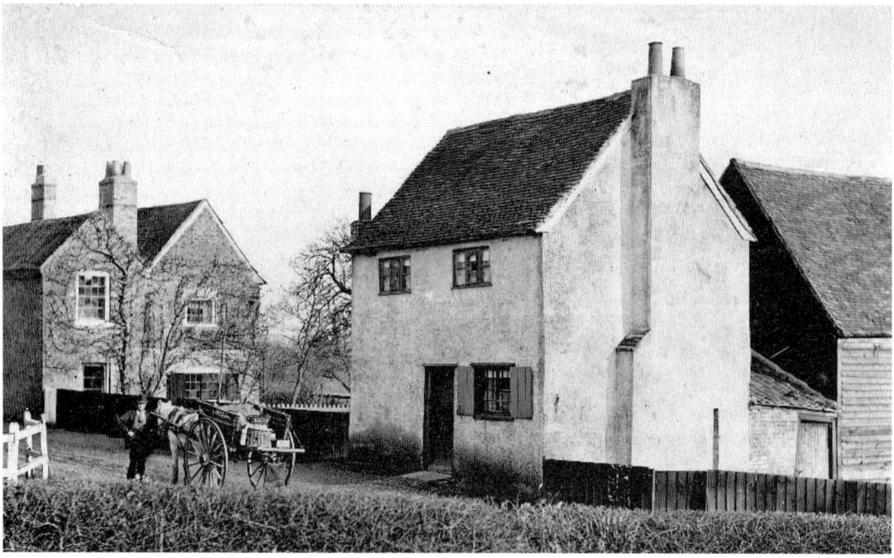

Cottage on the corner of Church Lane leading to Kingsbury Church, *c.* 1880. This is one of the cottages on the northern or upper yard site of Blackbird Hill Farm. Somewhat confusingly, on an 1875 map the upper yard is referred to as Blackpot Hill Farm and the lower yard is shown as Blackbird Hill Farm.

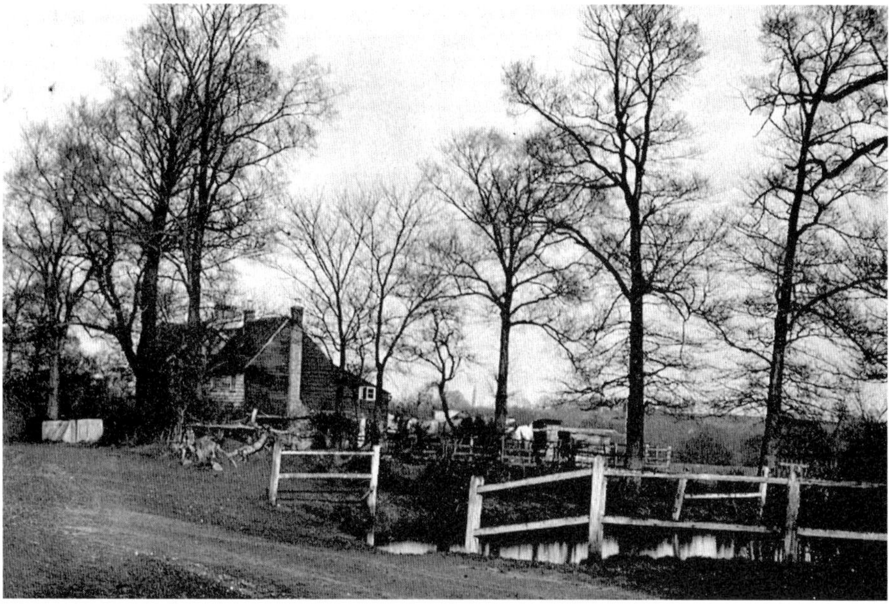

Hill Farm Cottages, 1920. The farm dates back to the fourteenth century when it was the home farm of Kingsbury Manor. When a barn collapsed in 1952 some fifteenth-century hammers were found. The 1861 census shows that the farmhouse was burnt to the ground, but had been rebuilt by 1871; it was not demolished until 1960.

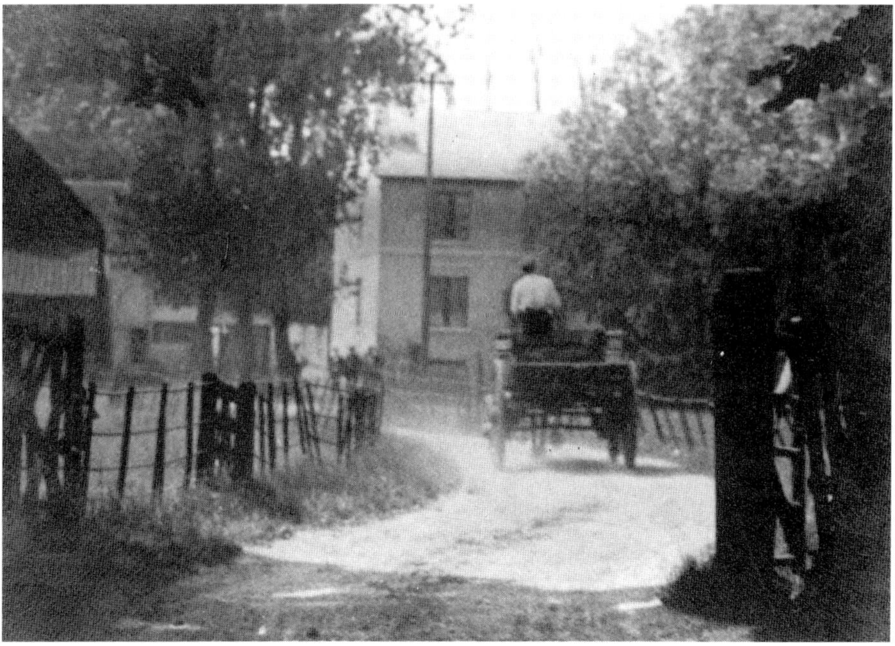

Big Bush Farm. The glorious picture above, taken in the summer of 1924, evokes the peaceful inter-war years, when the horse remained a major form of transportation. Below is another alluring image of the farm, this time a watercolour of 1927.

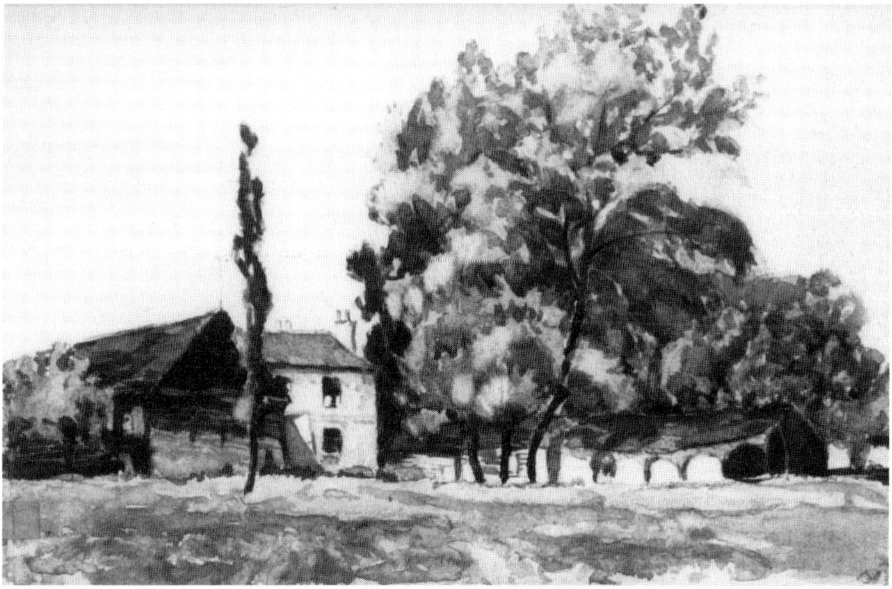

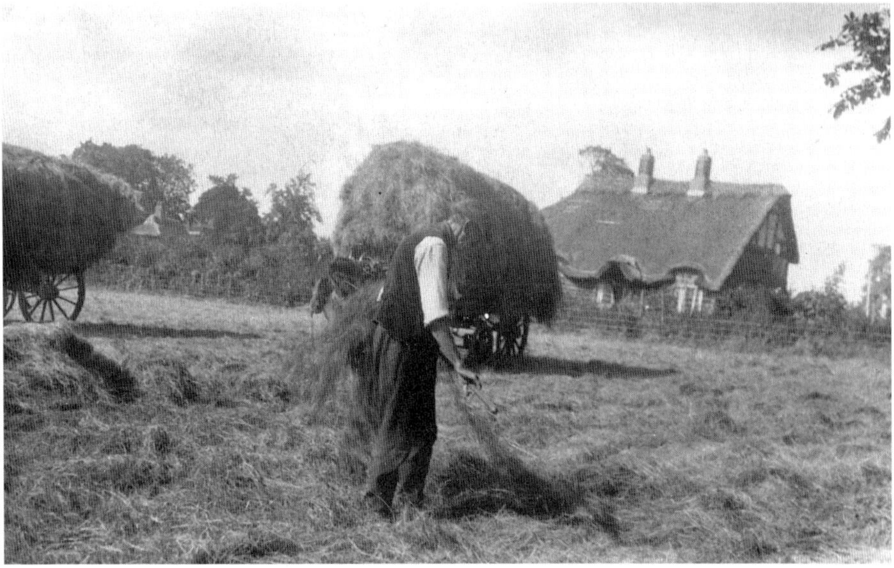

Hay-making at Pipers Green, 1930. Well within living memory hay was a staple crop of the fields of Kingsbury, as it had been from medieval times. This is a vision of a disappearing world as the agricultural idyll vanished beneath the sprawl of the urban jungle.

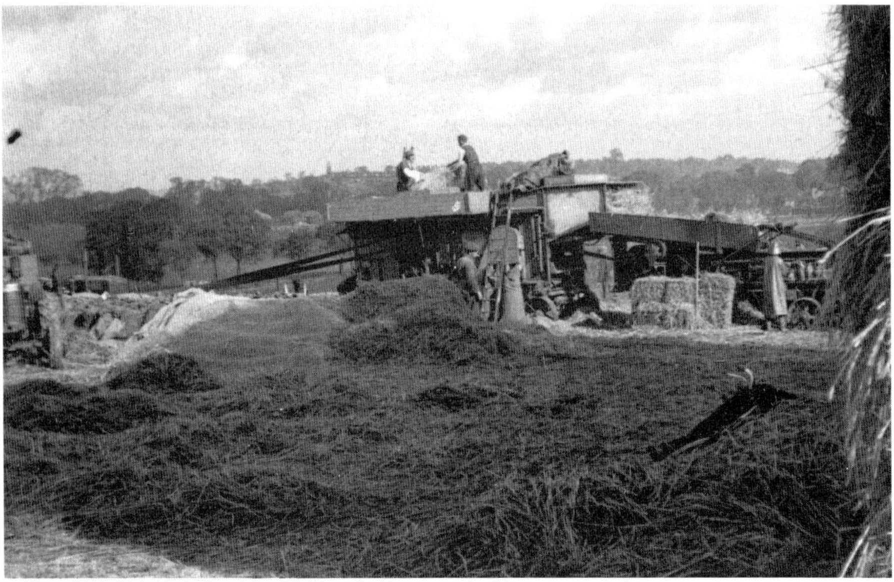

Threshing near Kingsbury, 1942. This is part of the collection of photographs taken by S.T. Hill. The subjects of the collection are wide ranging both topographically and chronologically, though sadly a number of prints almost certainly by this gentleman are unidentified; see pp. 91 (lower) and 95 (upper) for other photos from his collection.

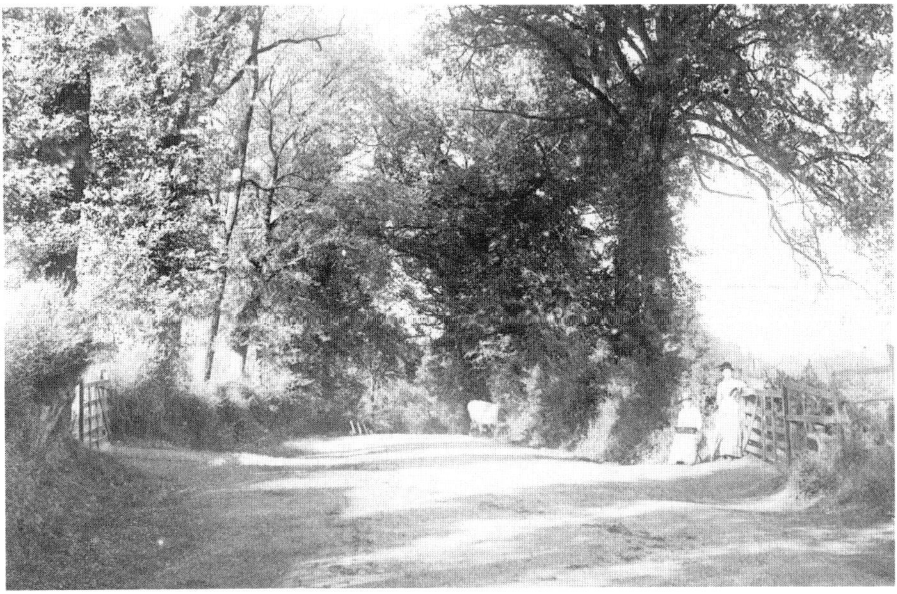

Old Church Lane, possibly as early as 1875. The photo was taken by F.A. Wood, the Willesden historian, local politician and latterly JP, who also had an interest in the parishes adjoining Willesden, including Kingsbury. The two ladies in the photograph are likely to be members of Wood's family, although neither looks like Mrs Mary Wood, his wife, who was buried in the churchyard at St Mary's, Willesden, in 1879.

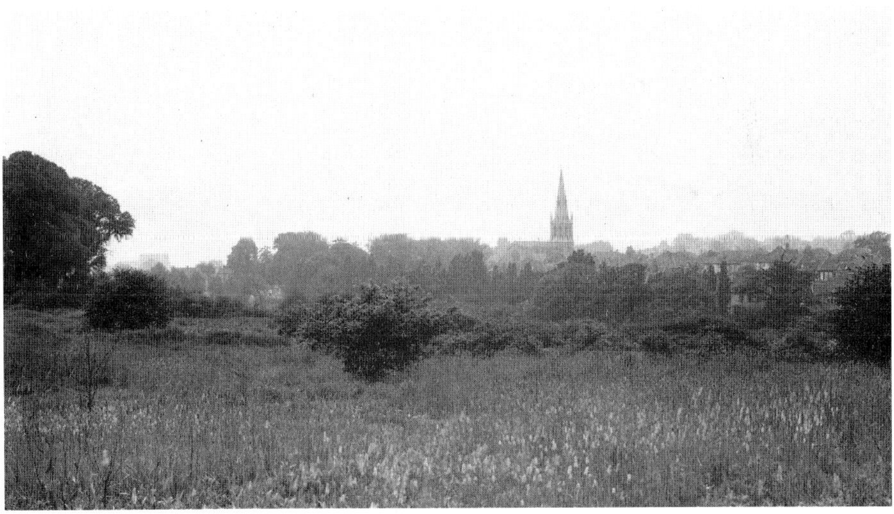

A peaceful view of new St Andrew's, looking over Birchen Grove, taken on 2 June 1950. In the 1930s this site was a source of acrimonious conflict between Wembley and Willesden councils as the latter intended to use it as a cemetery. The Second World War intervened and other delays resulted in less than one acre ever being consecrated.

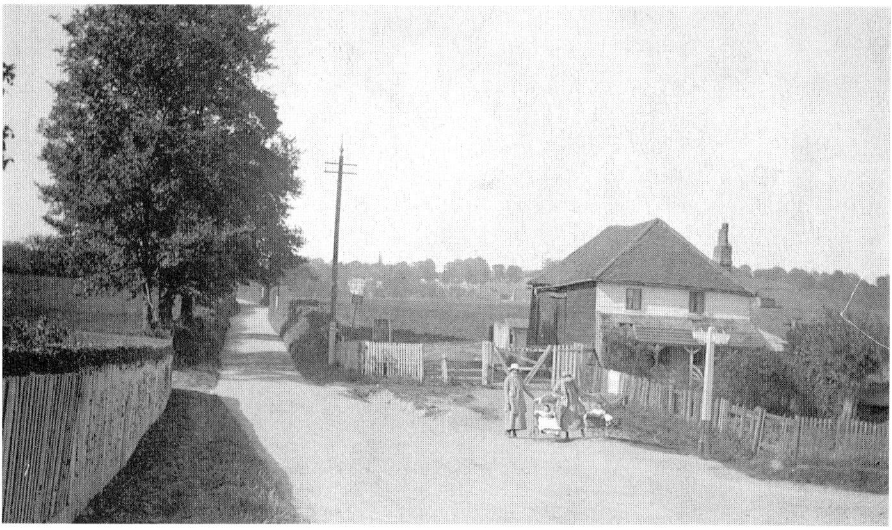

Church Lane, at its junction with Wood Lane (looking north), in the 1920s (above). The picture shows two ladies with perambulators on the road; the fence on the left belongs to Fryent Farm, with Fryent Cottages on the right, behind the women. Notice the quaint mile-post. The picture below has the inscription 'Opposite Cool Oak Lane, Church Lane, Kingsbury nr Old Farmhouse, *c.* 1920'. To pinpoint the precise place from this description is difficult on the Ordnance Survey map, but it is presumably only a few hundred yards away from the photo of Church Lane above. If this is the case the building just through the trees on the left middle distance would be Fryent Farm.

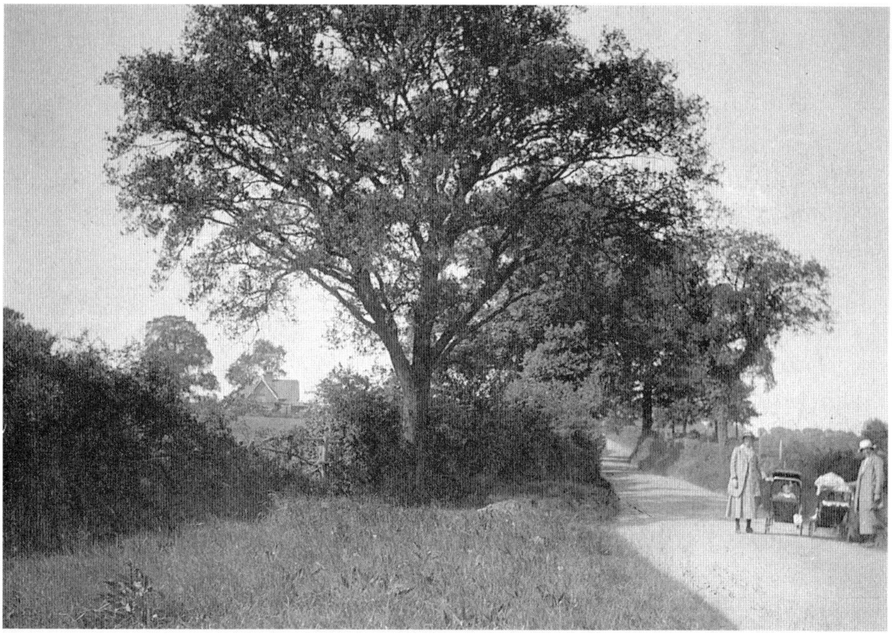

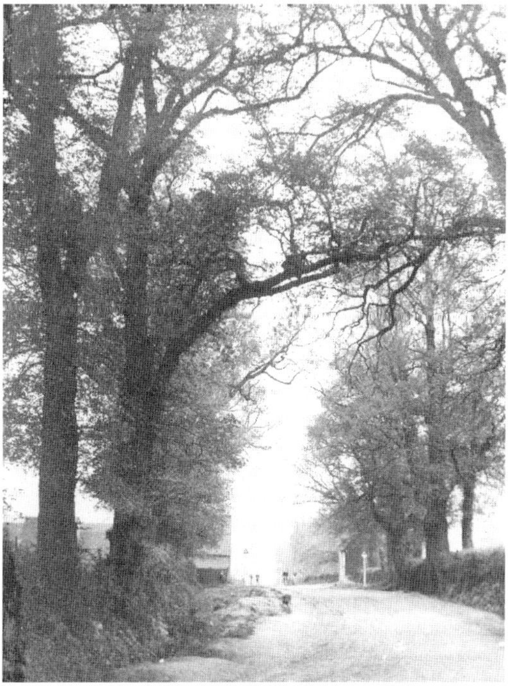

Blackbird Cross, *c.* 1920. Blackbird Hill originally had a steep gradient as it rose from the River Brent towards the lower yard of Blackbird Hill Farm. From there it took a gentler course up to the junction of Salmon Street and Forty Lane, seen in the background of this picture. Between 1919 and 1922 much work was undertaken to reduce the gradient of the hill and improve the road surface in preparation for the British Empire Exhibition (see pp. 72–4).

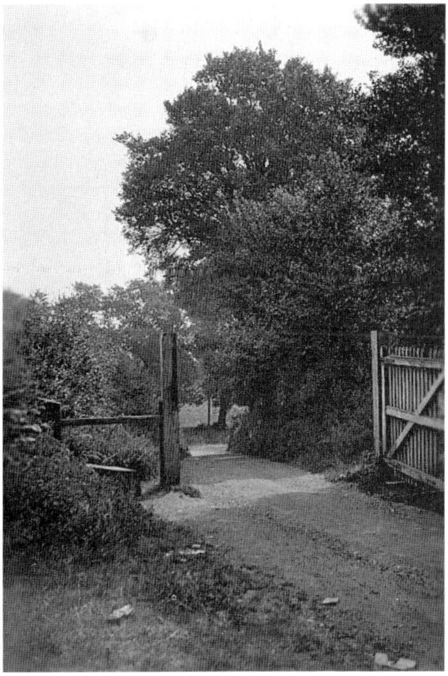

Kingsbury Lane in 1920. The continuation of Neasden Lane, after it crosses the Brent, was for centuries referred to as Blackbird or Blackpot Hill. Kingsbury Lane was a modern appellation, surviving only from the 1920s to the 1940s, being too easily confused with Kingsbury Road to the north. This image is almost certainly in the vicinity of the junction with Church Lane.

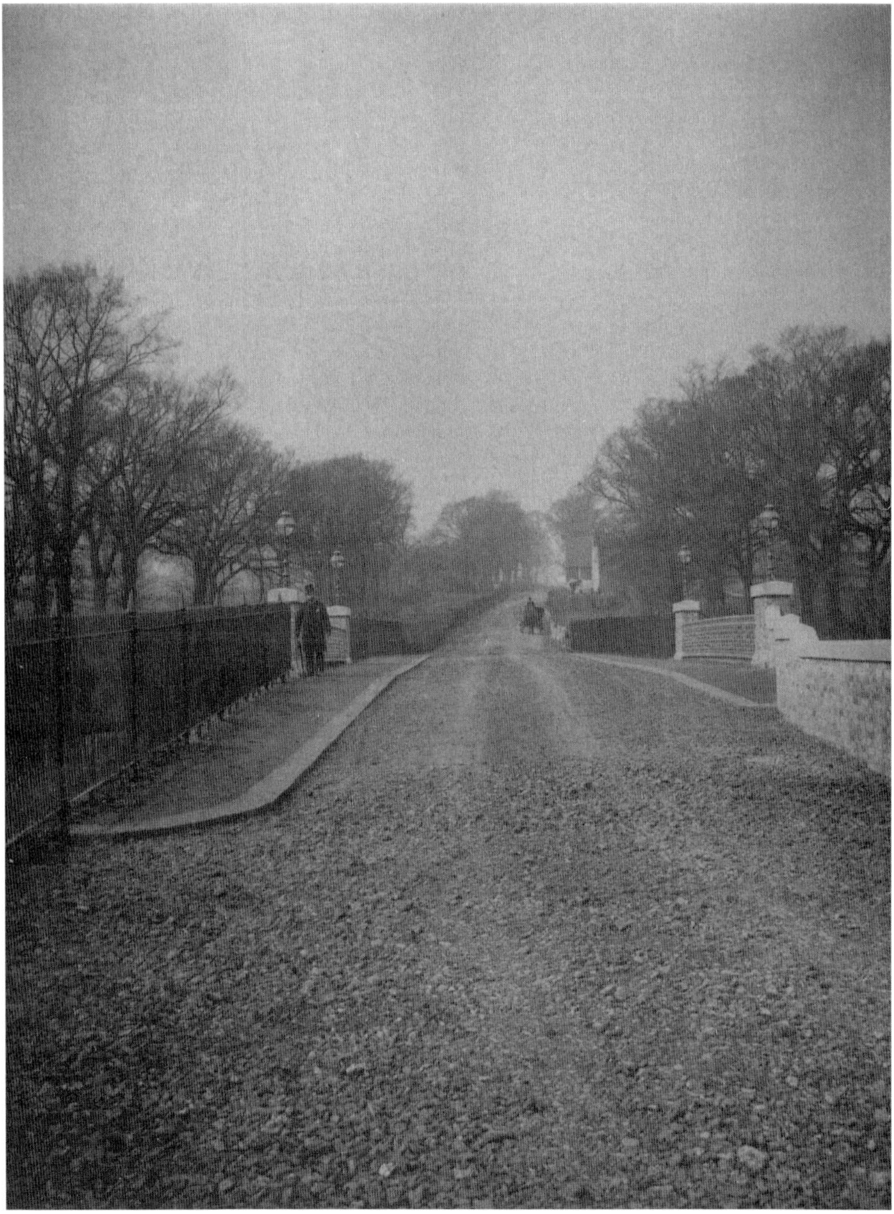

Another view of Kingsbury Lane, *c.* 1900. Compare this view to that on p. 86, taken about twenty years earlier. The only real differences between the two photos are the state of the road and the greater professionalism of the photographers. We are looking north over the River Brent to Kingsbury, the building in the middle distance on the right being the lower yard buildings of Blackbird Farm. This site was redeveloped as shops in the mid-1930s.

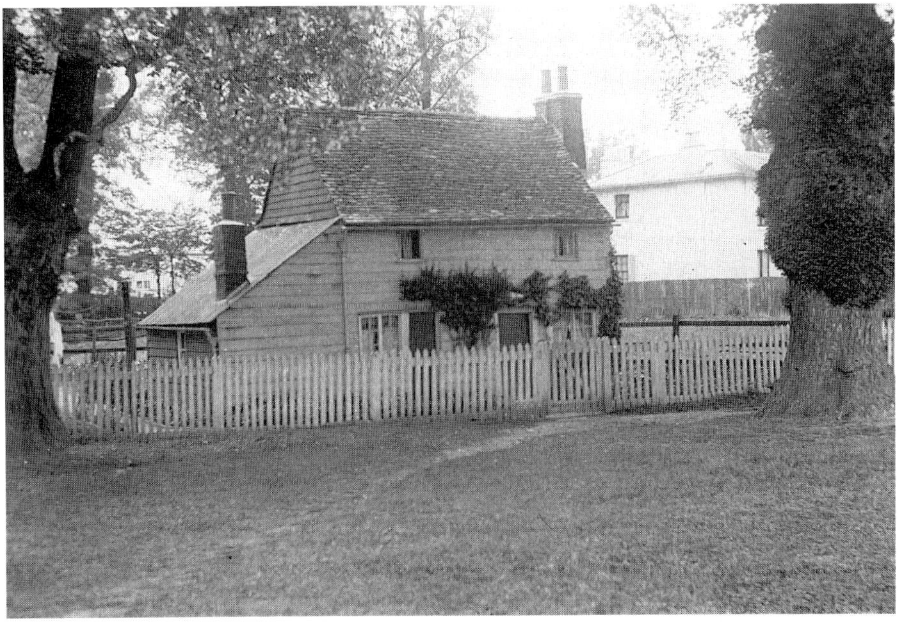

Kingsbury Green around 1905 (above). The complete lack of development has left the area intact and unspoilt. The location of The Plough (see p. 90) at a corner of the green is typical of English village layouts. The village green was an open area associated with children's games but was not immune to the onward march of progress: the green itself suffered during the widening of Church Lane in 1924. The picture below shows Kingsbury Road at the junction with Church Lane, looking over the remains of Kingsbury Green, *c*. 1950.

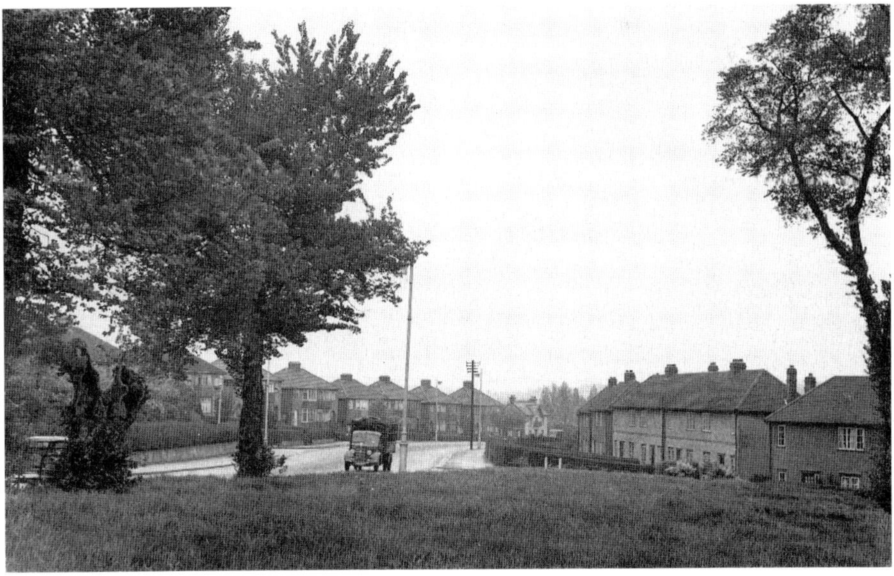

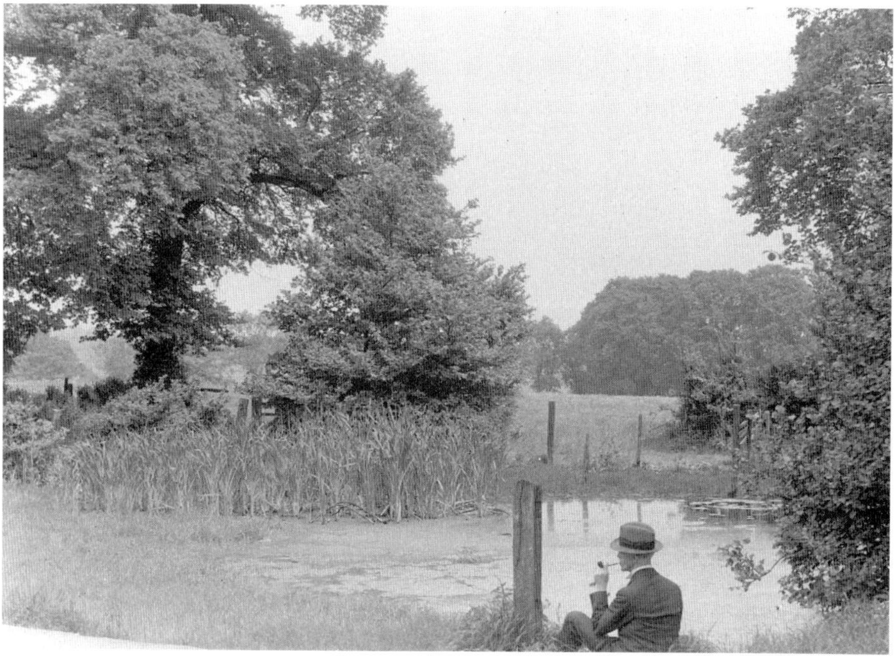

Salmon Street, Kingsbury. The view above is from *c.* 1934; that below was taken before the development of the 1950s. Known as Dorman Stone Lane in the fifteenth and sixteenth centuries, the old medieval street remains one of the most charming lanes in the borough. There is some evidence that the road is in fact pre-Roman, and fanciful theories suggest the name is derived from the fish, which was sacred in Celtic mythology. Others derive it from a family called Salomon or Solomon.

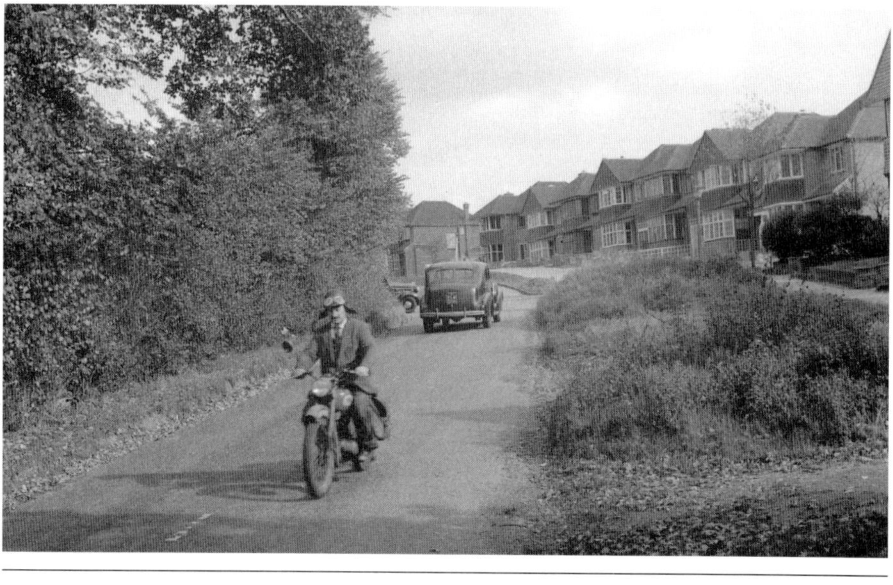

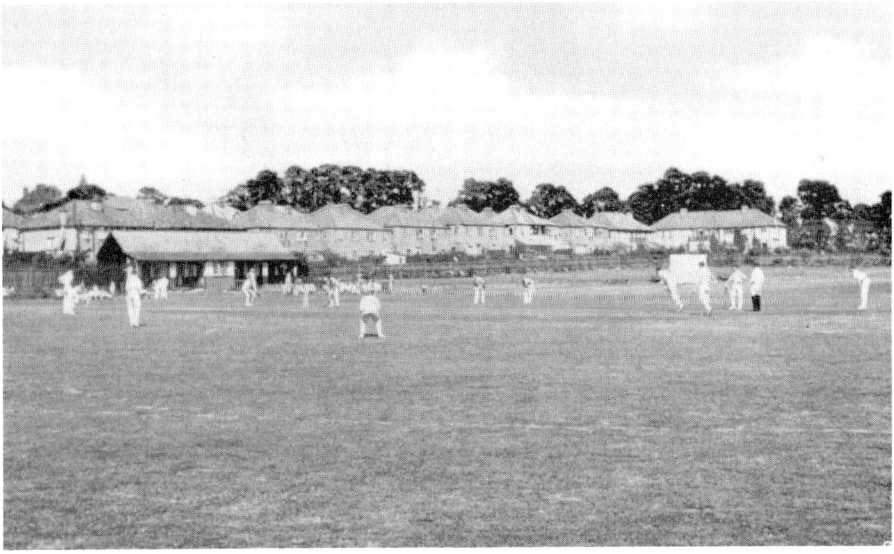

Church Lane recreation ground, Kingsbury (above). A cricket match is in progress. The photo, taken from the Wembley Official Guide for 1935, is another example of Kuno Reitz's craft (see p. 35). Roe Green Park, *c.* 1950 (below), once private polo grounds, was purchased for the community in two stages – in 1935 and 1938 – a total of twenty-six acres for a cost of £29,375. Both pictures give a good idea of the facilities available for sporting recreation in Kingsbury, although sporting activity is nothing new to the parish: the Kingsbury Cricket Club was established in 1828.

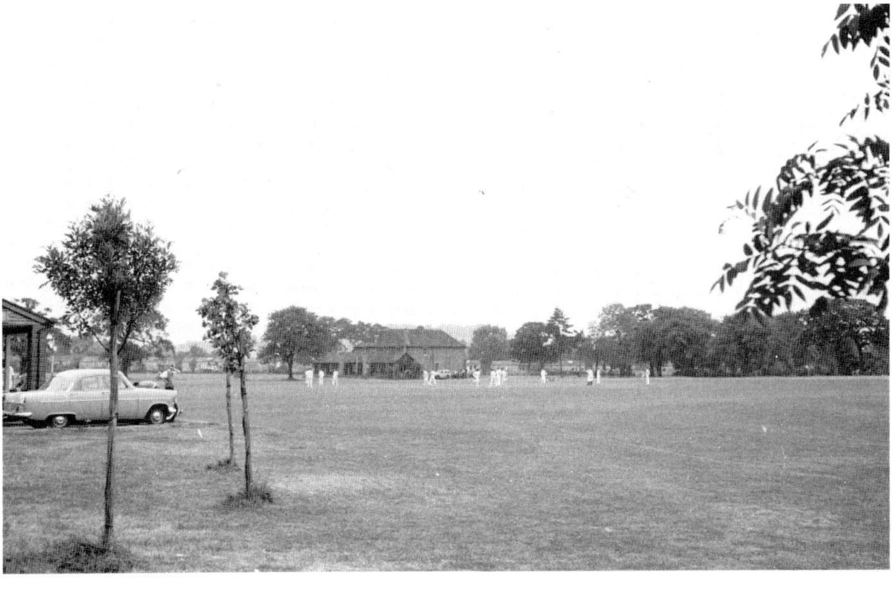

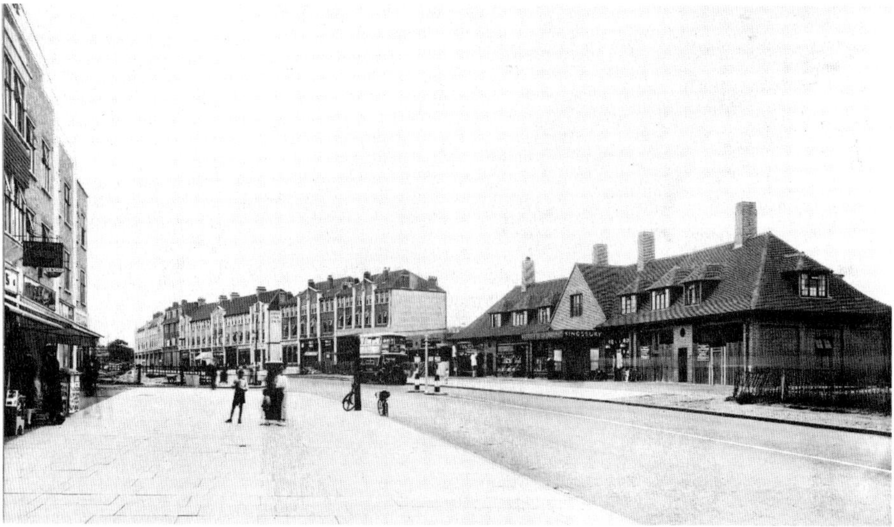

Two pleasant views of the shopping parade, Kingsbury, *c.* 1937. The station was opened in 1932 when the line was extended. Notice the fence made of chestnut pales to the right of the station in the picture above, a sure indication of the unfinished nature of development around the area. Notice also a No. 183 bus on its journey down the High Road. The view below, *c.* 1950, looks east from just outside the station to the far end of the shopping parade. The businesses then flourishing included A.W. Sommer radios, Kingsbury Café (proprietor R.G. Mills) on the south side, while on the north side were Barclays Bank Ltd and the Victoria Wine Co. Ltd, among others.

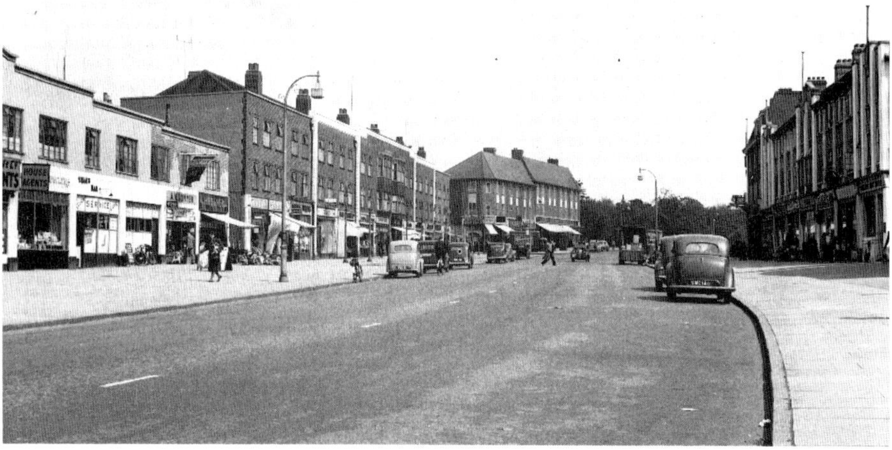

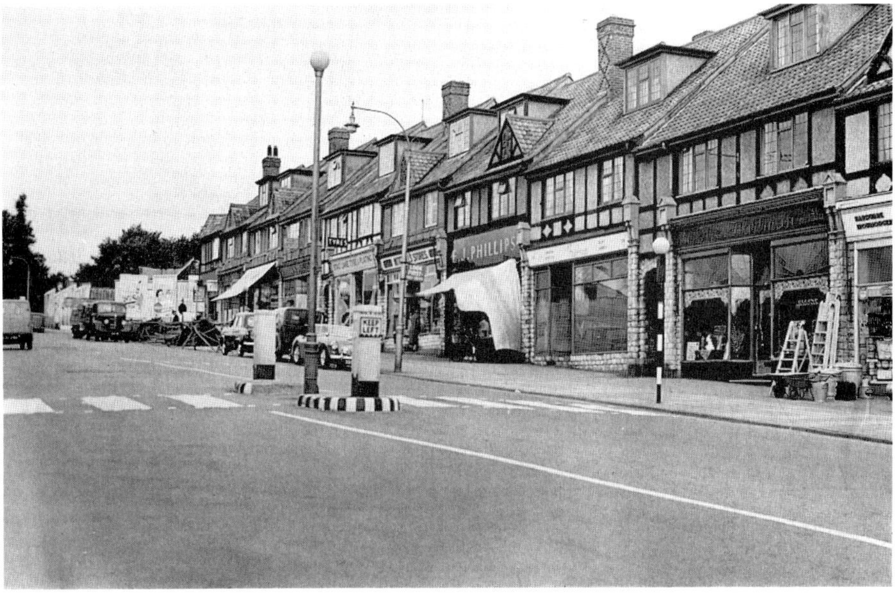

Blackbird Hill, *c.* 1950. Traders in business on the eastern side (above) at the time included Gilbert Reeves and Co. Ltd off-licence, Jack's Café, Eric Phillips butcher and S. Chandler hardware. At the top of this picture on the right-hand side is the site of Blackbird Farm (see pp. 93–4). Opposite here was Blackbird Hill Garage (below); this rather magnificent building became a victim of further redevelopment. Just beyond this we can see M.F. Ineichen newsagent and confectioner.

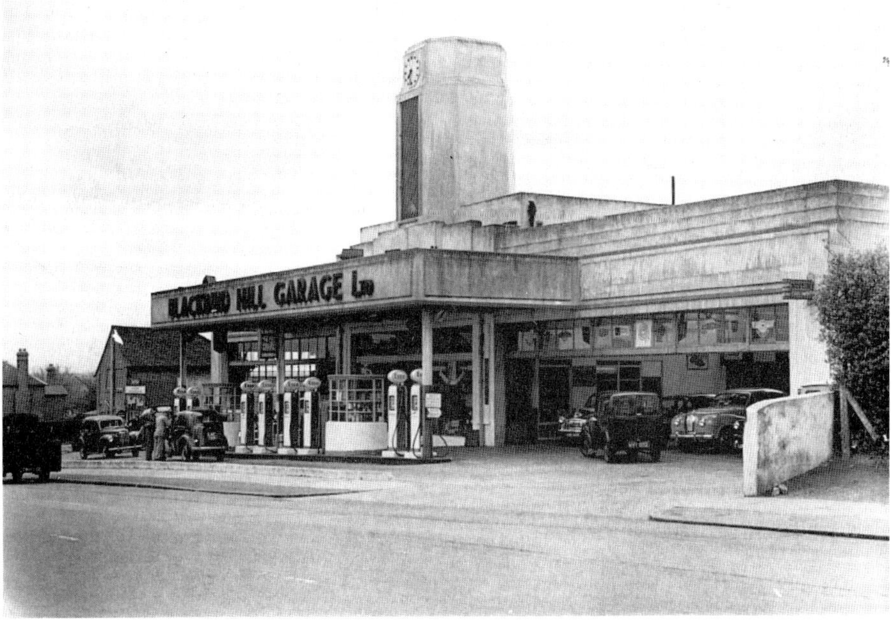

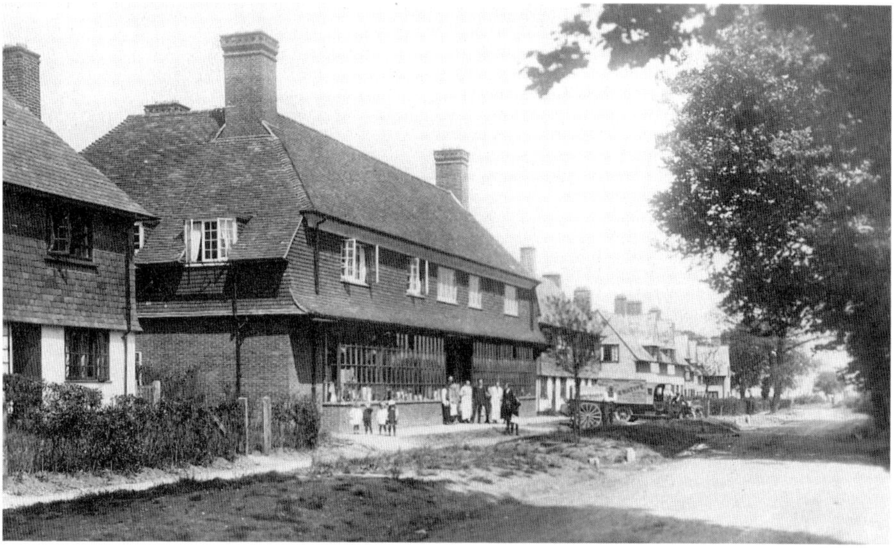

Stag Lane Village Store, Roe Green Village, *c.* 1920. These premises were at one time leased to Willesden Co-operative Society. The first floor served as a Co-operative hall, a Sunday school and, when Roe Green and Oliver Goldsmith schools were being built, as a temporary classroom. (See also p. 114.)

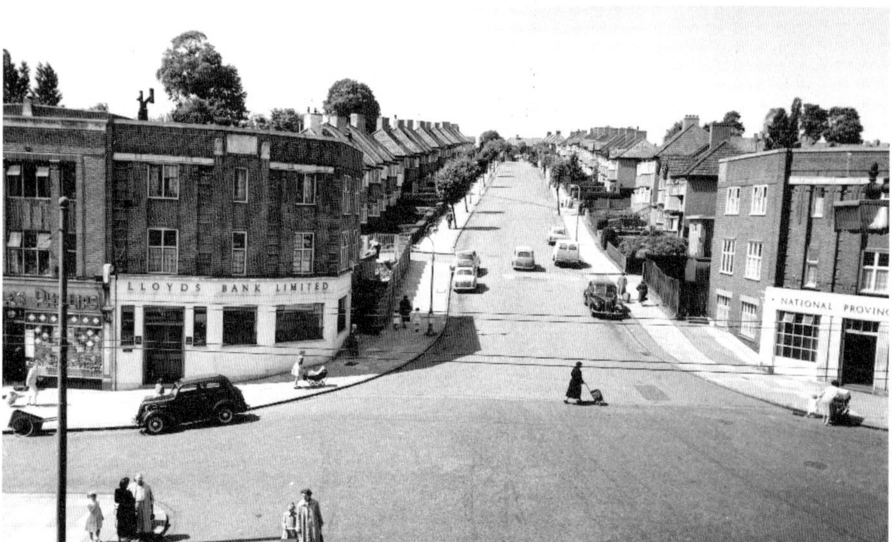

The junction of Wakeman's Hill Avenue with the Edgware Road, 1950. Notice the overhead trolley-bus wires and the preponderance of the wicker shopping trolley. A tranquil scene. The name Wakeman's Close appears on an All Souls College document, Oxford, of 1545.

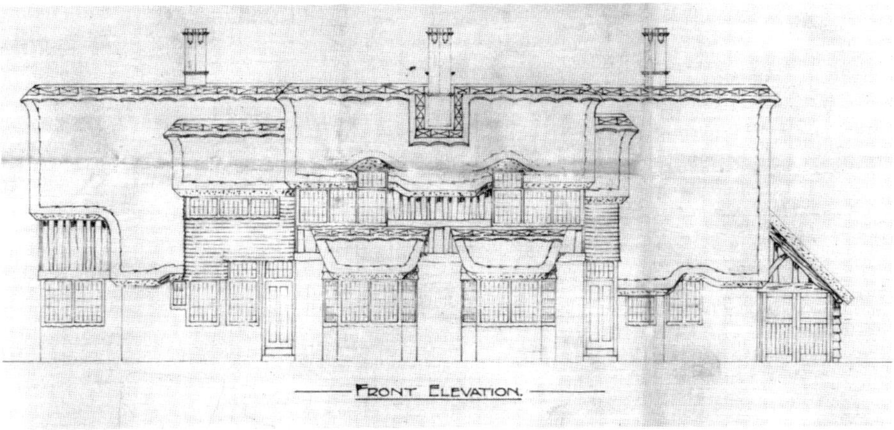

A pair of houses built by E.G. Trobridge at the junction of Hayland Close and The Old Way, Kingsbury, from the original drawing, March 1928 (above), and 142 Slough Lane (below), shown here in the late 1940s. Ernest Trobridge was born in Belfast in 1884, son of George Trobridge, a landscape painter. He was articled to a Belfast architect and won the Lanyon Memorial Fund Scholarship. This travelling scholarship took him to London and he had apparently settled at Highgate by 1908. His close involvement with the Swedenborg Church heavily influenced his life and career. Esher New Church was his first building, in 1909, following his successful renovation of Camden Road New Church. He moved to Kingsbury in September 1915. After the war the building boom enabled him to put his patented 'Compressed Green Wood Construction' designs to the Ministry of Health, who finally passed them so as to enable Trobridge to receive government subsidies. He began to work in brick in the 1930s but his designs remained unorthodox. Many other examples of his work remain, such as 12 and 15–18 Hayland Close (1926–7) and Rochester Court, Wakeman's Hill Avenue (1935–7).

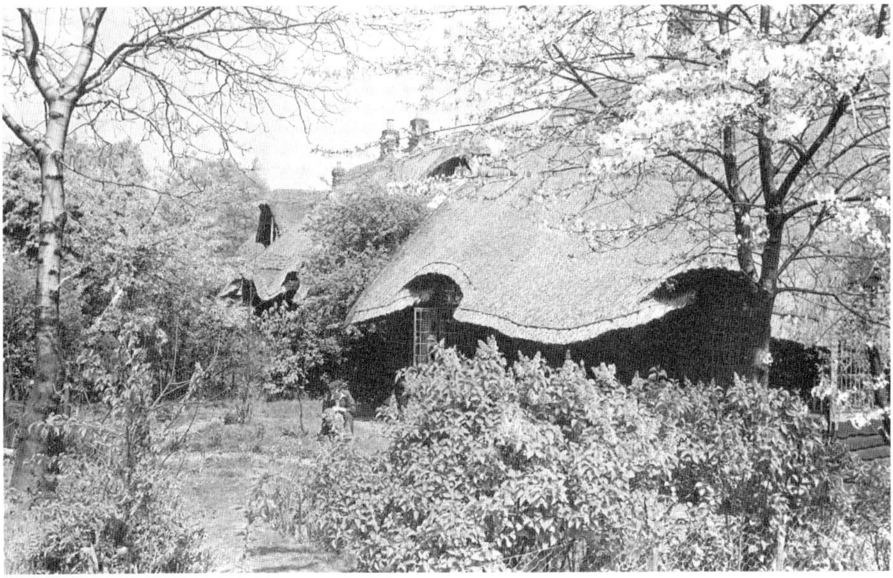

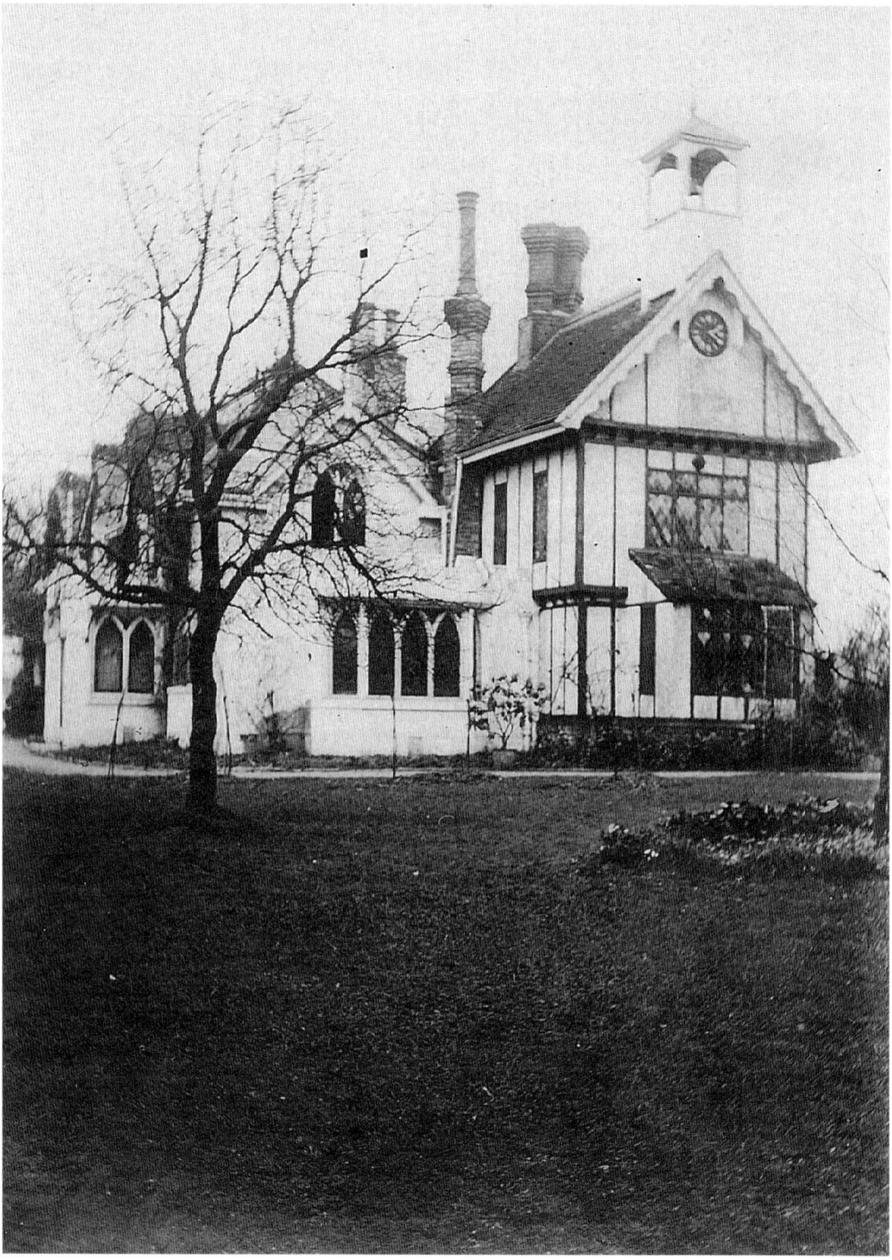

'Lewgars', Kingsbury, *c.* 1906. The property on this site was rebuilt in the eighteenth or early nineteenth century, although a house had probably existed here since the thirteenth century. In 1872 it was enlarged and decorated by Edward Nelson Haxell, an antiquary who ensured that materials from the renovation of St Andrew's (see p. 88) were incorporated into his own dwelling.

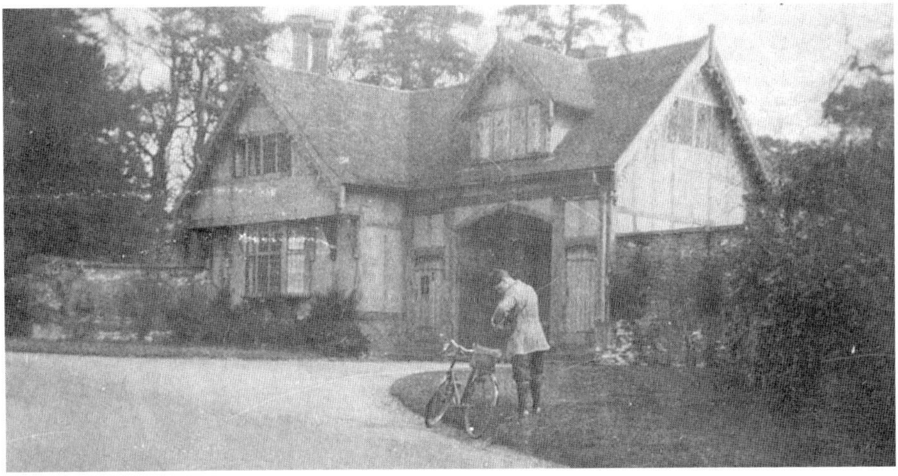

A second photo of 'Lewgars' in the 1920s, looking more like a sedate country mansion than the Gothic creation in the previous picture. By 1930 Henry Higinbotham was in residence. He was a Gore division magistrate and builder who developed a number of houses in the Townsend Lane area. He left 'Lewgars' vacant at the outbreak of the Second World War and its condition deteriorated to such an extent that in 1952 it was demolished to make way for new development.

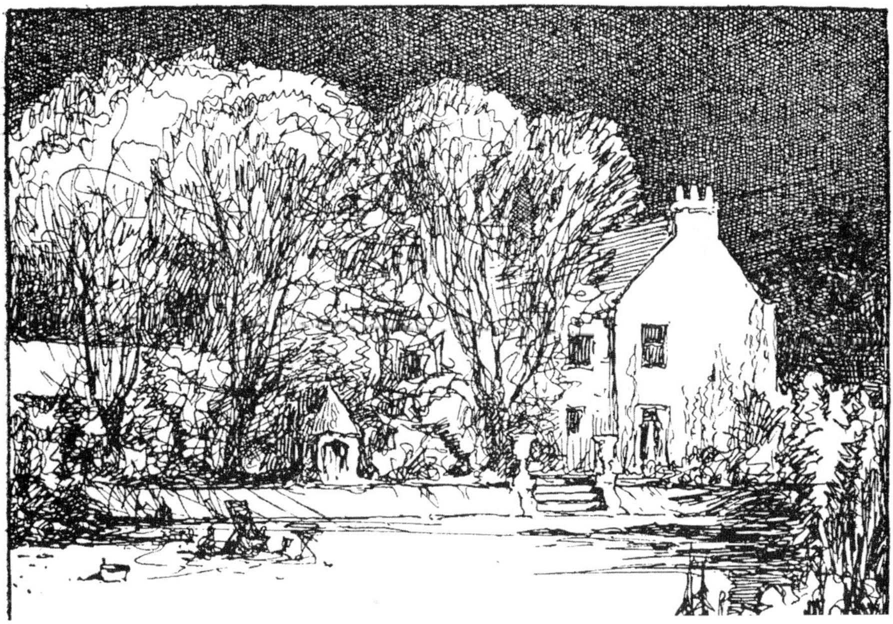

Hyde Farm House, Kingsbury, *c.* 1910. It was here that Oliver Goldsmith stayed from 1771 to 1774. He noted that he was 'almost wholly in the country in a farmer's house, quite alone trying to write a comedy'. During his time here he wrote *She Stoops to Conquer* and *Animated Nature*. The building was finally pulled down in 1932.

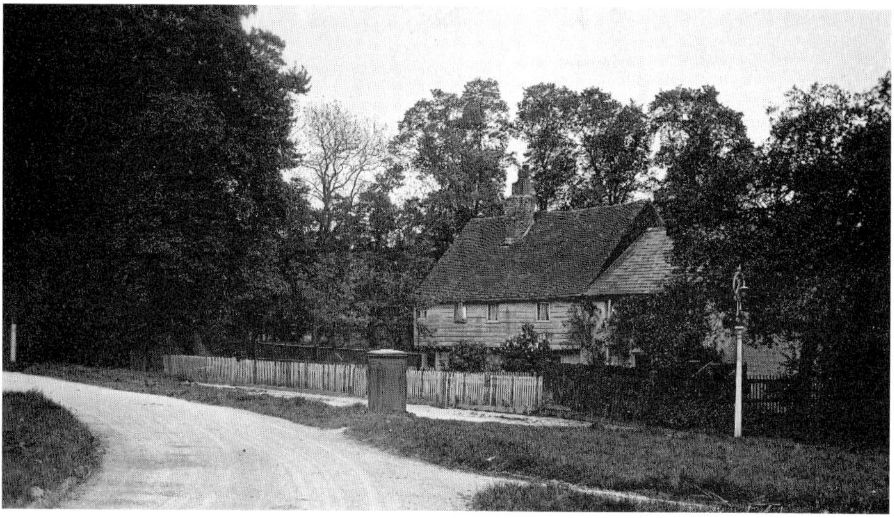

'Old Cottages, Kingsbury Green, Hendon', *c.* 1910, according to the address on this postcard. Apart from the simple proximity of Hendon to Kingsbury, there were a number of other ways in which the fortunes of the two places were intertwined. Hendon Union was the Poor Law Union into which Kingsbury, Wembley and indeed Willesden fell, and the poor house was sited in Hendon. Furthermore, under the census enumerators' returns Kingsbury was part of the Hendon registration district.

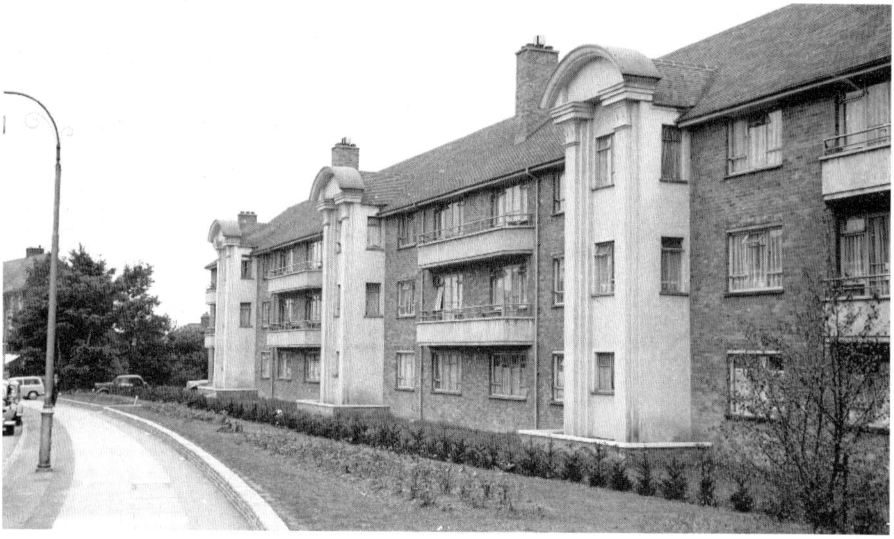

Sutherland Court, *c.* 1950. Off Kingsbury Road, near Roe Green Park, Sutherland Court was named after the Duchess of Sutherland who had the 'The Cottage' or Manor House built (see opposite). She was the second wife of George Granville Leveson-Gower, 3rd Duke of Sutherland, who died in September 1892, leaving her in possession of the family fortune. Obliged to leave Sutherland when a bitter dispute broke out over her inheritance, she built a number of properties around the country.

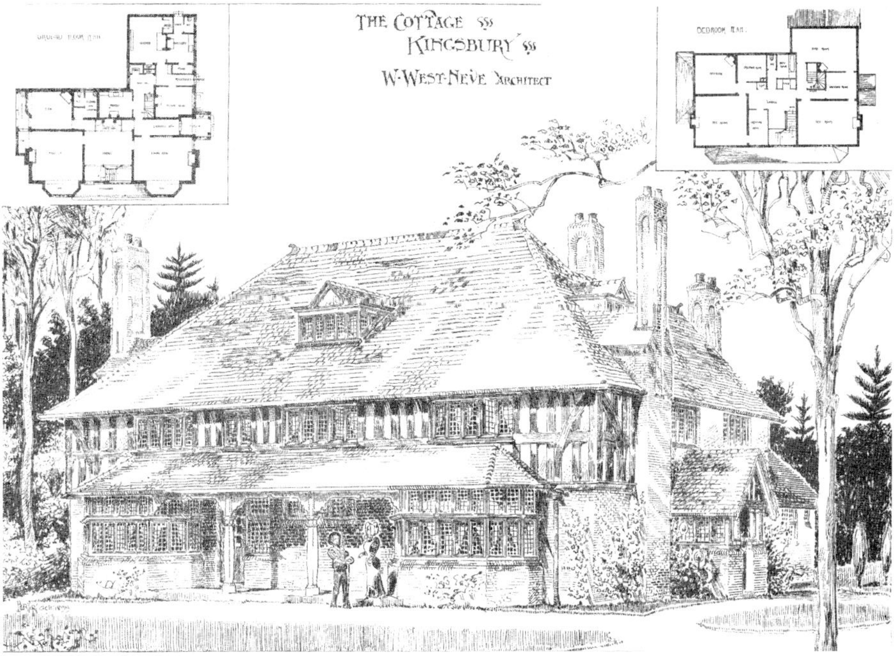

'The Cottage', Kingsbury, in 1899 (above) and Kingsbury Manor, as it became, in 1950 (below). Designed by W. West Neve (who was articled to Norman Shaw) for the Duchess of Sutherland, the large half-timbered property with a steeply pitched and hipped tiled roof was built in 1899. The name was changed to Kingsbury Manor by George Cloke around 1929. In July 1938 it was conveyed to Middlesex County Council and has been used as a home for the elderly. It also has a claim to fame as the site of John Logie Baird's experiments with television in 1928–30.

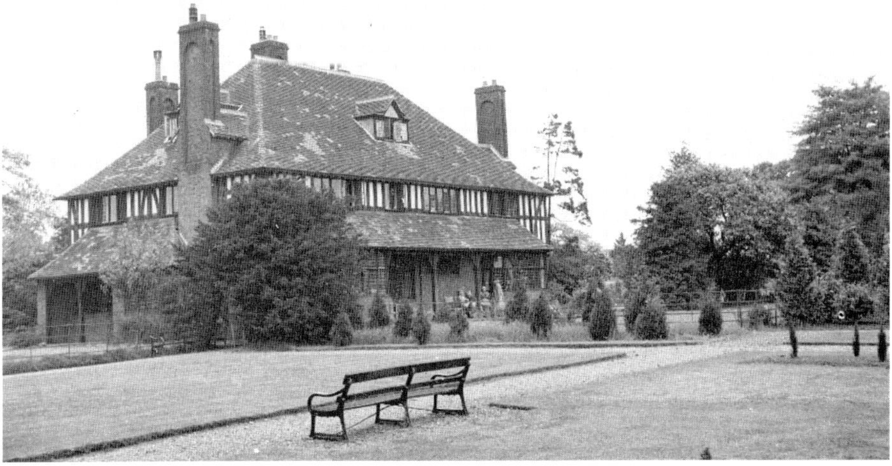

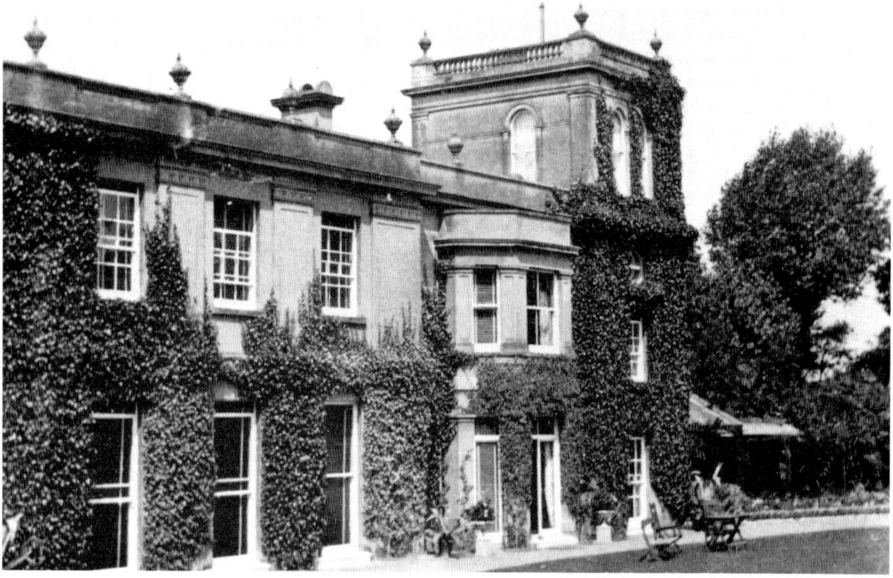

Grove Park House, *c.* 1900. The photo above shows the east front; that below shows a gymkhana in the park. Both photographs may have been taken during the residence of Lord Roberts of Kandahar, who lived here from 1893 to 1895. He insisted on taking an active part in the First World War but died in November 1914. The more likely possibility is that the photographs date from the period when the Walton family was in residence, for they certainly held gymkhanas as well as opened the grounds to the public. They had leased the building since 1882 and William Walton bought the house some time after 1892 when his father died. The property was demolished around 1947.

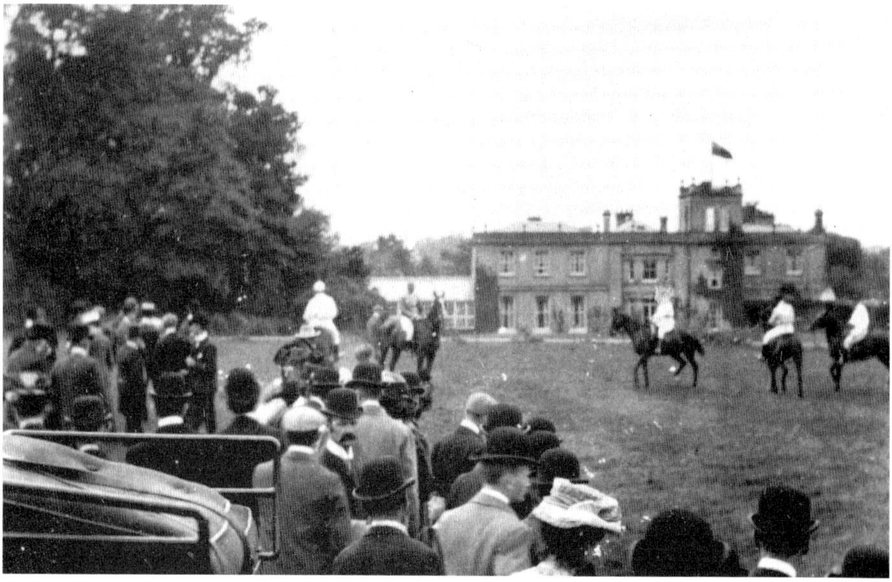

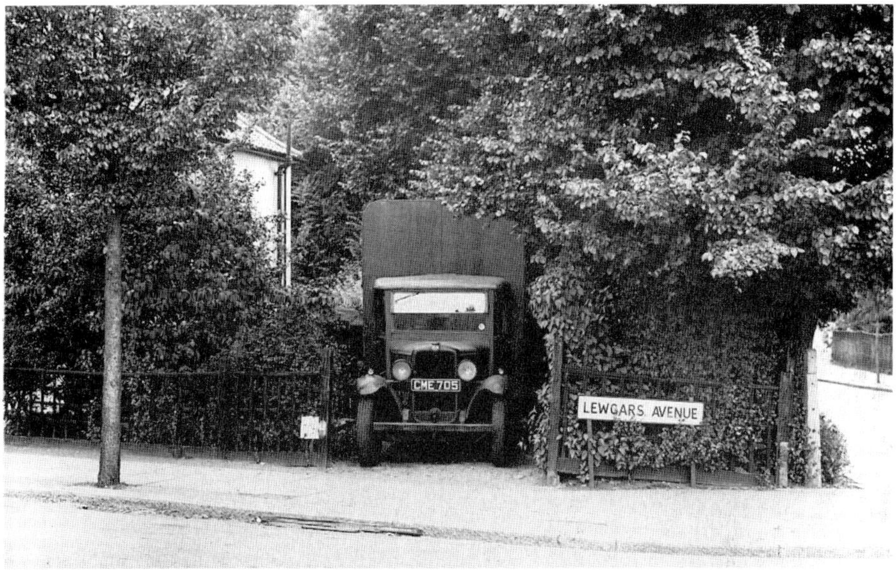

Lewgars Avenue (above) and Meadowbank Road (below), *c.* 1948. Lewgars Avenue was named after the house that stood in Slough Lane until 1952 (see pp. 108–9). The photographs are from the wonderful collection of material taken by the Wembley Borough Council Engineer and Surveyor, on this occasion as evidence for a proposed amendment to the Middlesex County Council Act 1944. Judging from other photographs in this collection, the common element seems to be the presence of lorries, to which the council was presumably intending to object.

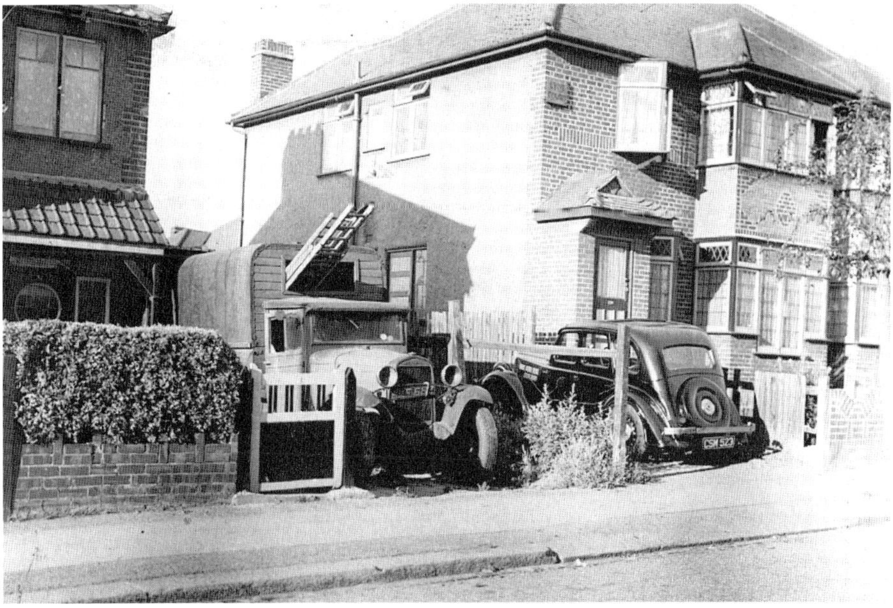

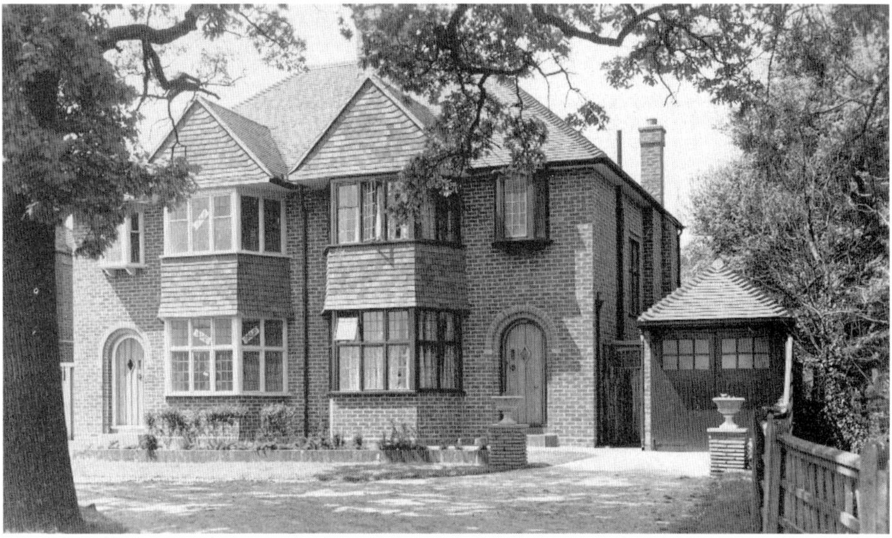

A 1930s postcard indicative of the majority of the housing stock built in the medieval lane of Salmon Street (see p. 102). Most of the properties were built in the 1930s by the Salmon Estate (Kingsbury) Ltd. By 1939 the houses were fetching £790.

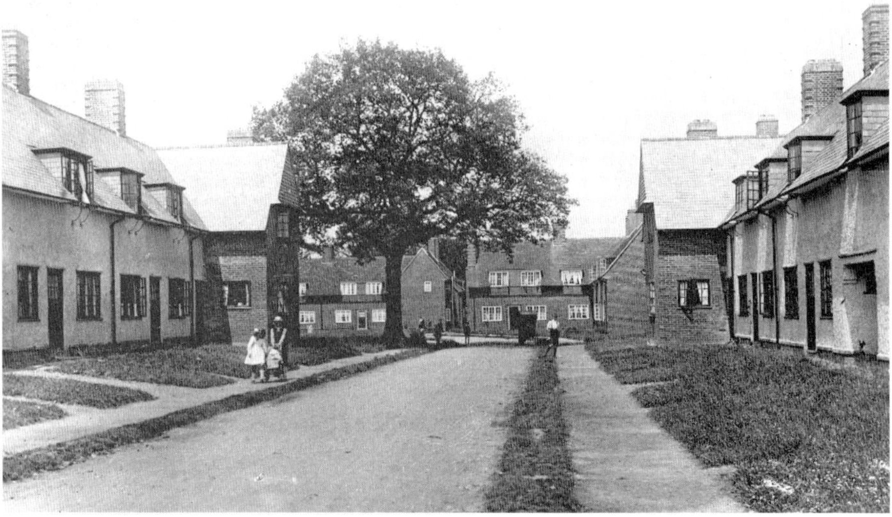

Roe Lane, Roe Green Village, *c.* 1920. The village was built on a twenty-four-acre pasture land site between Stag Lane and Bacon Lane. The land had previously been Buchanan's polo fields. The construction of the estate by contractors Holloway Brothers began in 1918, apparently with assistance from prisoners of war, and by 1919 some 150 houses had been built.

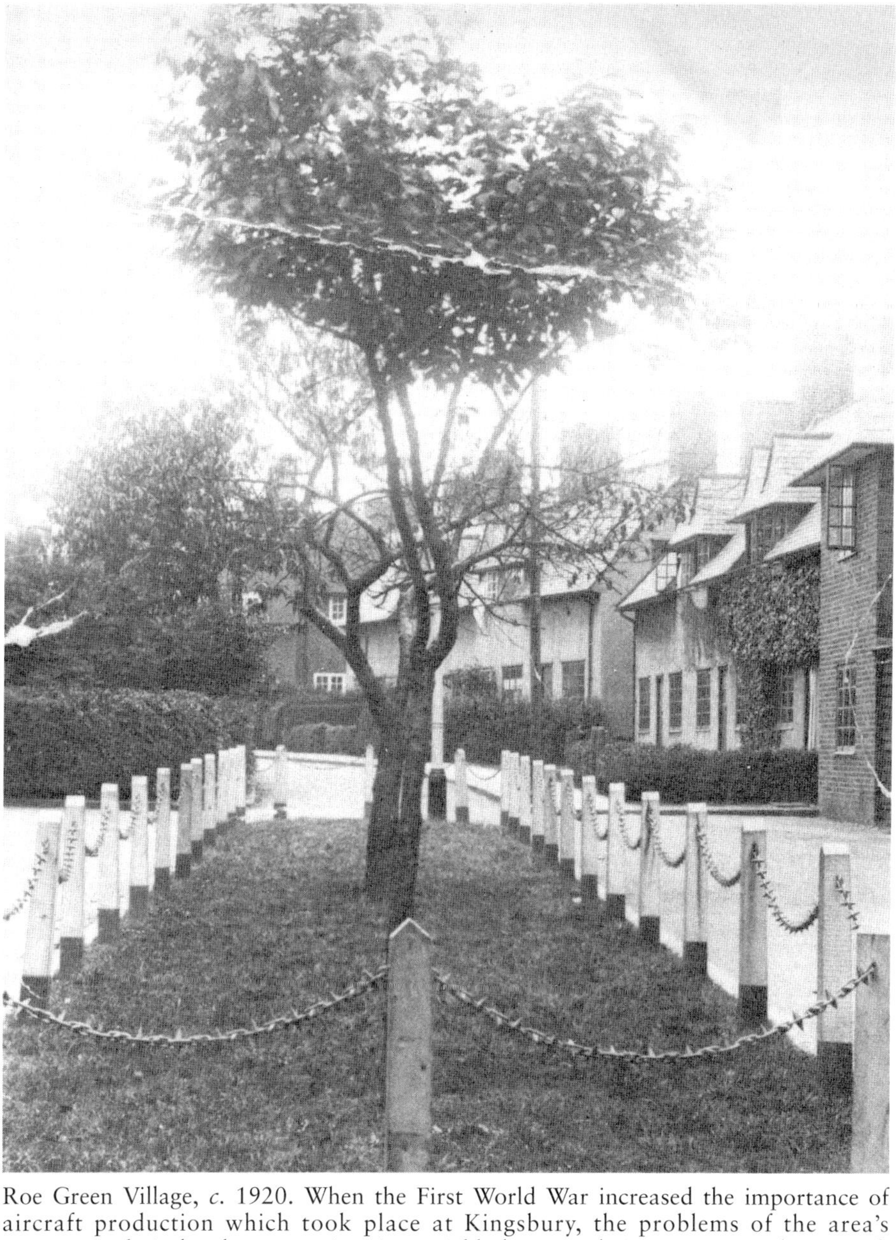

Roe Green Village, *c.* 1920. When the First World War increased the importance of aircraft production which took place at Kingsbury, the problems of the area's comparatively isolated country situation quickly became obvious. By 1915 the Aircraft Manufacturing Company (Air-Co) was employing around 600 people and had 100,000 square feet of factory space, but by 1918 this had increased to 4,400 employees and 730,000 square feet of premises. In 1916 the Office of Works commissioned its chief architect, Sir Frank Baines, to design houses for the aircraft workers. Roe Green Village, a 'garden village', was the result.

Queensbury Library (above) and Kingsbury Library (below), *c.* 1950. Queensbury Library was unusual in having a shop frontage. This is the original structure which was superseded in 1973 by a new building in Mollison Way. Despite an heroic effort to keep the library open (in which delicate negotiations with the London Borough of Harrow came to nought) it was closed in April 1989. Kingsbury Library was opened in 1940. This building was originally a clinic; the library was then housed in Roe Green Primary School.

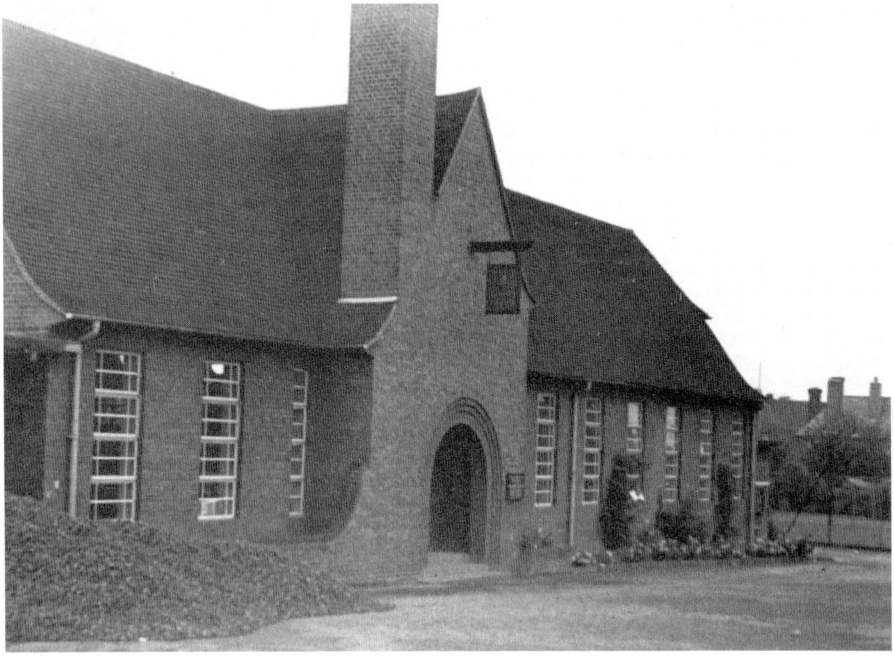

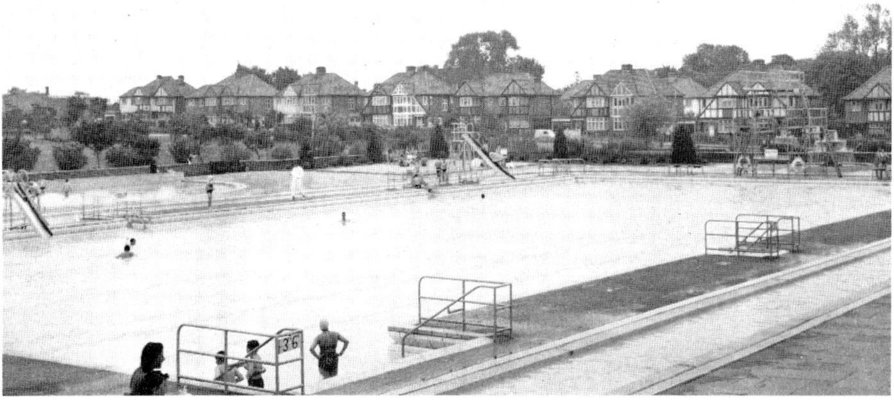

Kingsbury Swimming Pool in the 1950s. The pool was opened on 13 May 1939 at a cost of £42,628. After providing recreational activities for some fifty years it was officially closed in 1988 (it cost £100,000 a year to maintain but generated only £700 in admission fees) and eventually filled in during 1990. The site is currently being developed as a leisure centre to include a new library as well as at least two new swimming pools, a ten-pin bowling alley, six-screen cinema and gymnasium.

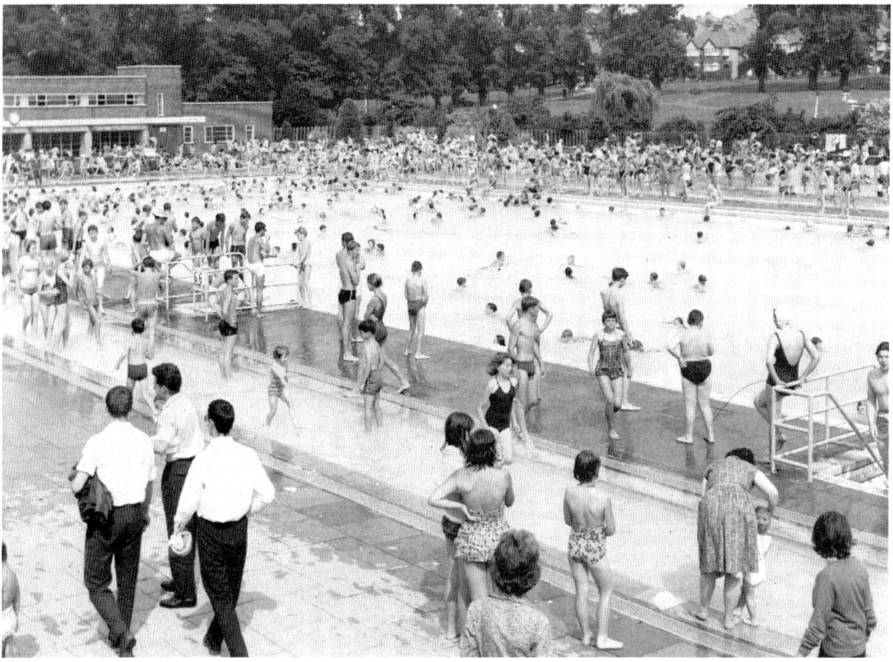

Mary born here 18/9/34

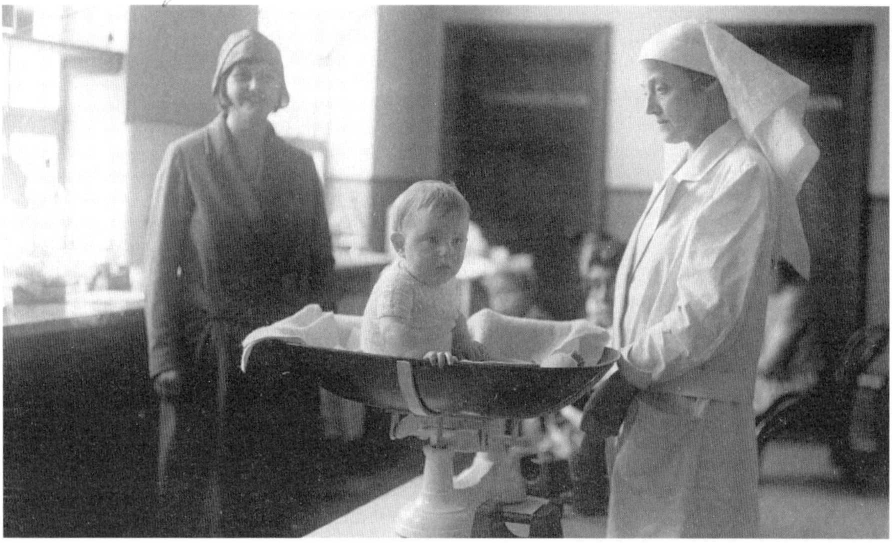

Weighing babies in the maternity hospital clinic at Kingsbury, *c.* 1930. Built as a smallpox hospital, in temporary buildings on land rented from Kingsbury Urban District Council, the hospital was converted to a maternity unit in 1931, shortly after its rebuilding in 1927. Its twenty-nine beds were increased to fifty-six in 1935. Under the National Health Act the hospital became part of the Central Middlesex group, but transferred to Charing Cross Teaching Hospital in 1952. The name was changed from Willesden to Kingsbury Maternity Hospital in 1949.

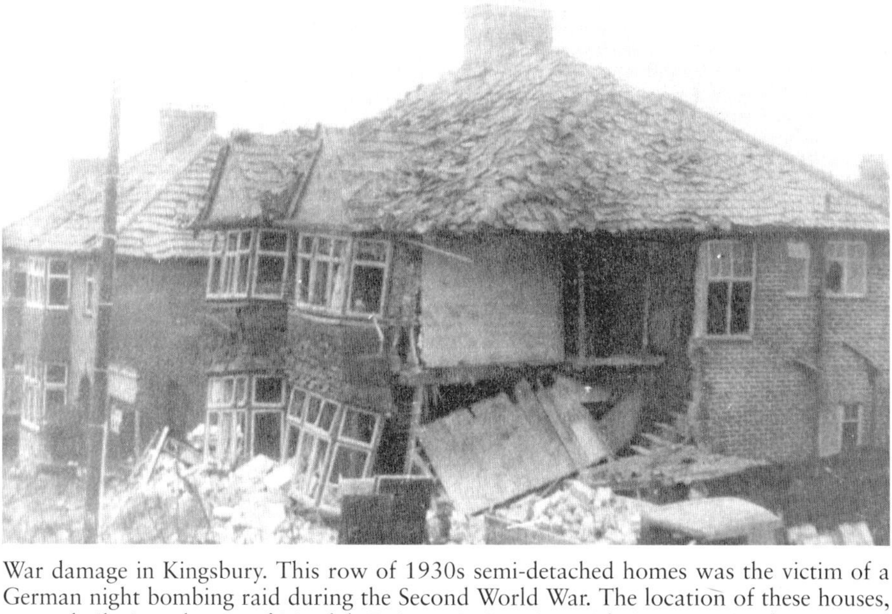

War damage in Kingsbury. This row of 1930s semi-detached homes was the victim of a German night bombing raid during the Second World War. The location of these houses, now rebuilt, is at the top of Mardale Drive at its junction with Coniston Gardens.

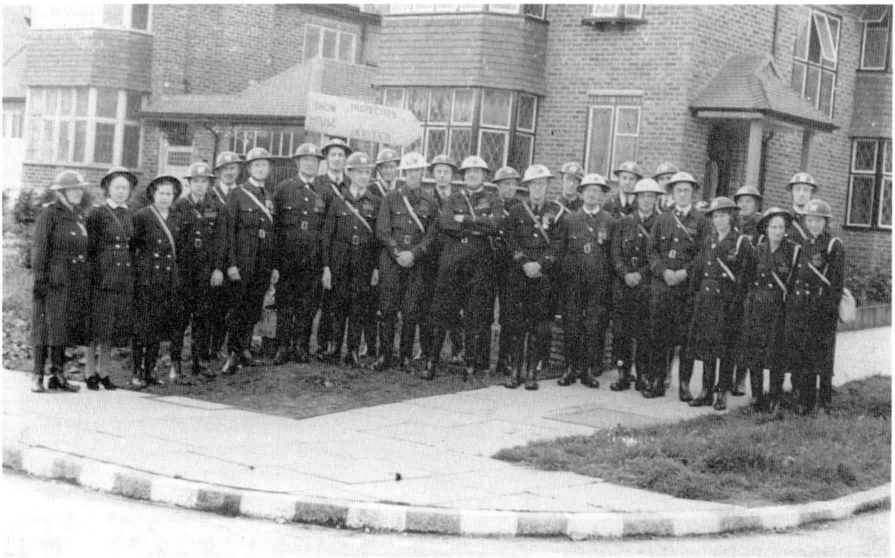

Two photos of Salmon Street A, Air Raid Precautions (ARP) patrol, 24 May 1941. War came to Kingsbury on the night of 27 August 1940 when incendiary bombs were dropped on Barn Hill and Salmon Street. The appointment of Jack Eddas as air raid protection officer for Wembley resulted in an ARP scheme that was felt to be second to none. The Home Office congratulated the council on the success of its ARP provision. At its peak there were 25,000 members of the Civil Defence in Wembley, including fire watchers. Note that milk deliveries continued despite the war – the horse-drawn milk float of Express Dairies is clearly visible in the background below.

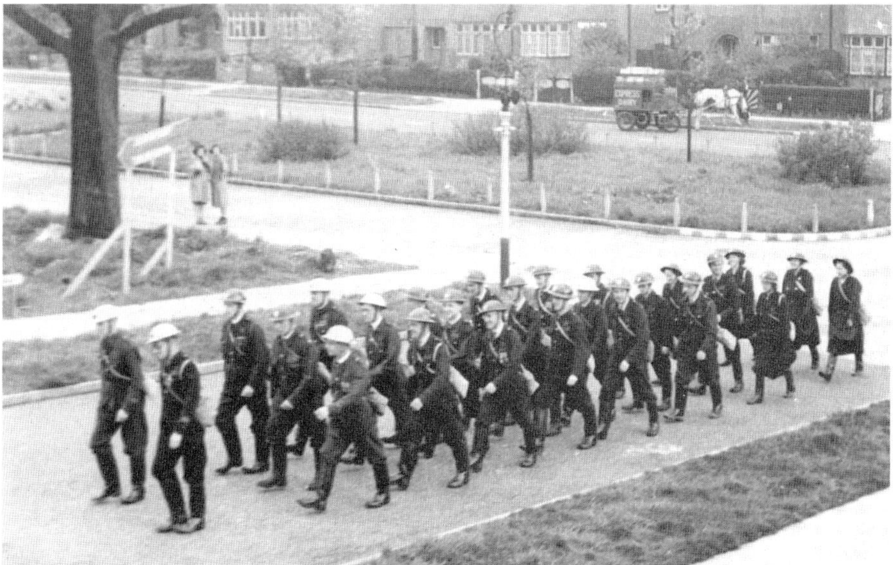

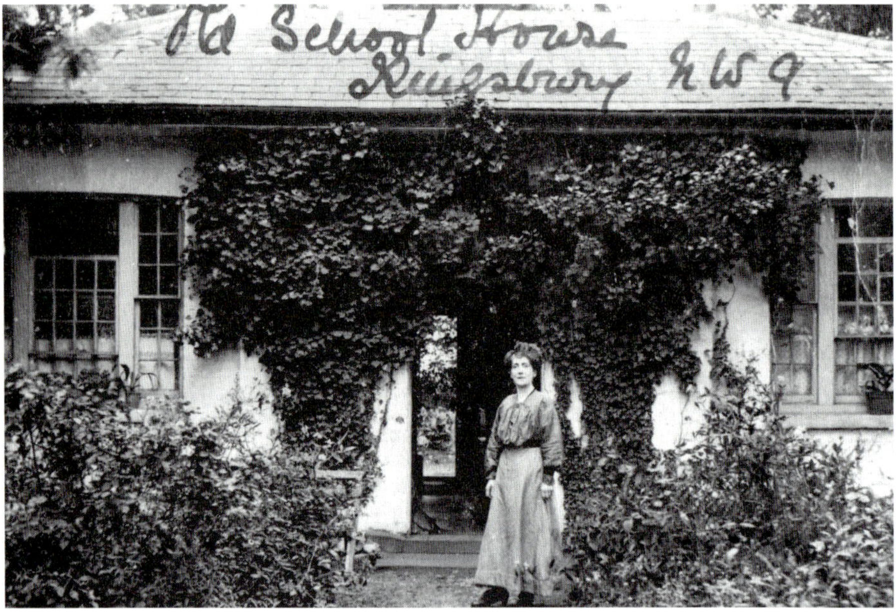

The old school house at the junction of Kingsbury Road and Stag Lane, *c.* 1920. Its use as a school house had apparently ended by the turn of the century. The woman in this picture is Mrs Laura Fox, the mother of the photo's original owner. She was described in an oral reminiscence as 'a kindly old-fashioned lady with a high lace collar with whalebone'.

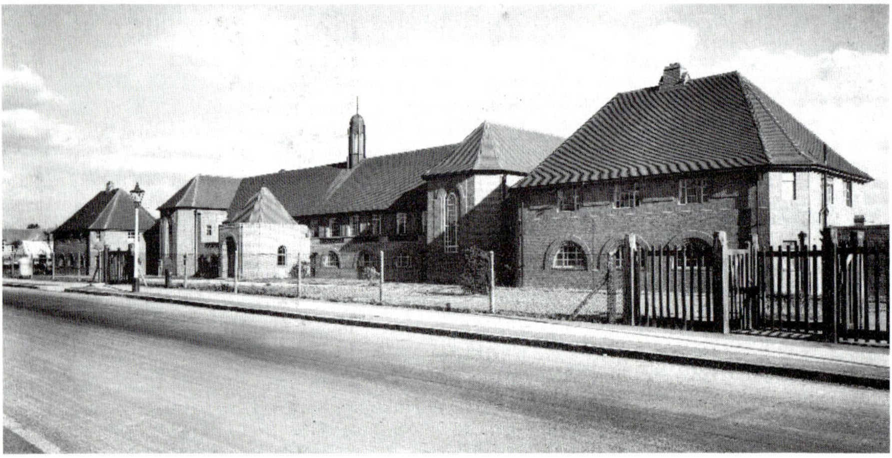

Kingsbury County School, Princes Avenue, Kingsbury, in 1931. In September 1925 a mixed secondary school was opened in a building once belonging to the Aircraft Manufacturing Company on the Edgware Road, which provided accommodation for some 380 pupils. The official opening took place in January 1926, and was attended by County Councillor J.H. Turner, Chair of the Board of Governors, and Sir Benjamin Gott, Secretary to the Middlesex Education Committee. The building above was completed and opened in 1931.

Mary started here in Sept 46 until ~~Dec~~ March 53

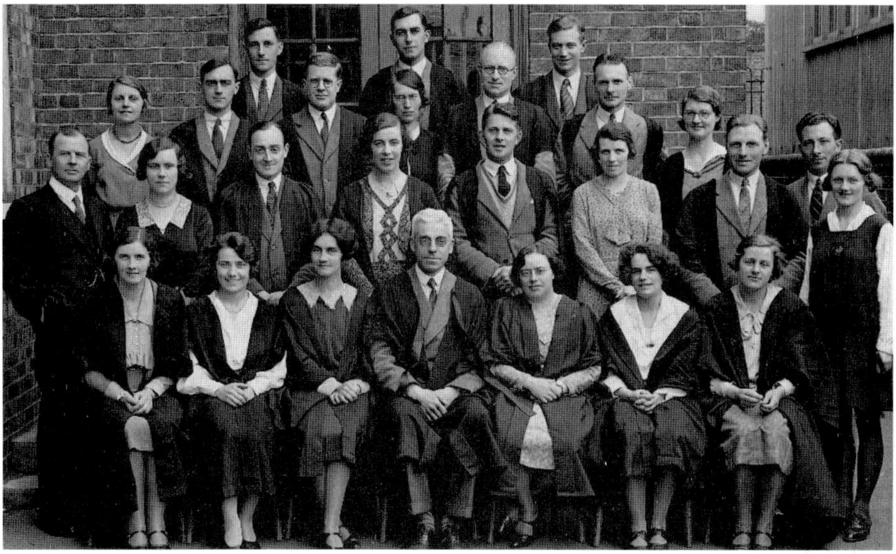

The staff (above) and the Netball 2nd XI (below) at Kingsbury County School, 1927–8. Just two from a series of excellent visual images indicative of the life of the school. The headmaster of the school at the time was Mr A.G. Tracey, BA, BSc. In a speech at the opening ceremony of the school in 1926 Mr Turner, the county councillor, declared that the boys and girls 'should remember that whatever might be their station in life, their character would always be their final capital'.

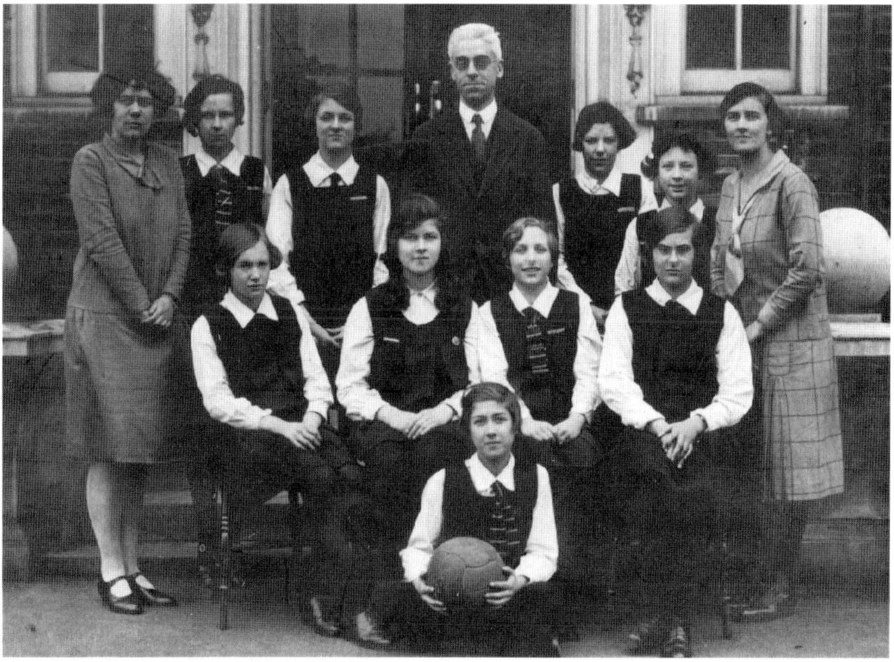

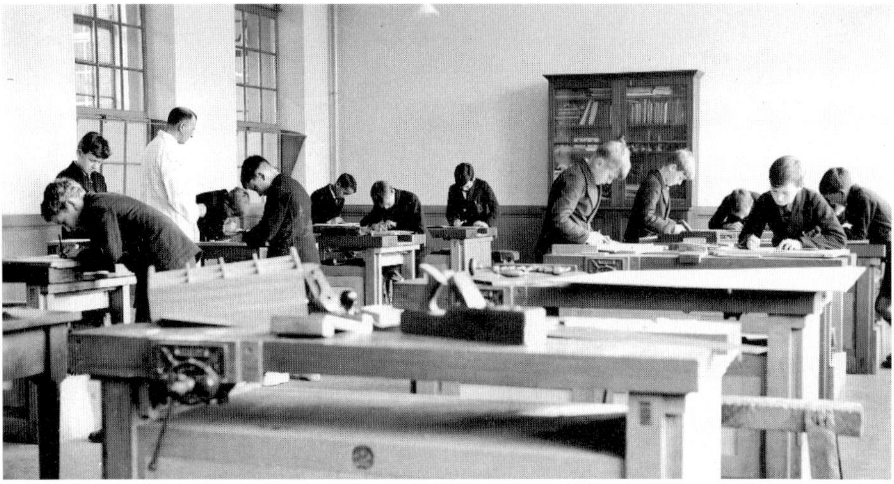

Instruction in woodwork at Kingsbury County School, *c.* 1928–9 (above) and the Frigidaire Division of General Motors, *c.* 1950 (below). An interesting juxtaposition of images showing hives of industry at two very different levels. The Frigidaire Division of General Motors opened its first branch in Britain in 1923. By 1926 offices and showrooms had been obtained in Kingsbury. Domestic refrigerators were being produced before the Second World War, but during the conflict air-conditioning units were built for tanks, and small refrigerators were designed for use on aircraft, including one used on Churchill's plane. After the war the company expanded, but had lost its connection with the locality by the 1980s.

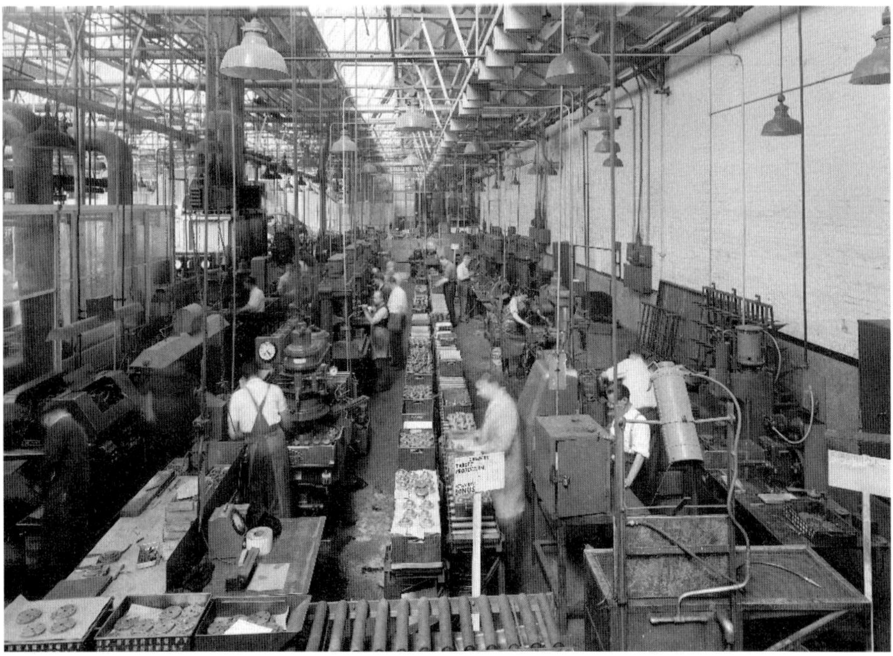

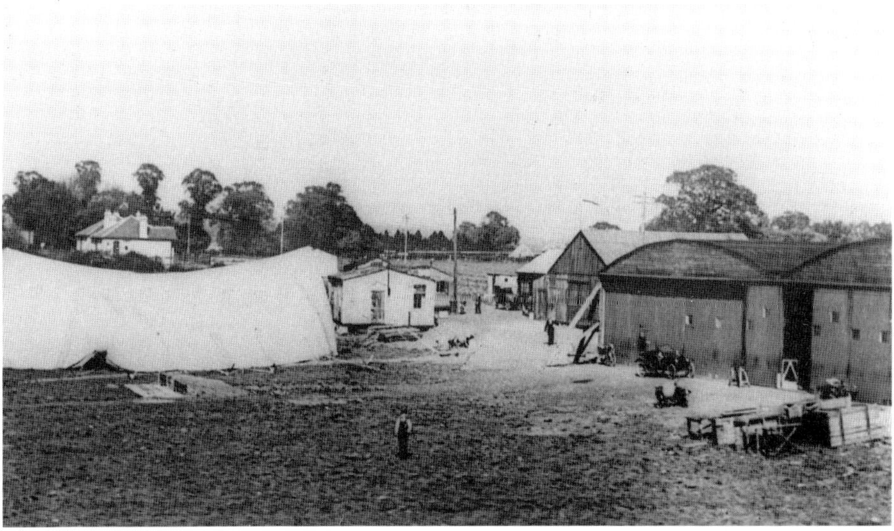

The de Havilland premises at Stag Lane, 1920 (above) and 1926 (below). Geoffrey de Havilland, whose services had been acquired by Air-Co (see p. 115) as chief designer in July 1914, registered his company on 25 September 1920. In 1921, with the help of financier Alan Butler, the company bought the Stag Lane aerodrome from which Amy Johnson and Jim Mollison flew.

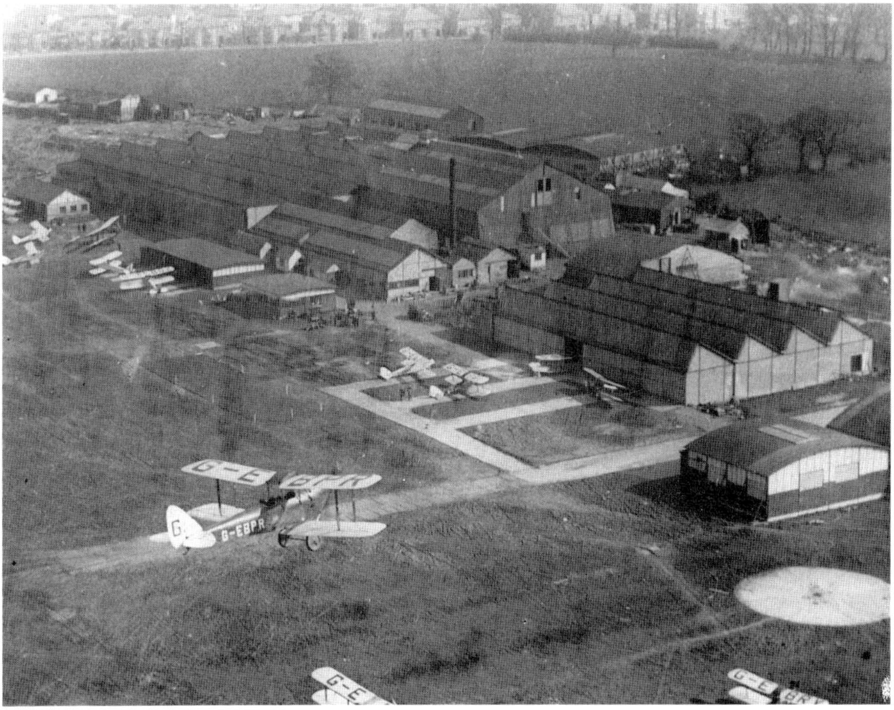

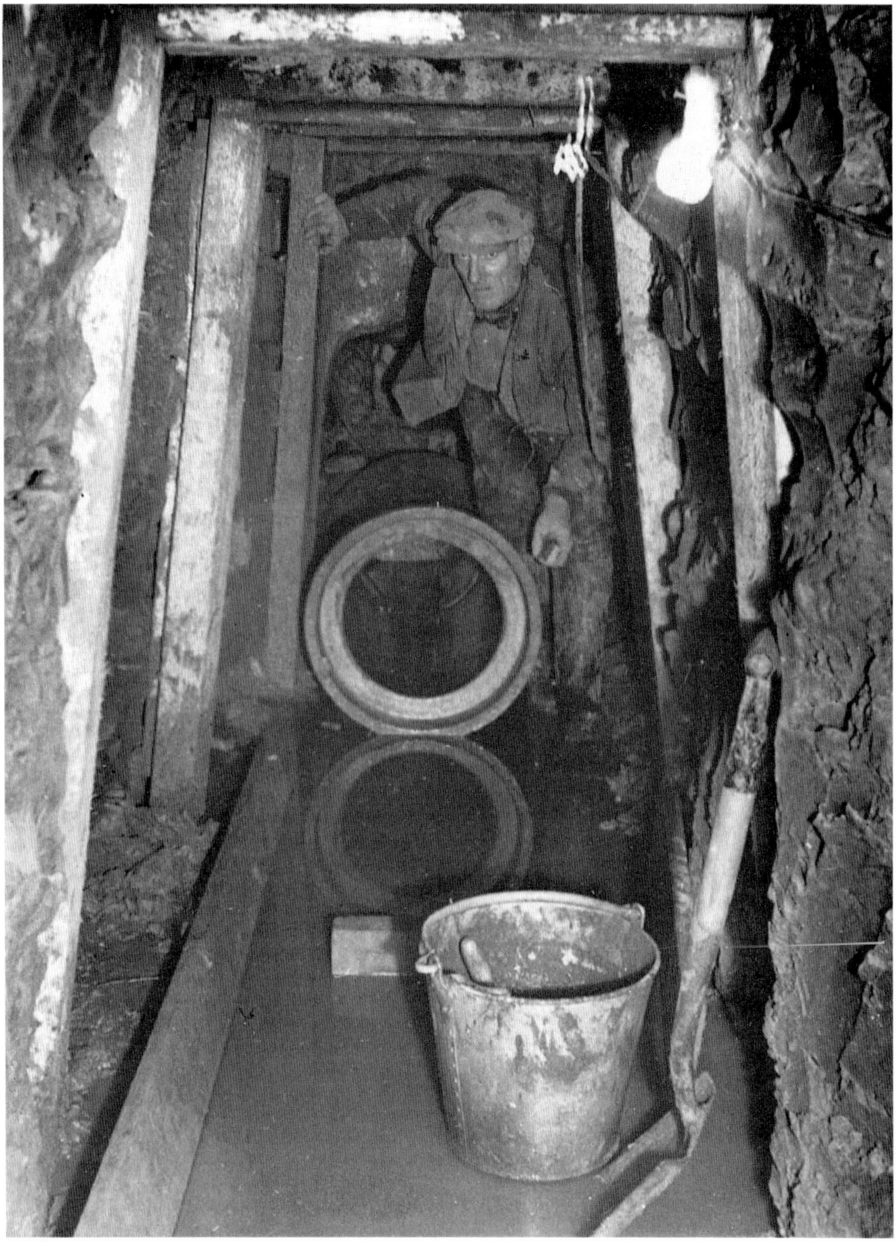

Construction of the de Havilland soil sewer in 1948. Not everything to do with the de Havilland works was romantic or airborne: this scene is more reminiscent of a colliery, and provides an idea of the conditions experienced by some members of the local workforce.

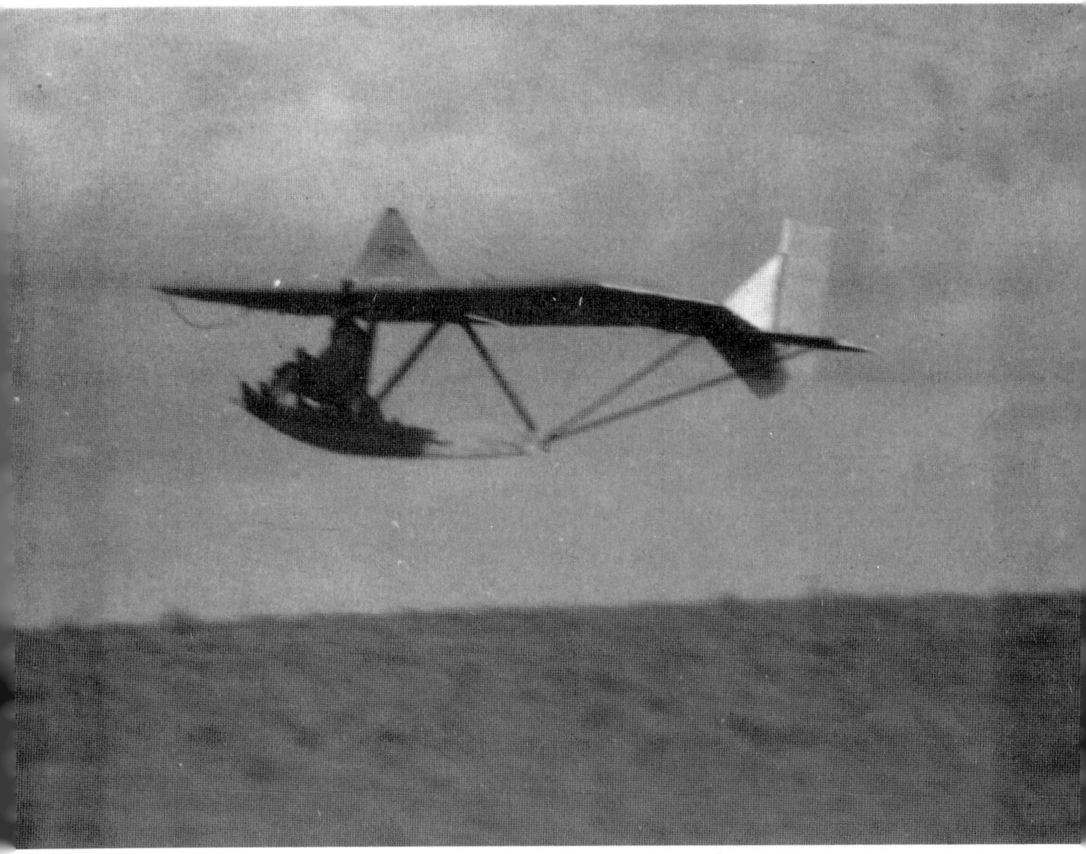

Gliding at Fryent Way in 1927. This picture may have a connection with de Havilland, but the only available information is that it came from the Director of Amenities and Works in 1977.

Acknowledgements

I feel it is important to acknowledge the many donations to the museum and archive, both documented and anonymous, that have enabled me to produce this work. I would also like to thank the Wembley History Society for allowing me to use some of their photos in this book. The few reproduced here are a small selection and there are many others that are worthy of inclusion in a book of this type. I should also like to acknowledge a personal debt to the many other organizations and individuals, both within Brent Council and beyond, who have helped in this venture, especially colleagues past and present at Cricklewood Library and the Grange Museum, and Bridget Keane and Ian Johnston for their contributions to this publication.

Finally I should like to thank my family, Lorraine, Laura and James, for their continual love, encouragement and support.

Bibliography

Dewe, D. and Sansom, A. *From Bacon Lane to Yuletide Road: A Guide to Brent Street Names*, London, Brent Library Service, 1975

Hewlett, G. *Aviation in and around Brent*, London, Brent Leisure, 1984

Hewlett, G. *An Historical Survey of Kingsbury*, London, 1982

Hewlett, G. (ed.) *A History of Wembley*, London, Brent Library Service, 1979

Victoria History of the Counties of England: *Middlesex*, vol. IV, Oxford University Press, 1971 (Harrow)

Victoria History of the Counties of England: *Middlesex*, vol. V, Oxford University Press, 1976 (Kingsbury)

Wembley News

Wembley Observer

Willesden (and Brent) Chronicle

BRITAIN IN OLD PHOTOGRAPHS

To order any of these titles please telephone Littlehampton Book Services on 01903 721596

ALDERNEY

Alderney: A Second Selection, *B Bonnard*

BEDFORDSHIRE

Bedfordshire at Work, *N Lutt*

BERKSHIRE

Maidenhead, *M Hayles & D Hedges*
Around Maidenhead, *M Hayles & B Hedges*
Reading, *P Southerton*
Reading: A Second Selection, *P Southerton*
Sandhurst and Crowthorne, *K Dancy*
Around Slough, *J Hunter & K Hunter*
Around Thatcham, *P Allen*
Around Windsor, *B Hedges*

BUCKINGHAMSHIRE

Buckingham and District, *R Cook*
High Wycombe, *R Goodearl*
Around Stony Stratford, *A Lambert*

CHESHIRE

Cheshire Railways, *M Hitches*
Chester, *S Nichols*

CLWYD

Clwyd Railways, *M Hitches*

CLYDESDALE

Clydesdale, *Lesmahagow Parish Historical Association*

CORNWALL

Cornish Coast, *T Bowden*
Falmouth, *P Gilson*
Lower Fal, *P Gilson*
Around Padstow, *M McCarthy*
Around Penzance, *J Holmes*
Penzance and Newlyn, *J Holmes*
Around Truro, *A Lyne*
Upper Fal, *P Gilson*

CUMBERLAND

Cockermouth and District, *J Bernard Bradbury*
Keswick and the Central Lakes, *J Marsh*
Around Penrith, *F Boyd*
Around Whitehaven, *H Fancy*

DERBYSHIRE

Derby, *D Buxton*
Around Matlock, *D Barton*

DEVON

Colyton and Seaton, *T Gosling*
Dawlish and Teignmouth, *G Gosling*
Devon Aerodromes, *K Saunders*
Exeter, *P Thomas*
Exmouth and Budleigh Salterton, *T Gosling*
From Haldon to Mid-Dartmoor, *T Hall*
Honiton and the Otter Valley, *J Yallop*
Around Kingsbridge, *K Tanner*
Around Seaton and Sidmouth, *T Gosling*
Seaton, Axminster and Lyme Regis, *T Gosling*

DORSET

Around Blandford Forum, *B Cox*
Bournemouth, *M Colman*
Bridport and the Bride Valley, *J Burrell & S Humphries*
Dorchester, *T Gosling*
Around Gillingham, *P Crocker*

DURHAM

Darlington, *G Flynn*
Darlington: A Second Selection, *G Flynn*
Durham People, *M Richardson*
Houghton-le-Spring and Hetton-le-Hole, *K Richardson*
Houghton-le-Spring and Hetton-le-Hole: A Second Selection, *K Richardson*
Sunderland, *S Miller & B Bell*
Teesdale, *D Coggins*
Teesdale: A Second Selection, *P Raine*
Weardale, *J Crosby*
Weardale: A Second Selection, *J Crosby*

DYFED

Aberystwyth and North Ceredigion, *Dyfed Cultural Services Dept*
Haverfordwest, *Dyfed Cultural Services Dept*
Upper Tywi Valley, *Dyfed Cultural Services Dept*

ESSEX

Around Grays, *B Evans*

GLOUCESTERSHIRE

Along the Avon from Stratford to Tewkesbury, *J Jeremiah*
Cheltenham: A Second Selection, *R Whiting*
Cheltenham at War, *P Gill*
Cirencester, *J Welsford*
Around Cirencester, *E Cuss & P Griffiths*
Forest, The, *D Mullin*
Gloucester, *J Voyce*
Around Gloucester, *A Sutton*
Gloucester: From the Walwin Collection, *J Voyce*
North Cotswolds, *D Viner*
Severn Vale, *A Sutton*
Stonehouse to Painswick, *A Sutton*
Stroud and the Five Valleys, *S Gardiner & L Padin*
Stroud and the Five Valleys: A Second Selection, *S Gardiner & L Padin*
Stroud's Golden Valley, *S Gardiner & L Padin*
Stroudwater and Thames & Severn Canals, *E Cuss & S Gardiner*
Stroudwater and Thames & Severn Canals: A Second Selection, *E Cuss & S Gardiner*
Tewkesbury and the Vale of Gloucester, *C Hilton*
Thornbury to Berkeley, *J Hudson*
Uley, Dursley and Cam, *A Sutton*
Wotton-under-Edge to Chipping Sodbury, *A Sutton*

GWYNEDD

Anglesey, *M Hitches*
Gwynedd Railways, *M Hitches*
Around Llandudno, *M Hitches*
Vale of Conwy, *M Hitches*

HAMPSHIRE

Gosport, *J Sadden*
Portsmouth, *P Rogers & D Francis*

HEREFORDSHIRE

Herefordshire, *A Sandford*

HERTFORDSHIRE

Barnet, *I Norrie*
Hitchin, *A Fleck*
St Albans, *S Mullins*
Stevenage, *M Appleton*

ISLE OF MAN

The Tourist Trophy, *B Snelling*

ISLE OF WIGHT

Newport, *D Parr*
Around Ryde, *D Parr*

JERSEY

Jersey: A Third Selection, *R Lemprière*

KENT

Bexley, *M Scott*
Broadstairs and St Peter's, *J Whyman*
Bromley, Keston and Hayes, *M Scott*
Canterbury: A Second Selection, *D Butler*
Chatham and Gillingham, *P MacDougall*
Chatham Dockyard, *P MacDougall*
Deal, *J Broady*
Early Broadstairs and St Peter's, *B Wootton*
East Kent at War, *D Collyer*
Eltham, *J Kennett*
Folkestone: A Second Selection, *A Taylor & E Rooney*
Goudhurst to Tenterden, *A Guilmant*
Gravesend, *R Hiscock*
Around Gravesham, *R Hiscock & D Grierson*
Herne Bay, *J Hawkins*
Lympne Airport, *D Collyer*
Maidstone, *I Hales*
Margate, *R Clements*
RAF Hawkinge, *R Humphreys*
RAF Manston, *RAF Manston History Club*
RAF Manston: A Second Selection, *RAF Manston History Club*
Ramsgate and Thanet Life, *D Perkins*
Romney Marsh, *E Carpenter*
Sandwich, *C Wanostrocht*
Around Tonbridge, *C Bell*
Tunbridge Wells, *M Rowlands & I Beavis*
Tunbridge Wells: A Second Selection, *M Rowlands & I Beavis*
Around Whitstable, *C Court*
Wingham, Adisham and Littlebourne, *M Crane*

LANCASHIRE

Around Barrow-in-Furness, *J Garbutt & J Marsh*
Blackpool, *C Rothwell*
Bury, *J Hudson*
Chorley and District, *J Smith*
Fleetwood, *C Rothwell*
Heywood, *J Hudson*
Around Kirkham, *C Rothwell*
Lancashire North of the Sands, *J Garbutt & J Marsh*
Around Lancaster, *S Ashworth*
Lytham St Anne's, *C Rothwell*
North Fylde, *C Rothwell*
Radcliffe, *J Hudson*
Rossendale, *B Moore & N Dunnachie*

LEICESTERSHIRE

Around Ashby-de-la-Zouch, *K Hillier*
Charnwood Forest, *I Keil, W Humphrey & D Wix*
Leicester, *D Burton*
Leicester: A Second Selection, *D Burton*
Melton Mowbray, *T Hickman*
Around Melton Mowbray, *T Hickman*
River Soar, *D Wix, P Shacklock & I Keil*
Rutland, *T Clough*
Vale of Belvoir, *T Hickman*
Around the Welland Valley, *S Mastoris*

LINCOLNSHIRE

Grimsby, *J Tierney*
Around Grimsby, *J Tierney*
Grimsby Docks, *J Tierney*
Lincoln, *D Cuppleditch*

Scunthorpe, *D Taylor*
Skegness, *W Kime*
Around Skegness, *W Kime*

LONDON

Balham and Tooting, *P Loobey*
Crystal Palace, Penge & Anerley, *M Scott*
Greenwich and Woolwich, *K Clark*
Hackney: A Second Selection, *D Mander*
Lewisham and Deptford, *J Coulter*
Lewisham and Deptford: A Second Selection, *J Coulter*
Streatham, *P Loobey*
Around Whetstone and North Finchley, *J Heathfield*
Woolwich, *B Evans*

MONMOUTHSHIRE

Chepstow and the River Wye, *A Rainsbury*
Monmouth and the River Wye, *Monmouth Museum*

NORFOLK

Great Yarmouth, *M Teun*
Norwich, *M Colman*
Wymondham and Attleborough, *P Yaxley*

NORTHAMPTONSHIRE

Around Stony Stratford, *A Lambert*

NOTTINGHAMSHIRE

Arnold and Bestwood, *M Spick*
Arnold and Bestwood: A Second Selection, *M Spick*
Changing Face of Nottingham, *G Oldfield*
Mansfield, *Old Mansfield Society*
Around Newark, *T Warner*
Nottingham: 1944–1974, *D Whitworth*
Sherwood Forest, *D Ottewell*
Victorian Nottingham, *M Payne*

OXFORDSHIRE

Around Abingdon, *P Horn*
Banburyshire, *M Barnett & S Gosling*
Burford, *A Jewell*
Around Didcot and the Hagbournes, *B Lingham*
Garsington, *M Gunther*
Around Henley-on-Thames, *S Ellis*
Oxford: The University, *J Rhodes*
Thame to Watlington, *N Hood*
Around Wallingford, *D Beasley*
Witney, *T Worley*
Around Witney, *C Mitchell*
Witney District, *T Worley*
Around Woodstock, *J Bond*

POWYS

Brecon, *Brecknock Museum*
Welshpool, *E Bredsdorff*

SHROPSHIRE

Shrewsbury, *D Trumper*
Whitchurch to Market Drayton, *M Morris*

SOMERSET

Bath, *J Hudson*
Bridgwater and the River Parrett, *R Fitzhugh*
Bristol, *D Moorcroft & N Campbell-Sharp*
Changing Face of Keynsham,
B Lowe & M Whitehead
Chard and Ilminster, *G Gosling & F Huddy*
Crewkerne and the Ham Stone Villages,
G Gosling & F Huddy
Around Keynsham and Saltford, *B Lowe & T Brown*
Midsomer Norton and Radstock, *C Howell*
Somerton, Ilchester and Langport, *G Gosling & F Huddy*
Taunton, *N Chipchase*
Around Taunton, *N Chipchase*
Wells, *C Howell*
Weston-Super-Mare, *S Poole*
Around Weston-Super-Mare, *S Poole*
West Somerset Villages, *K Houghton & L Thomas*

STAFFORDSHIRE

Aldridge, *J Farrow*
Bilston, *E Rees*
Black Country Transport: Aviation, *A Brew*
Around Burton upon Trent, *G Sowerby & R Farman*
Bushbury, *A Chatwin, M Mills & E Rees*
Around Cannock, *M Mills & S Belcher*
Around Leek, *R Poole*
Lichfield, *H Clayton & K Simmons*
Around Pattingham and Wombourne, *M Griffiths, P Leigh & M Mills*
Around Rugeley, *T Randall & J Anslow*
Smethwick, *J Maddison*
Stafford, *J Anslow & T Randall*
Around Stafford, *J Anslow & T Randall*
Stoke-on-Trent, *I Lawley*
Around Tamworth, *R Sulima*
Around Tettenhall and Codsall, *M Mills*
Tipton, Wednesbury and Darlaston, *R Pearson*
Walsall, *D Gilbert & M Lewis*
Wednesbury, *I Bott*
West Bromwich, *R Pearson*

SUFFOLK

Ipswich: A Second Selection, *D Kindred*
Around Ipswich, *D Kindred*
Around Mildenhall, *C Dring*
Southwold to Aldeburgh, *H Phelps*
Around Woodbridge, *H Phelps*

SURREY

Cheam and Belmont, *P Berry*
Croydon, *S Bligh*
Dorking and District, *K Harding*
Around Dorking, *A Jackson*
Around Epsom, *P Berry*
Farnham: A Second Selection, *J Parratt*
Around Haslemere and Hindhead, *T Winter & G Collyer*
Richmond, *Richmond Local History Society*
Sutton, *P Berry*

SUSSEX

Arundel and the Arun Valley, *J Godfrey*
Bishopstone and Seaford, *P Pople & P Berry*
Brighton and Hove, *J Middleton*
Brighton and Hove: A Second Selection, *J Middleton*
Around Crawley, *M Goldsmith*
Hastings, *P Haines*
Hastings: A Second Selection, *P Haines*
Around Haywards Heath, *J Middleton*
Around Heathfield, *A Gillet & B Russell*
Around Heathfield: A Second Selection,
A Gillet & B Russell
High Weald, *B Harwood*
High Weald: A Second Selection, *B Harwood*
Horsham and District, *T Wales*
Lewes, *J Middleton*
RAF Tangmere, *A Saunders*
Around Rye, *A Dickinson*
Around Worthing, *S White*

WARWICKSHIRE

Along the Avon from Stratford to Tewkesbury, *J Jeremiah*
Bedworth, *J Burton*
Coventry, *D McGrory*
Around Coventry, *D McGrory*
Nuneaton, *S Clews & S Vaughan*
Around Royal Leamington Spa, *J Cameron*
Around Royal Leamington Spa: A Second Selection,
J Cameron
Around Warwick, *R Booth*

WESTMORLAND

Eden Valley, *J Marsh*
Kendal, *M & P Duff*
South Westmorland Villages, *J Marsh*
Westmorland Lakes, *J Marsh*

WILTSHIRE

Around Amesbury, *P Daniels*
Chippenham and Lacock, *A Wilson & M Wilson*
Around Corsham and Box, *A Wilson & M Wilson*
Around Devizes, *D Buxton*
Around Highworth, *G Tanner*
Around Highworth and Faringdon, *G Tanner*
Around Malmesbury, *A Wilson*
Marlborough: A Second Selection, *P Colman*
Around Melksham,
Melksham and District Historical Association
Nadder Valley, *R. Sawyer*
Salisbury, *P Saunders*
Salisbury: A Second Selection, *P Daniels*
Salisbury: A Third Selection, *P Daniels*
Around Salisbury, *P Daniels*
Swindon: A Third Selection, *The Swindon Society*
Swindon: A Fourth Selection, *The Swindon Society*
Trowbridge, *M Marshman*
Around Wilton, *P Daniels*
Around Wootton Bassett, Cricklade and Purton, *T Sharp*

WORCESTERSHIRE

Evesham to Bredon, *F Archer*
Around Malvern, *K Smith*
Around Pershore, *M Dowty*
Redditch and the Needle District, *R Saunders*
Redditch: A Second Selection, *R Saunders*
Around Tenbury Wells, *D Green*
Worcester, *M Dowty*
Around Worcester, *R Jones*
Worcester in a Day, *M Dowty*
Worcestershire at Work, *R Jones*

YORKSHIRE

Huddersfield: A Second Selection, *H Wheeler*
Huddersfield: A Third Selection, *H Wheeler*
Leeds Road and Rail, *R Vickers*
Pontefract, *R van Riel*
Scarborough, *D Coggins*
Scarborough's War Years, *R Percy*
Skipton and the Dales, *Friends of the Craven Museum*
Around Skipton-in-Craven, *Friends of the Craven Museum*
Yorkshire Wolds, *I & M Sumner*